A House Called

MORVEN

by Alfred Hoyt Bill *in collaboration with* Walter E. Edge
*Revised by* Constance M. Greiff
*with a Postscript by* Bolton F. Schwartz

PRINCETON UNIVERSITY PRESS, PRINCETON, NEW JERSEY

# A House Called Morven

*Its Role in American History*

Published by Princeton University Press, Princeton, N.J.
In the U.K.: Princeton University Press, Guildford, Surrey

LCC 76-53641
ISBN 0-691-04641-7

Special Printing for the New Jersey American
Revolution Bicentennial Celebration Commission

# CONTENTS

# ILLUSTRATIONS

# FOREWORD

*There can be no foreword without a past.*

IN JUNE 1922 I first had the privilege of visiting Morven. President Warren G. Harding was the main speaker at the dedication of the War Memorial Monument across the lawn from the mansion.

The President had invited a number of guests to accompany him from Washington, including myself and my colleague in the United States Senate, Joseph S. Frelinghuysen; Senator Frederick Hale, of Maine; and Speaker of the House of Representatives The Honorable Frederick Gillette, of Massachusetts. The special guests were entertained at luncheon at Morven.

The house was then occupied by Mr. and Mrs. Bayard Stockton. She was a gracious hostess, and I was greatly impressed by the simplicity and charm of the historic mansion.

Twenty-odd years later, while I was serving my second term as governor of New Jersey, Mrs. Edge and I were motoring through Princeton and on passing the premises it occurred to me that my wife would enjoy looking through the old house. We drove in and the caretaker willingly permitted us that privilege. The property had been leased to General Robert W. Johnson, but at the time he was not in residence.

We were endeavoring to locate a temporary home in or near Trenton, and Mrs. Edge was so charmed with Morven that I immediately made enquiries as to the possibility of securing it. George A. Brakeley, Vice President of Princeton University, came to the rescue, and General Johnson kindly agreed to transfer his lease to me.

It then occurred to me that if this shrine could be purchased, I would eventually present it to the state to be used as a governor's mansion or a museum, thus preserving all its historical associations for posterity.

# Foreword

The Stocktons then in possession, members of the family that had owned Morven for two hundred and forty years, accepted my offer without any conditions. I then publicly stated that I would ultimately present the property to the state.

On June 18, 1951, Governor Alfred E. Driscoll approved a legislative joint resolution accepting the gift for the state, which graciously provided that the Edge family should remain in possession as long as they desired. However, while appreciating the offer of the state, Mrs. Edge and I have now turned the property over, and we hope it will be occupied by successive governors.

Stratford, Monticello, and other residential shrines have glorious pasts, but I greatly doubt if any American manor can claim more interesting incidents and historical associations than can Morven.

The following pages will recite the entrancing part Morven has played in the history of New Jersey and the nation.

WALTER E. EDGE

Princeton, New Jersey
September 28, 1953

# PREFACE

THE traveler entering or leaving Princeton, New Jersey, by way of Stockton Street (Route U.S. 206) may easily miss seeing the fine colonial mansion that stands on the north side of the road two or three hundred yards to the west of the junction of that street with Nassau. His glance will be caught by the tall, white monument that rises above the double row of Japanese cherry trees to the east of the house and will be distracted from it by the lofty tower of Trinity Church and the ornate front of Thomson Hall opposite. Standing some hundred yards back from the roadway, moreover, on the far side of a broad lawn, the mellow front of yellow brick, with its white shutters and hospitably broad, white portico, is obscured by the umbrageous branches of many splendid trees.

But the mansion deserves much more than the slight glimpse that the passer-by can get of it. It has stood there since the days when the road in front of it had only lately changed its name from the Old Dutch Trail to the King's Highway—two hundred and fifty years. It is, with possibly one exception, the oldest house in the Borough of Princeton, and for close to two centuries it has borne the name of Morven, which was given to it by the most distinguished of its mistresses.

Situated about midway between New Brunswick and Trenton on the overland link of the old amphibious route between New York and Philadelphia, the wealth, enterprise, intelligence, and public spirit of its owners made it not only the nucleus of the settlement that was to become Princeton but a center of civilization, culture, and statesmanship from its earliest days. For more than two hundred years the house was owned by the Stockton family, passing from father to son for five generations from the Richard Stockton who built it, and returning to the direct line of inheritance after an interval of possession by a collateral descendant in the sixth generation. In colonial days its owners were judges of the supreme court, members of the Royal governor's council, and frequently his hosts when he toured the province. Under Morven's roof were made the plans that brought the College of New Jersey (now Princeton University) to the little eighteenth-century village, and much of the money for that purpose was pledged there.

There, too, the cause of American Independence was anxiously debated and finally wholeheartedly embraced; and from its door the Richard Stockton who was its owner at that time went forth to the Continental Congress to sign the Declaration of 1776. He lost his liberty and his health in the cause, and the British revenged themselves upon him by reducing one wing of his home to smoking ruin. His son, grandson, and great-grandson sat in the United States Senate: one of these in the House of Representatives also. His grandson, Robert Field Stockton, developed for the United States navy the first propeller-driven warship in the world and shared with Frémont the glory of the conquest of California. It was he also who pioneered the project of the canal that linked the Raritan River with the Delaware, and he had a large part in the construction of the railroad that soon followed it.

Such men naturally attracted distinguished visitors, and Morven was always famous for its hospitality. Washington was a guest there both as commander in chief of the Continental armies and as President. The family papers record the visits of seven other Presidents of the United States while they were in office; and there were several, James Madison among them, who were probably entertained there as private citizens.

Other guests not less notable were the Marquis de La Luzerne, King Louis XVI's ambassador to the infant United States, and Lafayette, who revisited the scenes of his youthful exploits after a stormy interval of more than forty years. Among others who were entertained there were the first ambassador from the Netherlands, Major Aaron Burr and Alexander Hamilton, Light Horse Harry Lee, Generals Nathanael Greene, Israel Putnam, and John Sullivan, the painter Sully, Daniel Webster repeatedly, such assorted divines as Jonathan Edwards and Bishop George Washington Doane, every president of the College of New Jersey and of Princeton University, Eliot of Harvard and Butler of Columbia. Doctor Benjamin Rush, the famous physician, and Elias Boudinot, President of the Continental Congress, were frequent visitors as brothers-in-law of the family.

A considerable part of the following narrative, like much of what has already been written of Morven, rests necessarily upon oral tradition. The fire by which the British destroyed the east wing of the house consumed almost all of the papers related to its history up to that time. Much of its life for the past hundred and seventy years is reflected in letters and documents that have been accumulated in the Princeton University Library and elsewhere; a few remain in the possession of various members of the family. But for a number of episodes that have the ring of truth I have been able to find no documentary evidence and I have accepted them at their face value.

The record of the genealogy of the family becomes confused here and there. The two historians of the family occasionally disagree both with each other and with local historians of Princeton. The genealogical tables that I have been able to examine are sometimes in disagreement. When such cases became involved in the story of the house, I have done my best to accept what seemed to me the most probable solution of the difficulty. If my judgments have been contrary to the accepted belief of any of the present members of the family, I can only plead the excellence of my intentions and beg them to accept my profound apologies.

For valuable suggestions and information, and for invaluable encouragement, in the writing of this book, I am deeply indebted to Professors Julian Parks Boyd, Walter Phelps

# Preface

Hall, William Starr Myers, Duncan Spaeth, and Thomas Jefferson Wertenbaker, of Princeton University;

To Princeton neighbors: Governor and Mrs. Walter E. Edge, Mrs. Walter Lowrie, Mr. Howard Russell Butler, Jr., Mr. Edward L. Pierce, Mr. James R. Sloane, Mrs. Richard Stockton 3rd, Mrs. Bayard Stockton 3rd, the Misses Stockton, and Mrs. Richard T. Anderson, who gave me the benefit of their personal memories of Morven and were otherwise helpful;

Also to Doctor L. H. Butterfield, of the Institute of Early American History and Culture, Judge Sidney Goldman, of Trenton, General Robert W. Johnson, of New Brunswick, Mr. and Mrs. J. Potter Stockton, of Spring Lake, Mr. R. N. Williams 2nd and Mr. N. B. Wainright, of the Historical Society of Pennsylvania, Mr. Roger H. MacDonough, of the New Jersey State Library, Mrs. Maud H. Greene, of the New Jersey Historical Society, Mr. Howard I. Hughes, of the Trenton Free Public Library, and the members of the staff of the Manuscripts Room of the New York Public Library.

My hearty thanks are also owing to Doctor Colton Storm, of the William L. Clements Library, Ann Arbor, Michigan, for the photostat of a letter from Richard Stockton to Doctor Benjamin Rush; to Mrs. C. Welles Little, of Hagerstown, Maryland, and Doctor Spaeth for the loan of Stockton papers and documents in their possession; and to Mr. Arthur Conger, of Princeton, for allowing me to examine his collection of Morven and Stockton memorabilia.

And I have the pleasure of recording my gratitude to Doctor Henry L. Savage, Doctor Howard C. Rice, Jr., Mr. Alexander P. Clark, Mr. Malcolm O. Young, and Mr. Alexander Wainright, of the Princeton University Library, and Professor Henry A. Jandl, of the School of Architecture, for their expert, untiring, and friendly assistance.

ALFRED HOYT BILL

Princeton, New Jersey
September 28, 1953

# PREFACE TO THE REVISED
# EDITION

AS ONE means of celebrating the nation's 200th birthday, the New Jersey American Revolution Bicentennial Commission has supported a new edition of this book about a house where a good deal of New Jersey's history was, and is still being, made. In so doing, it was decided to make a number of changes to accommodate new information and new interpretations that have come to light in the more than twenty years since *A House Called Morven* was first issued. At the same time, no one wished to alter the narrative style of a book that has delighted so many readers.

Most of the passages requiring alteration were based on insufficient knowledge about the early history of the Stockton family in New Jersey and about the dating of Morven and the sequence of changes in its fabric. Accordingly, the first chapter was revised extensively, and a new essay on the architecture was substituted for the one prepared for the first edition by George B. Tatum. The remaining chapters stand largely as first published, except for changes necessitated by the finding of fresh evidence. Some readers may find Mr. Bill's interpretations of the actions of some members of the Stockton family overly generous. It was not, however, my intention to alter his viewpoint, but only to correct errors where the changes could be supported by documentation.

When Mary W. Gibbons, Elizabeth G. C. Menzies, and I first began the research on local buildings for *Princeton Architecture*, we were struck by the discrepancy between the traditional date for the construction of Morven and its stylistic characteristics. Having questioned this early date, we looked hard at the available documentation on the Stocktons' landholdings and buildings, and published our conclusions in that volume. Subsequently Miss Menzies illustrated, in *The Millstone Valley*, the striking similarity between the stair at

Morven and those in other Princeton buildings by Charles Steadman.

Over the years since these books were published, I continued to collect evidence leading to some changes in the interpretation of Morven. New and more conclusive documentation may still come to light, which will alter our perception of the building further. Until it does or until a thorough physical investigation of its inner structure is undertaken, it is impossible to arrive at a definitive analysis of Morven's evolution.

For assistance in searching out the elusive fragments of fact about Morven's past, I owe an enormous debt to Howard C. Rice, Jr. of the Princeton University Library (now retired) and M. Halsey Thomas, Archivist Emeritus of Princeton University, who were generous in sharing their encyclopedic knowledge of local documentary sources. I am also grateful to the late Kenneth Richards, his successor William Wright, and other members of the staff of the Bureau of Archives and History, New Jersey State Library, and to Mrs. Rebecca Meulich of the Trenton Free Public Library.

For research assistance in preparing this revision, I wish to thank Mrs. Alma R. Field. I am particularly indebted to her for calling to my attention the letter from Anthony Wheelock to Richard Stockton about the care of war prisoners, which led to the conclusion that the name of The Barracks was derived from its use as a jail during the French and Indian War. I am also grateful to Mrs. Susan Bradman for information about the Stocktons in Burlington County.

Particular gratitude is due to Charles E. Peterson of Philadelphia, from whom I learned a good deal of what I know about American architecture, and who contributed advice and assistance in the analysis of the fabric of Morven, particularly in pointing out the discrepancy between the plan of the basement and that of the first floor. I also wish to thank Lee Nelson of the National Park Service for confirmation of a structural detail, and Herbert Wettstein of the Division of

## Preface to the Revised Edition

Building and Construction, New Jersey State Department of the Treasury for assistance in obtaining a set of drawings prepared for the State by Edgar I. Williams, AIA, in 1954. The plan and conjectural view of the south façade of Morven were prepared for this edition by Michael J. Mills, based in part on Mr. Williams' drawings.

CONSTANCE M. GREIFF

Princeton, New Jersey
October 20, 1976

# NOTE ON SOURCES

Most of the major publications and manuscript sources referring to the Stockton family were utilized in preparing the first edition of this book. What were evidently not consulted then, and what form the basis for many of the conclusions about the Stocktons' architectural activities cited here, are New Jersey's early public records, including deeds, wills, and inventories, most of which are to be found in the Bureau of Archives and History, New Jersey State Library, and in the early maps of the area. Most of the latter are in the collections of the Princeton University Library. Four maps were published by the library in 1964 in a pamphlet entitled *New Jersey Road Maps of the 18th Century*, edited by Howard C. Rice, Jr. Early newspaper advertisements published in the *New Jersey Archives* series and the files of nineteenth-century local newspapers in the New Jersey State Library and Princeton University Library also yielded valuable information.

Useful documentation on the early activities of the Stockton family is contained in the records of the Chesterfield Monthly Meeting of Friends, available on microfilm at the Trenton Free Public Library, and in Orra Eugene Monnette's *First Settlers of ye Plantations of Piscataway and Woodbridge*, which reprints the Piscataway town records.

The letter from Anthony Wheelock to Richard Stockton concerning French prisoners at Princeton in 1760 was printed in the *Historical Magazine* for 1862; Annis Stockton's inventory of Morven appears in *The New Jersey Genesis* for July 1965. Nineteenth century views of Morven were published in Benson Lossing's *Field Book of the Revolution*, *Appleton's Journal* for December 25, 1875, and a large volume of collected articles, *Princeton*, which appeared in 1879.

C.M.G.

A House Called

MORVEN

# CHAPTER I

## By the "Light Within" and
## the "New Lights"

THE STOCKTON family had been established in the area for over half a century before the house was begun. By then there were finer and larger houses in New Jersey, but none in Princeton, where the recently built college rose starkly over the few straggling inns and houses that composed the village. In size and in comfort it undoubtedly rivaled the new house completed for the President of the college.

On the crest of the long ridge that rises gradually from the crossing of the Millstone River to drop steeply to Stony Brook some five miles to the west, the house stood foursquare, its two-and-a-half stories rising above the surrounding fields, which had been virgin woodland two generations before. The road in front of it—once the Assanpink Trail of the Lenni Lenape, the Delaware Indians—had been known as the Old Dutch Trail after 1655, when Peter Stuyvesant seized the Swedish forts on the lower Delaware; and, after England acquired the colony and English settled the area, as the King's Highway. The quickest route between the Delaware and New Amsterdam, it had served the Dutch couriers and the few travelers with strength and courage to face its difficulties.

By the time the grandfather of Richard Stockton, the Signer, settled in Princeton, there had been peace with the Indians for a quarter of a century. The Dutch had spread from Manhattan across the Hudson to the hills of Bergen. Emigrants from New Haven had founded New Ark in 1666. Colonists from Long Island had crossed Arthur Kill to build Elizabeth Town, where the trail began. But once these outposts of civilization had been left behind, the traveler plunged into dense forests, stumbled down steep and sudden slopes to brawling brooks or the treacherous fords of swampy creeks,

3

and was confronted mid-way in his journey by the wide Raritan, where tide and current combined to imperil his passage.

Less than twenty years before the Stocktons came to Princeton, William Edmundson, a Quaker missionary who crossed the Jerseys on his way to Maryland in 1675, had found the country a howling wilderness. Benighted and deserted by his Indian guide, he made his way back some ten miles next morning to the "Rarington River" and "a small landing place from New York, whence there was a small path to the Delaware Falls." By that path and "by the good hand of God" he reached the falls next day but saw "no tame creatures by the way." For some *wampampeg* an Indian, his squaw, and his boy took him and his companions across the Delaware in a canoe. They swam their horses over and traveled along the west bank of the river for several miles but even thus far found no inhabitants.

Not long after this, by order of a court at New Castle, a ferry replaced the Indian canoes at the falls. In 1686 John Inian established his ferry across the Raritan where New Brunswick now stands, and owing to Inian's efforts for the opening of the country, ax and mattock transformed the old trail, which had been "nothing but a footpath for men and horses between the trees," into a road that could be used by wheeled vehicles. That same year Robert Fullerton, the first English settler in the region north of the Raritan, established himself on his farm. By that time Henry Greenland had already been settled for three years within what is now Princeton Township, northwest of the point where the road crossed the Millstone at Kingston. His future son-in-law, Daniel Brinson, had, in 1686, bought a tract of approximately four hundred acres some three miles to the west. Within the next decade, these two pioneers would be joined gradually by a half-dozen other families, all of Quaker background.

Clarke, Olden, Fitz Randolph, Horner, Worth, and Stockton were their names. They were as far as possible from being the traditional pioneers, homesteading a small farm, clearing the land with their own hands, while musket and powder lay ready on a convenient stump. They were people of substance. The desire to live among their fellow Friends and the rich opportunities available in the virgin soil of central New Jersey, not dire economic need, seem to have impelled them to seek new homes in the wilderness. Most, if not all, of these families had been in America for more than one generation, and they had not been poor when they landed.

Benjamin Clarke's father, formerly a stationer in London's Lombard Street, had an excellent bookshop in the flourishing port of Perth Amboy in 1683 and died six years later, leaving his son a very considerable estate. Benjamin Fitz Randolph, who came from Nottingham in England, had made his first American home at Barnstable, Massachusetts. Richard Stockton's father, also a Richard, had arrived at New Amsterdam from England sometime before 1656.

Guided by that "inner light" that governed all their doings, and blessed, like the great champion of the Society of Friends, William Penn, with the ability to make friends of the mammon of unrighteousness, the settlers on the brook the Indians called Wapowog, and the white men Rocky, or Stony, Brook, prospered greatly on the rich clay loam of their holdings. Slaves and indentured servants made their rapid progress possible. Worth built a mill, or, more exactly, two grist mills and a bolting mill under one roof; with the help of the Friends of Burlington, Chesterfield, and Little Egg Harbor, they built a small frame meeting house.

The Richard Stockton who settled in Princeton was born in England. According to family tradition—the family records were probably among the papers burned by the British when they occupied Morven in December 1776—his father, also named Richard, was one of the Stocktons who had dwelt in Cheshire since the time of the Conquest. Many of that family's epitaphs are to be found under their coat of arms and the motto, *Omnia Deo Pendent*, in the parish church of Malpas near the river Dee. "Here is buried," reads one of them, "Owen Stockton, Gentlemen, who deceased ye second day of December 1610, and John Stockton, his eldest sonne, who deceased ye eighteenth day of June 1643." From this Owen and this John, the family holds that Richard, the founder of the family in America, descended. Despite this tradition of gentle descent, both emigrant Richards, father and son, firmly styled themselves, on all legal documents as "yeoman," not "gentleman." Their descendant, the Signer, however, seems to have assumed the use of a family crest.

Why or when Richard Stockton came to the Dutch colony in New York is uncertain. He brought with him his wife and sufficient funds to establish himself as a landholder in the predominantly English village of Flushing on Long Island, in what is now the Borough of Queens. The first of a family that was to be distinguished in America for its love of liberty and strong religious convictions, it is significant that the earliest record of him here is his signature on a petition for the release of one William Wickenden, who had been fined and imprisoned by Peter Stuyvesant, the Governor of New Amsterdam, for preaching without a license in 1656.

When the English took over the colony in 1664, he became active in public affairs. The new governor made him a lieutenant of the Flushing company of light horse. He became one of the freeholders of Flushing. He prospered in other ways as well, fathering at least three sons and six daughters. But he was evidently not totally satisfied with his way of life. By 1686 he was buying what were generally stigmatized as "Quaker books," and by 1691 he had become a member of the Society of Friends. A year later he moved to Burlington County in West Jersey, where Friends from London and Yorkshire had founded a settlement fifteen years before.

His Flushing property—about seventy acres or more at home and about sixty acres a mile or two away, with as much meadow as would yield twenty or twenty-five loads of hay, "being by the coast on the Bay commonly known as Mattagaseson Bay, within the bounds of Flushing"—he sold for three hundred pounds. With twenty-five pounds added to that sum, he bought almost fourteen hundred acres, a strip almost two miles long and a mile wide, in an area known by the Indian name of Onianickon or Annannicken. His new

The Stockton coat of arms

holdings lay, adjoining land of such Burlington families as Schooley and Hutchinson, along North Run, in what is now the eastern part of Springfield Township, extending into North Hanover Township. There he lived until his death fifteen years later. His widow, Abigail, three sons, and six daughters survived him, and a thousand acres of his land were still owned by his descendants more than a century after his death.

His eldest son, and namesake, Richard, had preceded his father in the move from Flushing to Burlington County by a year. In 1691 he and a young widow, Susannah Witham Robinson, brought before the Chesterfield Friends Meeting their intention of marrying. The matter was debated seriously by both the Women's and Men's Meetings. In September the Men's Meeting rendered its decision, reluctantly concluding "by Reason of Report Conserning their unseemly and foolish Carriage which is owned by them and for which they are sorry[.] But yet friends Cannot have unity with them but leaves them to Prosede in their Marriage as they Shall see meete."

The couple evidently took the Chesterfield Friends at their word, removing from Burlington County to Piscataway Township in Middlesex County. The birth of their first child, another Richard, was duly recorded in the Piscataway records in April 1693. They may already have been living on the farm of over four hundred acres bought from Daniel Brinson some time before 1696, the year in which Richard agreed to pay an annual quit rent on the land to the Proprietors of East Jersey. This parcel lay in that part of Princeton south of Nassau Street which was part of Piscataway Township until 1730, when New Windsor Township was formed.

The present Nassau and Stockton Streets mark the northern boundaries of the tract, Stony Brook its southern limit. From east to west it extended between the present Washington and Springdale Roads. In 1697 Richard and Susannah diminished their holdings by selling a little over a hundred acres to Richard Ridgeway. But by 1701 Stockton had become by far the largest landholder in the vicinity. On the 20th of October in that year he bought from William Penn, for nine hundred pounds, a tract of 5,500 acres (reserving 1,050 acres therein, which evidently had been deeded already to others) that stretched from Stony Brook northward to Rocky Hill and westward from the Millstone River to the Province Line, the line surveyed by Keith to divide East from West Jersey.

Since the mid-1670s Penn had been one of the proprietors of West Jersey and this land was a part of his share at the division among the proprietors in 1693. Penn's settlement in Pennsylvania, his "Holy Experiment," was now nineteen years old, and this month he was bringing to a close his last visit to America. For two years he had been wrestling with his cantankerous colonists. Between 1682 and 1685 their number had increased from 2,000 to 7,200; by 1700 it had doubled, with a corresponding deterioration of moral standards. Penn had found piracy prevalent in the region and the inhabitants by no means unfriendly to its existence among them. The Philadelphia Yearly Meeting had endorsed slavery as Biblical, and Penn had met with opposition when he insisted upon the marriage and education of the slaves and regulations for their trial and punishment.

Slaves and a large family made possible the management of so sizeable an estate as Richard Stockton had acquired. The inventory taken at the time of his death listed among his possessions "one Negro woman and six children." He, too, had fathered six children, all boys. Of these the eldest, another Richard, was only sixteen when his father died. His brothers—Samuel, Joseph, Robert, John, and Thomas—had followed him into the world punctually at two-year intervals. To house his growing family, Richard had constructed a sturdy stone house, part of which still stands on Edgehill Street. For some two hundred years it has been known as "The Barracks," a name probably dating back to the aftermath of the French and Indian War. In 1760 another Richard Stockton, his grandson, was in charge of French prisoners at Princeton, housing them in a building then in his possession, undoubtedly the ancestral house he held in trust for his younger brothers.

When the first Richard died in 1709, he left his family well provided for. Six hundred acres of land east of the present Harrison Street went to his eldest son, Richard, another six hundred to Samuel, 500 acres each to Joseph, Robert, and John, and to Thomas, his youngest, 140 acres of his Stony Brook holdings together with 400 acres of the Annannicken property that had come to him at his father's death two years before. His meadow lands were divided among the five older boys, and twenty shillings a year was bequeathed to his mother, who had already been well provided for by his father's will.

John's inheritance was made up partly of woodland, partly of his father's "dwelling plantation," which included the house. But his mother held the dwelling plantation until John should come of age; and after that she was to retain the use of half of the house and its improvements during her lifetime. She was also to have the use of all the Negro slaves, until her sons came of age, at which time each was to receive one. One slave, Dinah, was excepted, being willed to the testator's brother-in-law, Philip Phillips, his sister Hannah's husband.

Richard must have respected his wife's head for business. He not only left her the residue of his estate, encompassing approximately half his land, but named her his sole executrix, both unusual acts in the eighteenth century. As executrix she caused one William Emley to make a survey of the estate within six months of her husband's death, and to her sons' properties she added generously from her own share. Evidently attractive as well as businesslike, Susannah eventually married for a third time. The groom was Thomas Leonard, a man several years her junior. Together with Samuel's brothers, Susannah and Thomas Leonard signed the wedding certificate when he married Amy Doughty in 1719. Her death left Thomas Leonard as the largest landlord in the neighborhood.

The area was growing rapidly, and the value of landed property grew with it. For fifty years immigrants from New England and Long Island, from Wales and Scotland, French Huguenots, Quakers, and Baptists fleeing from persecution, and others who sought only cheaper land or a milder climate, had been pouring into the country. By 1700 East Jersey had the nine towns of Perth Amboy, Middletown, Freehold, Piscataway, Woodbridge, Elizabeth Town, New Ark, Acquackanoak, and Bergen. By that year lumbering had begun in the Pines; sawmills were built; there was mining for iron in the southern swamps as well as in the northern hills, and a few iron forges and furnaces had been established.

In 1714 William Trent laid out his town at the falls of the Delaware. As the work of wheelwrights replaced the sections of tree trunk that had furnished the first wheels for the settlers' carts, wagons appeared more and more frequently among the strings of freight-laden pack horses that jogged past the Stockton house each day, and settlers followed. Four miles to the west the village of Maidenhead, now Lawrenceville, was founded, and Kingston at a like distance to the east; and the little settlement at Inian's Ferry on the Raritan grew large enough to receive a charter as New Brunswick in 1730.

By 1740 there were bridges across the Millstone at Kingston, and across Stony Brook at Worth's mill. The Old Dutch Trail had in fact become the King's Highway. Whereas in 1715 the traveler saw from it only four or five houses, fifteen years later he followed an almost continuous line of fences, with numerous substantial farmhouses and barns behind them. From the rich, virgin soil came crops of an abundance that astonished settlers fresh from Europe or New England. Jonathan Belcher, who had passed the first sixty years of his life in comparatively bleak Massachusetts, and had spent many months in England, was delighted by the Jersey fruit, including peaches as good as the English ones; vegetables even better; and on the wild lands, oaks, black walnut, elm, maple, birch, white cedar, pine, hickory, sassafras, wild grapes, and a profusion of wild flowers.

In 1748, when Professor Kalm, of the University of Abo in Swedish Finland, made the journey from Trenton to New Brunswick, he found the country mostly cleared, broad wheat fields bordering the roads, peach, apple, and cherry orchards laden with more fruit than the people could eat, and at the farms, great barns, each of whose wide, gently sloping shingle roofs sheltered wagons, stalls for horses and cows, a pig sty, a threshing floor in the center, and a hayloft above.

The village of Princeton had come into being by that time. James Leonard had built its first house about half a mile east of the Stockton house in 1724 and had given the place its name, perhaps because the village of Kingston, and Queenston, a hamlet a mile or so up the highway towards New Brunswick, already existed. Professor Kalm was storm-bound in Princeton for a whole day and night and noted that most of the houses were built of wood and stood at a distance from one another, with gardens and pastures between, but that thereabouts the woods had been so cut away and the land so well cultivated that one might have imagined himself to be in Europe.

Trenton still had only about a hundred houses at this time —most of them, the Professor observed, built only of boards. But the inhabitants did a large business in forwarding to New Brunswick by wagon travelers and freight that were brought up the river from Philadelphia in vessels that were locally known as "yachts." New Brunswick, the center of a flourishing and growing country and located at the head of deep-water navigation, had become a busy port. Warehouses had sprung up along the waterfront, and hardly a day went by without a sloop dropping down the river loaded with flour, grain, meat, finished lumber, and, by 1750, Jersey linen, bound for New York or Perth Amboy, while cargoes of

British merchandise and sugar and molasses from the West Indies were unloaded on the New Brunswick wharfs.

At the mouth of the Raritan, Perth Amboy's magnificent harbor had made it a flourishing port. So deep was the water at the foot of its high bluffs that ships of three hundred tons could be moored to the trees within a plank's length of the buildings of the town. Its commerce with Europe and the West Indies was as considerable as fluctuating regulation by the governor and council of the province would permit; and it had barracks to house the lately imported Negro slaves until they were distributed throughout the country.

On the crest of the wave of this rapid material growth John Stockton came of age in 1722 and lived his whole life. Yet not every man shared in the general prosperity. Why Richard Stockton passed over his older sons to leave the dwelling plantation to John will never be known, but he chose wisely. Richard and Samuel both eventually went through bankruptcy proceedings, and their estates were sold at Sheriff's sale. Much of Thomas Leonard's property was also sold at Sheriff's sale, including the lot on Nassau Street where the building now known as Bainbridge House was to rise. But John Stockton flourished. Where and how he got his education can only be surmised. There is no record of a school in Princeton before 1757, when a Latin school was opened in association with the college. Still it is unlikely that the education of the young Stocktons was neglected; and one must infer the employment of tutors, especially for John, whose wide and enlightened activities and whose friends among the highest persons in the province indicate a well-trained mind and excellent attainments.

In 1729, when he was twenty-eight years old, John married his cousin Abigail Phillips, the daughter of his father's sister Hannah and her husband Philip, to whom the slave Dinah had been bequeathed by his father. Young Abigail and her family were Presbyterians and John, despite his Quaker

13

background, became active in the affairs of that church. He also took part in the affairs of the province. He became and continued to be for many years one of the presiding judges of the Court of Common Pleas under the Royal government. At home four sons and four daughters, along with the care of the homestead farm and other properties, occupied his energies and those of his wife.

In John's time the old stone house was considerably larger than it is now, ninety feet wide although only twenty-five feet deep. It was surrounded by cultivated fields, an orchard, and numerous outbuildings including a large Dutch barn, a stable, a wagon house, and a cider house. Within were five rooms on the first floor, each with a fireplace, and six on the second, not counting rooms for the servants. It was an informal, but comfortable house, with plenty of space for a growing family and room to spare for the accommodation of guests, among whom were often John Hamilton, the Deputy Governor, and Colonel Cosby, Cornelius Van Horn, and John Wills. Managing a large farm required conscientious attention, but it also left time for entertaining and discourse with friends on the issues of the day. One might raise crops and also pursue politics, religion, or scholarship. A year after John's death, Andrew Burnaby, a young English traveler, wrote of such Jersey farmers: "They live together on their estates, and are literally gentlemen farmers."

It was a day of heavy drinking. The discrepancy between theological belief and the personal conduct of people of wealth, light, and learning was more obvious than it is today, but they were little disturbed by it. In 1757 Edward Shippen, a trustee of the College of New Jersey, wrote to its president, Aaron Burr, suggesting that the president caution the students against the dangers of alcoholic excess and described gentlemen who "have taken a dram or two in the morning, a quart of punch or Tiff before dinner, and maybe a glass or two of wine and bitter into the bargain rather than appear impolite at a friend's house where they may happen to dine, and drank five or six glasses of wine at table in Loyal healths." But he is not inclined to be censorious and quotes a chorus from "M. Boileau" as follows:

Enfin grand j'ay bien bu, rien vu me fait la Loi
Je brave le peril, je ris de la Tempete.
   Il ne point de Roi
   Plus Heureux que moi
   Rien me donne de l'Effroi
   J'ai du Bien par dessus la tete.

Often the discussion of the most serious matters was well lubricated by the product of the grape. At a dinner for the trustees of the College in 1772, the forty guests consumed 37 bottles of wine, 14 of beer, 12 bowls of punch, and 8 bowls of toddy. The products of John's cider house were undoubtedly supplemented by wine and punches, even when his guests had come to discuss important issues. When the time of the "Great Awakening" came and the "New Lights" in the lately formed Presbytery at New Brunswick defied the "Old Side" and were expelled by the Synod, he frequently entertained both David and John Brainard, who were leaders in the movement. Another sort of guest was the Honorable John Belcher, Esquire, Commander in Chief and Governor of His Majesty's Province of East and West Jersey.

Having made the governorship of Massachusetts and New Hampshire too hot for himself, Belcher had wangled that of New Jersey and married a Burlington girl. He would arrive from his home in Elizabeth Town in an elegant coach and four. He was noted for his capacity for sound Madeira, but he too entertained David Brainard and also Whitefield, the most distinguished of the "New Lights," and he drove twenty miles to hear the Reverend Mr. Tennent preach. He was well liked by people of substance. When he was accused of being friendly to certain "scandalous riots" which had "perplexed the province," a no less respectable body than the Presbytery of New Brunswick met at Princeton in December of 1751 for the sole purpose of addressing the British government in his favor.

Belcher gave whole-hearted support to what was the greatest and most lasting accomplishment of John Stockton's life: the leading part that John played in bringing the infant College of New Jersey to Princeton. Opened at Elizabeth Town under the presidency of the Reverend Jonathan Dickinson in 1747, the college had been moved in the same year to New Ark under the Reverend Aaron Burr, its second president, whose son gave the name its unenviable notoriety. But its location was generally felt to be not sufficiently central. Its removal to New Brunswick was considered, but in 1752, while the people of that town procrastinated about making the required provision for it, John Stockton and two other wealthy men of the Princeton neighborhood, Thomas Leonard, who was one of the trustees of the college, and John Horner, signed a bond for a thousand pounds to secure its establishment at Princeton; and Nathaniel Fitz Randolph "gave four acres and a half of land to set the college on." Plans were drawn for a college building that would be the largest structure in the colonies; on July 29, 1754, the foundation was begun; and in November two years later President Burr and his seventy students moved in.

The village had grown during the past thirty years. It now had at least one tavern, and probably more than one, since its position made it the most convenient stopping place between New Brunswick and Trent's Town. Where the highway passed through the village the houses now stood close enough together to cause it to be called Main Street by the inhabitants. Since 1720 the mail had been sent over once a week from the post office at Trent's Town, at least during the summer. But there was still no place of public worship nearer than the Stony Brook Meeting House, and good Presbyterians had to go to church at either Maidenhead or Kingston.

Above the little string of shops and houses lining the village street, which ran at a considerably lower level than it does today, the four-story brown stone walls of the college, one hundred and seventy-six feet in length, towered majestically. The trustees, grateful for the support of the Governor, who called the college his "adopted daughter," proposed to name the building Belcher Hall. But Belcher's modesty forbade. He suggested that it be named Nassau Hall after King William III, of the illustrious house of Nassau, who had delivered the British nation from those "two monstrous furies," Popery and Slavery, and the suggestion was adopted.

The building represented a considerable act of faith on the part of its sponsors, and an almost equal generosity. In addition to the thousand-pound bond, ten acres of cleared land for the building and two hundred acres of woodland had been required of them. The college had received gifts to the amount of twelve hundred pounds sterling, eighteen hundred pounds in the provincial currency. But these funds yielded hardly enough to support the president and tutors; and further sums had to be raised. The year after the completion of Nassau Hall the college lost by death both its able president, Aaron Burr, and its powerful friend the Governor. A year later, in 1758, both Burr's successor, Jonathan Edwards, and John Stockton died.

Fortunately John's eldest son, Richard, had already begun to take a part in the work his father left unfinished. Already he had assumed responsibility for dispensing certain sums to carpenter-builder Robert Smith for the construction of Nassau Hall. By this time he had been established for four years on the land deeded to him by John and Abigail in 1754, the property to which his new wife would give the name "Morven."

# CHAPTER II

## "In a State of Splendor"

BY THE time of his father's death, this Richard may have already begun building the fine house he called Morven. It faced the road squarely, northeast of the more modest stone homestead that had sheltered the first two generations of Stocktons in Princeton. For the next two decades Richard and his wife lavished on it both their money and their loving care.

Born in 1730, Richard had been sent to Nottingham in Maryland for his preparatory education at the academy of the Reverend Samuel Finley, who later became president of the College of New Jersey. After two years at Nottingham Richard entered the college as one of its first students and was one of the six who made up its first class to graduate, in 1748, while it was still at New Ark. He then read law with David Ogden, a distinguished New Ark lawyer, and six years later, at the age of twenty-four, was admitted to the bar.

He was devoted to his profession, eloquent and persuasive. For a time he may have maintained an office in New Ark, but by 1754 he was established at home in Princeton. So widespread was his reputation that clients came to him not only from the Jerseys but from the neighboring colonies. He was licensed a counsellor in 1758, and became a sergeant at law when he was thirty-four. Among his students were William Paterson, who was to be a justice of the Supreme Court of the United States, Elias Boudinot, President of the Continental Congress in 1782, and General Joseph Reed, of the Continental army.

But undoubtedly his most fortunate achievement was his marriage. His wife was Annis Boudinot. Her father was Elias Boudinot, who was also the father of Richard's law student of the same name. He was of a Huguenot family that had fled from France at the promulgation of the Edict of Nantes in 1685. After an apprenticeship with a New York goldsmith he had gone into business for himself in Philadelphia, where he had been next door neighbor to Benjamin Franklin and had evidently prospered during the 1730's and 1740's. For in 1750 he organized a company to exploit a copper mine near New Brunswick and a couple of years later moved with his family to Princeton.

He had a daughter and two sons by this time: Annis, born at Darby, Pennsylvania, in 1736; Elias, born in Philadelphia in 1740; and Elisha, also born in Philadelphia, in 1749. But the copper mine proved to be a failure, and his son Elias had to gaze enviously at the students of the college, to which his father could not afford to send him. The elder Elias was forced to combine his silversmith trade with a business of general merchandise and the position of postmaster in order to make a living. In 1757 he moved to "a pleasant and agreeable situation opposite the College, being 46 ft. front and 36 deep with ten rooms, eight with fireplaces, a large new stable, 40 feet long and 20 broad with a good well and large garden with a variety of fruit trees, a large bed of asparagus, etc. all enclosed with a good boarded fence, fit for a Merchant or a Tavern"—and to his other activities he evidently added that of tavern keeper.

Annis was probably married from this house. No record of the wedding date survives, but Julia, their first child, was born in 1759. Perhaps some clue to the date may be found in the tale of the unrequited love of a young tutor, Benjamin Prime. Wooing a pious local poetess, Prime addressed her as "Aemilia," the literary name Annis used in writing to her husband and closest friends. Surely in a town of fifty to seventy-five families, it is unlikely that there were two romantic versifiers using that *nom de plume*. In any event, Prime left "N–ss–u H–ll and all its joys" in September 1757, citing the wish to protect his correspondent's innocence and reputation. In worldly terms, Annis had certainly chosen the more desirable suitor. The daughter of a relatively poor man, she was marrying one of the richest landowners in town.

But although the bride's father might be described as a tradesman of decaying fortune, there was no denying that the Boudinots traced back to Elias, or Elie, Seigneur de Cressy, a prosperous merchant living near La Rochelle, who had come to New York in 1687. The first Richard Stockton, indeed, may well have known him in Flushing days, for he was made a "free man" of New York in 1688 and was imprisoned for opposing Leisler in the following year. The marriage, moreover, was based on much more than youthful ardor, though the bride was perhaps only nineteen and the bridegroom twenty-five. Profound affection and a community of tastes made the basis of a happiness that endured through good times and bad until Richard's tragic death brought it to a close twenty-six years later.

In "The Dream," one of her early poems, Annis wrote with a frankness a less forthright girl might have shrunk from:

"Methought without restraint you lean'd your head
On this fond breast, and rested every care:
My hand you took and from the circle led
My willing steps to breathe the vernal air."

But she wrote also:

"Thro' various scenes we rov'd, lovely and gay:
Of books we talk'd, and many a page compared:
Thy works of genius softened by the lay
Of *her* who all thy leisure moments shared."

Her father-in-law, John Stockton, died on the 20th of May, 1757. By his will his second son, John, received that portion of his landed estate lying on the north side of the village Main Street, and the land on the south side was left in Richard's trust to provide for the education of his third and fourth sons, Philip and Samuel. To Richard himself he had already deeded, three years before his death, the eastern part of his holdings, on which the walls of Morven were to rise.

Handsome, highly intelligent, with a cultivated mind and inexhaustible mental and physical energy, Annis Stockton brought to her new home an enthusiasm for its development and beautification, in which her husband, a man of taste and feeling equal to hers, shared heartily. Though his profession kept him often long absent, they worked out together the improvements of house and grounds. One of their first acts of this sort appears to have been the planting of two tulip poplars at the entrance as "bride trees," with which it was the custom of the time to commemorate a marriage.

They planted along the King's Highway in front of the house the row of catalpas which are said to have burst into full bloom on the Fourth of July each year from the first Independence Day until, at a great age, they finally died. The famous chestnut walk, of which more hereafter, sprang from French horse chestnuts that Samuel Pintard, at that time a captain in His Majesty's Twenty-fifth Foot Regiment, and his brother Lewis brought with them when they came courting Richard's sisters Abigail and Susannah; and from the same stock grew the gigantic tree behind the house, which measured eleven feet in girth, with—it is said—a hundred-foot spread of branches, when an ice storm brought it down some hundred and sixty years later.

John Stockton had left a numerous family of children, and Annis must often have found her new house filled with visiting brothers-in-law and sisters-in-law, seven in all, of whom only Hannah was as old as she. The youngest of the four girls was Rebecca, who was only nine; and the three boys, John, Philip, and Samuel Witham, were aged thirteen, eleven, and six. Seven years later Hannah married Annis's brother Elias and went to live at Elizabeth Town, where Elias had established a prosperous law practice. The Pintard brothers claimed Abigail and Susannah as their brides in due course, and Rebecca grew up to marry James Cuthbert, of Berthier House in Canada. John entered the Royal navy and was lost at sea when still quite young; Philip became a Presbyterian minister; and Samuel Witham left home to begin a distinguished career in public life.

## "In a State of Splendor"

As her father-in-law's children went out into the world, Annis brought into it children of her own: Julia, her eldest, in 1759; twin girls, Mary and Susan, two years later; Richard, after a three-year interval; then Lucius Horatio in 1768; and finally Abigail in 1773. But these maternal and quasi-maternal cares—difficult and delicate though they must have been—were not enough to absorb the attention and energy of Annis Boudinot Stockton. As a girl she had evidently read widely and with discrimination. She continued to do so, and to produce verses which, though they echoed the poetry of Pope, Young, Thomson, and Gray, were quite as good as the verse in the magazines of the time.

She never took her versifying seriously, had no aspirations to become a bluestocking. But her lines "Addressed to Col. Schuyler on his return to Jersey after two years Captivity in Canada" were published in Gaine's *New York Mercury*, January 9, 1758, and promptly reprinted in *The New American Magazine* for that same month, though they were written, it was stated, "in the few minutes Colonel Schuyler stayed at Prince-town . . . in his way to Trenton." And this was by no means the only one of her poems to appear in the provincial papers.

Following the fashion of the day, she gave herself and her husband the literary names of Emelia and Lucius, and it was thus that they signed their letters to each other. Perhaps it was to sustain this romantic pose that she adopted the white myrtle for her special flower and had herself painted with a spray of it in her hand. According to local legend the white myrtle in her garden died at her death, and attempts to grow it there since then have always failed. Under her influence her home became what Doctor L. H. Butterfield has well called it, "an outpost of sensibility."

When the *Poems of Ossian*, James Macpherson's successful forgery appeared, Annis read them with delight, as thousands of others did, including Thomas Jefferson. *Fingal, An Epic Poem in Six Books* was published in 1762. It purported to be translations of heroic lays of the Gaelic bard Ossian, narrating the exploits of his father, Fingal, king of the northwestern Caledonians. Fingal's home was Morven, and Annis gave the name to her husband's house, which has borne it ever since. It signifies, or so she believed, a range of hills, and was thus appropriate to the location. Earnest Presbyterian though she was, there was nothing dismal about her religion, and the lines of the poem that appear to have particularly commended the name to her were:

"Sons of Morven, spread the feast,
Send the night away with song."

In all of this she had her husband's complete cooperation. The income from the farms and from his lucrative law practice were spent freely on his home both within doors and without. The house was filled with fine furniture and pictures; the library was large and well chosen. He became interested in discovering the family coat of arms—one of those vanities, doubtless, that his Quaker grandfather had allowed to be forgotten, and of which he retained only a memory of the motto: *Omnia Deo Pendent*. And when his student Joseph Reed went to London to polish his legal education at the Inns of Court, Richard wrote to "Dr. Josy" to hunt it up for him over there, bearing in mind that the name had ever been Stockton, never Stockdon.

For the first ten years of his married life Richard devoted himself chiefly to the law and to his family. Politics had little appeal for him. "The publick is generally unthankful," he wrote to Joseph Reed in 1764, "and I will never become a servant of it, till I am convinced that by neglecting my own affairs, I am doing more acceptable service to God and Man." But a man of ability, wealth, and position such as his can hardly avoid public service of many kinds, especially when it is in the tradition of his family. The mantle of John descended upon the shoulders of Richard and fitted them per-

23

fectly. Some years before Morven had been given its name the house had become a center of culture and influence, not only for the community but in the whole province. Even before his father's death Richard appears to have been active in raising funds for the college. Two years later, as one of its trustees, he is writing in urgent need of two hundred and twelve pounds, for which he will give a mortgage, to meet a payment due on the college land.

There were repair bills to be audited and paid, and more than once a new president to be secured with the promise of a salary of two hundred pounds in "proclamation money," about thirty pounds in perquisites, a large house, pasture, and firewood. For the college presidents died off in rapid succession in these years. Moreover, when the Royal governors visited Nassau Hall, as they did in 1758 and 1760, what house in the neighborhood was so fitting for their entertainment as Morven?

When permission was obtained from the New Brunswick Presbytery for the building of a church in the village, the subscription paper for its erection was written in a hand believed to be that of Richard Stockton and dated January 20, 1762, and he contributed "one acre of land to set the church on." A total of three hundred and twenty-nine pounds was raised in gifts ranging from three pounds up to fifty. The college cooperated in the project and took title to the building, which was eventually built on college land and became, upon its completion, a "sort of College Chapel Church," the president and professors acting as pastor and preachers.

Space for the students was reserved in the gallery that ran around three sides of the building, and it was agreed that the college should have free use of the church for three days each year for commencement. The building was of brick and stood on the present site of the First Presbyterian Church, but with its side to the street. The pulpit stood against the wall, opposite the two entrances, and the rest of the floor was occupied by pews that were owned by the townspeople, one of the two most expensive being the property of Richard Stockton, for which he paid twenty-two pounds, ten shillings.

With the French and Indian War came the nuisance, if not the hardship, of soldiers quartered on the inhabitants of the Princeton locality: sometimes as many as fifteen to a one-room house. In 1758 Richard drew up a petition against this practice and signed it along with his Stockton relatives Job, Joseph, Robert, and Samuel, and Elias Boudinot, his father-in-law. The war brought in its train the Stamp Act; and with it began to flow that tide which was to bring Richard Stockton lasting fame and final misfortune.

His legal attainments made it inevitable that he should be consulted on such a point of constitutional law as taxation without representation. His position on the subject was characterized by moderation and patience, and reflected the mood of his province, which had not suffered from a tyrannical Royal governor as New England had. The year before the Stamp Act Congress was held in New York Richard had suggested to Joseph Reed that American members be elected to Parliament. The next year he gave his opinion that Parliament had no authority whatever over the American colonies, since they were not represented in it.

When the question of sending delegates to the Stamp Act Congress was discussed at a session of the supreme court at Perth Amboy, certain lawyers resolved on a policy of passive resistance: to refrain from buying the stamps and to cease doing business. But Richard wrote to Speaker Ogden that delegates ought to be sent; otherwise "we shall not only look like a speckled bird among our sister Colonies, but we shall say implicitly that we think it [the Stamp Act] no oppression." It was he who drafted the provincial assembly's petition to the King on the subject that November—a document that appears never to have been presented, since the hated act was repealed the following March. And he was soon to become so much of a republican that he considered William Pitt, the Great Commoner, to have been degraded by his elevation to the House of Lords as Earl of Chatham.

Though he was now only thirty-six years old, his health had suffered so severely from steady application to business both public and private that he was advised by his physicians to seek recuperation in a trip abroad. He left his wife at home, for she was unwilling to leave her children; and one has only to read Benjamin Franklin's "Precautions for a Sea Voyage" to understand the risks she would have run in taking them on a trans-Atlantic crossing.

"To begin with," the sagacious author of *Poor Richard's Almanac* advises, "do not tell people you are going, or callers will prevent your making proper preparations." Next, be careful to choose a good captain. The traveler should bring his own supply of water in bottles, to keep it sweet; also his own tea, chocolate, cider, and his favorite wine; also dried raisins, almonds, sugar, citrons, rum, eggs dipped in oil, and bread that has been sliced and twice baked. Live poultry gets tough during the voyage, Franklin warns, for the sailors stint the fowls of water. So it is better to take along sheep or hogs. And since the worst sailor is generally made the cook, it is well to have a lamp and a broiler, with spirits of wine for fuel, and a small tin-plate oven, and cook for one's self. A two-pound shot, he adds, will mash the dried peas by rolling in the kettle.

Doubtless Richard neglected none of these precautions: the Stocktons never stinted themselves of creature comforts, and his devoted wife surely saw to it that he was well provided with them. His voyage was a prosperous one of only twenty-six days. But trans-Atlantic mail service had still to be established. The transmission of letters was still dependent on the good offices of some accommodating sea captain. On one occasion, though Richard made the rounds of the American coffee houses in London, a vessel bound for Boston was the best he could find for that purpose. So Annis doubtless waited long and anxiously before his first letter, dated August 7, 1766, came to her.

In it he told her of what he had seen of the sights of London, and under the same cover he forwarded a letter to Governor Franklin—Benjamin Franklin's illegitimate son William—which he left unsealed, so that she could read it. Several weeks later came a letter written on the 20th of August. His health and appetite were now excellent, he wrote. He had been to Dublin and Cork and had bought a supply of Irish linen for her and for Governor Franklin's lady.

The Governor had given him a letter to a London publisher, introducing "Mr. Stockton . . . a considerable lawyer," and asking that he might be given "a sight of Samuel Johnson and a few more of your authors . . . for we Americans, when we go to England have as much curiosity to see a live Author, as Englishmen have to see a live Ostrich or a Cherokee Sachem." Richard went to the play at Covent Garden or Drury Lane about once a week, doubtless saw Garrick in *Hamlet*, probably heard Chatham and Burke speak in Parliament; and certain commissions that had been entrusted to him brought him into contact with the great world and high society.

He presented to King George III in person an address by the trustees of the College of New Jersey, was consulted by Rockingham and other prominent statesmen about colonial affairs, and, with Benjamin Franklin, who was in London as colonial agent for Pennsylvania, conferred with the London merchants on the issue of paper money by the colonies and an act of Parliament forbidding it. A plan to raise more money from the colonies made him "exceedingly fear," he wrote, "that we shall get together by the ears." But when he was questioned about America by one of the secretaries of state, he rejoiced that he had nothing to ask of the government "and therefore dare speak my sentiments without cringing. Whenever I can serve my native country," he went on, "I leave no occasion untried."

Of all that he saw and did he wrote copiously to his "Emelia," signing his letters "Lucius." And it probably did not astonish her to gather that, wherever he went, he was well received. Tall and of a commanding presence, with the carriage of the accomplished swordsman and horseman that he was, his handsome features and dignified and simple but "highly polished" manners made him generally acceptable. He had an interesting interview with Lord Chesterfield. The Marquis of Rockingham entertained him at his country seat in Yorkshire. He was a guest at several other great country houses, and attended the Queen's birth-night ball and other brilliant social functions.

Stories of his social successes reached Philadelphia in due course, and Annis, who had been there on a visit, wrote of how people had teased her about them. He replied that she should have laughed at "those idle people . . . who would persuade you that I prefer the elegance of England to the sylvan shades of America. No, my dearest Emelia, the peaceful home that God has blessed me with at Princeton, you and the sweet children you have brought me are sources from which I receive my highest earthly joys. . . ."

"I see not a sensible, obliging tender wife," he wrote in another letter, "but the image of my dear Emelia is full in view. I see not a haughty imperious ignorant dame, but I rejoice that the partner of my life is so much her opposite. . . . Kiss my dear sweet children, and give the hardest squeeze to my son. . . . Tell Dick I will bring him a laced hat and each of the girls something. Adieu, my dearest Emelia, may Heaven protect you and your dear little family until I meet you." Of the birth-night ball he wrote: "Here I saw all your Duchesses of Ancaster, Hamilton, etc., so famous for their beauty. But here I have done with this subject. For I had rather ramble with you along the rivulets of Morven or Red Hill and see the rural sports of the chaste little frogs, than again be at a birth-night ball."

She and his home, indeed, seem to have been seldom out of his thoughts. He can have overlooked few opportunities for the embellishment of the house, its grounds, and its gardens. From this trip presumably came the Morven state china of dark blue willow-ware, now so rare. For the garden he sent home "a little box of flower seeds and the roots that will do at this season, with the hope that these will please you for the present, but I really believe you have as fine tulips and hyacinths in your little garden as any in England." He was making "a charming collection of bulbous roots" to send when the danger of freezing was over. "Suppose, in the next place," he went on, "I inform you that I design to ride to Twickenham . . . to view Mr. Pope's garden and grotto . . . and that I shall take with me a gentleman who draws well to lay down the exact plan of the whole." The garden was much as the poet had left it, and the consequences of that excursion were to affect Morven in one way and another for generations to come.

To all this Annis replied in long and frequent letters filled with news about the children and domestic matters, which he read eagerly. She wrote him verses, of which he wrote to her: "Your verses to me give me great pleasure." And well they might, if "An Epistle to Mr. Stockton" may be assigned to this period. The concluding stanza runs as follows:

"But if the powers of genius ever heard
A votary's prayer, and e'er that prayer prefer'd,
On me may wit and elegance bestow
Some emanation bright, some softer glow,
Some sweet attractive that my heart may twine,
Stronger than beauty, with each nerve of mine.
For, oh, I find on earth no charms for me
But what's connected with the thought of thee."

From London Richard traveled to Edinburgh, where his experiences ranged from a public dinner at which he was the guest of the Lord Provost and council and received the freedom of the city, to one night in the blind and filthy streets of "auld reeky," when he routed with his small sword a ruffian who attempted to rob him. The purpose of this northern journey was to secure a new president for the College of New Jersey. Since Richard's departure from America his old friend and former teacher, President Finley, had died. The trustees had elected the Reverend John Witherspoon, D.D., of Paisley, to succeed him, and had sent the letter informing him of his election to Richard with the request that he present it to Doctor Witherspoon in person and urge him to accept.

The mission was not an easy one. At Paisley Richard had the freedom of the town conferred upon him, but neither Doctor Witherspoon nor his friends knew anything of the importance of the College of New Jersey. Back in London, on March 17, 1767, Richard wrote to Annis that the reverend doctor might, moreover, have been completely discouraged by "an artful, plausible, but wickedly contrived letter, sent from Philadelphia to a gentleman in Edinburgh." And when Doctor Witherspoon appeared to be persuaded, his wife remained obdurate. She refused even to discuss the matter, though Richard traveled the fifty miles from Edinburgh to Paisley for that express purpose. She was, her husband explained, "owing to a certain greatness of mind, averse to changing place."

But, Richard continued in his letter to Annis, "I have taken most effectual measures to make her refusal very troublesome to her. I have engaged all the eminent clergymen in Edinburgh and Glasgow to attack her in her intrenchments, and they are determined to take her by storm, if nothing else will do." To this epistolary bombardment and the persuasions of Benjamin Rush, who took time out from his medical studies at Edinburgh for the purpose, the lady capitulated. When Richard returned home the following September, the new president of the College of New Jersey and his stubborn helpmeet were not long in following him.

## "In a State of Splendor"

Richard brought home with him presents that must have required care and thoughtfulness in their selection. There was the promised "laced hat" that little Dick had set his three-year-old heart upon, and "something pretty for the little girls." For his wife he had been at pains to find the best paste for making floral designs out of shells, an art that was occupying the leisure of the ladies of the time. And among other commissions, he had executed for her one that would have been maddening to a less devoted spouse. This concerned a gown which she had sent over with him to be dyed green but which, since the English ladies had persuaded him that green would make it look "badly watered," he had ordered to be dyed "a pompadour" crimson.

But best of all, perhaps, was the plan of Alexander Pope's garden at Twickenham. This entailed the construction of a grotto, and for its decoration he had collected such rare and curious items as a Roman brick from the top of Dover Castle, a piece of wood from the five-hundred-year-old effigy of Archbishop Peckham at Canterbury, a piece of the King's coronation chair, and "the best cement for sticking shells in a large way."

Annis was delighted with the plan. Morven and its surroundings promised to lend themselves nicely to its application to them. The King's Highway—the present Stockton Street—corresponded to the Thames before the house at Twickenham. The Chestnut Walk, extending from the present Bayard Lane to the present Library Place, ran like the road from London to Hampton Court, which separated Pope's villa from his garden. The position of the slave quarters answered to that of the poet's garden house; and in the same relative positions as at Twickenham lay the vineyard, the kitchen garden, "the groves," and the orchard.

Work on the project began as soon as the season made it possible. The shade trees that they planted were the same as Pope's: cedars of Lebanon, cypresses, royal walnuts, Spanish chestnuts, yews, mulberries, and boxwood; and there were willows that sprang from cuttings of the willows that Lady Mary Wortley Montagu had presented to Pope and thus made a fashionable adornment in the design of embroidery, mourning jewelry, and the background of miniatures. Though there was no lack of servants for the work, both Richard and Annis made it a labor of love as far as their time and strength permitted, and after Richard's death Annis was to write sorrowfully of the "fragrant bowers planted by his hand."

Their good life together, busy, prosperous, and happy, began again. They lived, as one historian of the family has described it, in "a state of splendor." But it was a splendor that was graced by a warm and open hospitality, and they seem to have been better able than most wealthy people to avoid becoming the slaves of their possessions. Among their pleasures were visits to Philadelphia, where Annis had made a friend of bluestocking Elizabeth Graeme, of nearby Graeme Park. Elizabeth had been to England and met Lawrence Sterne and other literary celebrities, and on her return had set up the earliest American salon. She wrote verses which she was not alone in taking seriously. Annis was among the ardent admirers of them and, addressing her as Laura, wrote on one occasion:

> "Permit a sister muse to soar
> To heights she never tried before,
> And then look up to thee."

To Annis, addressed as Emelia, Laura reciprocated in the fashion of the day with literary extracts and a journal of her thoughts, which helped Annis through a severe illness.

But as the months slipped by, Richard had less and less time to devote to his home life. In addition to the task of picking up the law practice necessarily neglected in his absence, public honors brought with them public duties. The year after his return Governor Franklin made him a member of the Supreme Royal Legislative, Judiciary, and Executive Council of the province, and in 1774 he, who had always dressed with quiet elegance, donned the splendid robes of a judge of the provincial supreme court. But although he enjoyed the favor of the Royal government and the confidence of his friends on both sides of the quarrel, his position on the council became more and more difficult as relations worsened between the colonies and the mother country.

To Elizabeth Graeme, Annis had written in January 1769 complaining of a cold she had caught by getting her feet wet on the ferry boat on her return from a visit to Philadelphia, and had added that she was sorry to see that "we are in very Bad Bread the other side of the water." British troops had already occupied Boston. Seventeen-seventy saw the "Boston Massacre" and Lord North prime minister. By 1773 John Hancock, Samuel Adams, and Patrick Henry had come out for separation. The Boston Tea Party provoked the passage of the Boston Port Bill and the first Continental Congress met at Philadelphia a year later.

It was in this very year that Richard accepted his judgeship on the supreme court. A vigorous upholder of the rights of the colonies, he was nevertheless an equally strong advocate of moderate measures by both parties. But he received little support from other members of the council. Of these, three followed the Governor in his subservience to the Crown; four were neutral; only two, John Stevens and Francis Hopkinson, stood with Richard in his championship of the American cause. On December 12, 1774, he drew up and sent to Lord Dartmouth, Secretary for the Colonies, "An Expedient for the Settlement of the American Disputes," which was in fact a plan for the self-government of America, independent of Parliament but still owing allegiance to the English Crown. If something of the kind were not done, he warned the noble lord, the result would be "an obstinate, awful, and tremendous war."

When the general assembly and the council met at Perth Amboy early in the following year, he and William Livingston drew up a conciliatory answer to the speech of the Governor, which had itself been conciliatory. But by March Governor Franklin was complaining that Livingston and Richard's brother-in-law, Elias Boudinot, were stirring up the members of the assembly to get official approbation of delegates for the second Continental Congress and thus influence the New York Assembly.

Even in his own town Richard's moderate attitude must have made his position difficult. Within sight and earshot of Morven's windows the spirit of revolution flamed and crackled. In July 1770 James Madison, then an undergraduate, wrote of the students' demonstration against "the base conduct of the merchants of New York in breaking through their splendid resolutions not to import. . . . The letter to the merchants of Philadelphia requesting their concurrence was lately burned by the students of this place in the college yard, all of them appearing in their black gowns and the bell tolling," and "all of them in American cloth." Four years later New Jersey echoed the Boston Tea Party with a similar function at Greenwich, and the Princeton students burned the college steward's whole winter supply of tea, together with an effigy of Governor Hutchinson with a tea canister about his neck, in a fire on the campus, to the tolling of the college bell.

Spending an August Sunday at Princeton that year, John Adams sent a card to John Dickinson Sergeant, a rising young lawyer, son of the college treasurer, and Sergeant came to the Hudibras Inn and drank coffee with him. "I heard Witherspoon all day," Adams recorded; and he may well have found both men sympathetic with his belief that the colonies ought to be independent. For next May Sergeant became secretary of the provincial congress that met at Trenton, and Witherspoon, who had been a Jacobite prisoner after Prince Charlie's rebellion, was ardently for revolution.

Both Sergeant and Witherspoon remained warm friends of Richard's, however. So did Frederick Frelinghuysen, though both he and Sergeant were members of the Committee of

Safety, which began its sessions at Princeton in August 1775. April of that year had brought news of Lexington, but Richard was not one of the five influential Princeton citizens who attended the provincial congress. Bunker Hill was fought; the second Continental Congress rejected Lord North's tardy "conciliatory measures" and elected George Washington commander in chief of the Continental armies. Boston was besieged. The expeditions of Arnold and Montgomery set out for Canada. In November the First New Jersey Continental Regiment, under the command of William Alexander, who claimed the title of Lord Stirling, occupied Elizabeth Town. But Richard continued to hold his offices in court and council until the revolution put an end to those institutions, as it shortly did.

This, however, made no breach between him and his brother-in-law. Their difference of opinion, like that between him and most of his other friends, was one of degree rather than kind. Boudinot, a member of the Committee of Correspondence, had managed to send Washington a shipment of powder that was desperately needed by the army besieging Boston. He became Lord Stirling's aide-de-camp. But he still hoped that Britain and the colonies might come to terms without further bloodshed, and as late as April 1776 he so successfully opposed Witherspoon in an informal debate at New Brunswick that of the thirty-six present at the meeting all but three or four voted against a resolution favoring separation from Great Britain.

Meanwhile that force that neither war nor any other calamity can long resist had lighted with a brief gleam of old-time gaiety the menacing gloom that had begun to lower over Morven. Daughter Julia, not yet seventeen years old but precocious both mentally and physically, heiress to her mother's brains and charm, and already acknowledged to be the beauty of the family, had won the heart of the distinguished Philadelphia physician Benjamin Rush.

Rush had been graduated from the College of New Jersey

at fifteen, the year after Julia was born. After several years' apprenticeship to a doctor in Philadelphia he had taken his medical degree at the University of Edinburgh in 1768 and had returned to Philadelphia to establish himself in a highly successful practice there. A favorite of Richard and Annis in his undergraduate days, he had been a frequent visitor at Morven in the years that followed, and had first held Julia in his arms when he had carried her, a little girl of four, home from a college commencement where she had fallen asleep. One August day eleven or twelve years later, Richard and Annis drove to an outlying tavern to welcome him on a visit of special significance and, in spite of the fourteen years' difference between his age and their daughter's, emphasized their approval of the match by giving them a brilliant wedding in January 1776.

Six months later, the bride's father, the bridegroom, and Doctor Witherspoon, the officiating minister, signed the Declaration of Independence. Exactly a year after the wedding Doctor Rush was dressing wounds on a battlefield within cannon-shot of Morven; Doctor Witherspoon was a refugee; Richard Stockton, his health ruined by imprisonment, had been forced to relinquish the cause for which he had suffered; Princeton had been ravaged by fire and sword; Morven had been pillaged and its east wing left a roofless, blackened ruin. Six troubled, dreary years were to pass before any such happy times as Julia's wedding were to return to Annis's and Richard's beloved home—and he would not be there to share them with her.

Richard Stockton, Jr., the Old Duke, 1764-1828. By Edward
Ludlow Mooney. Princeton University.

Richard Stockton, the Signer, 1730-81. Probably by
John Wollaston. Princeton University.

Annis Boudinot Stockton, 1736-1801. By an unidentified artist.
Princeton University.

Robert Field Stockton, the Commodore, 1795-1866. By Thomas Sully. Princeton University.

# CHAPTER III

## "The End of All Perfection"

IN later years, Benjamin Rush, forthright and untroubled
by legal niceties, said that his father-in-law was "timid
where bold measures were required," but that he was always
devoted to his country's liberties. Richard's course, until he
felt himself compelled to withdraw from the struggle, proved
that he meant every word when he wrote to Annis from England in 1766: "Whenever I can serve my native country I
leave no occasion untried"; and the year 1776 brought one
occasion after another that could not be met with half measures.

January saw Governor Franklin actually, though not formally, a prisoner in his house at Perth Amboy, guarded by
Lord Stirling's soldiers. In February Stirling's regiment
marched to garrison New York, which was obviously General
Howe's next major objective. The British were forced to
evacuate Boston in March. In the early summer Sir Henry
Clinton's expedition against Charleston was beaten off by Fort
Moultrie, and by mid-June the ships of Howe's great fleet
had filled the Lower Bay at New York.

By that time a provincial congress was in session at Burlington. It ordered the Governor to be placed under arrest
and brought before it under military guard. "The Governor,"
according to the Reverend Doctor Ashbel Green, "treated the
Congress with marked indignity," which so aroused the ire of
Doctor Witherspoon that he let loose upon Franklin "a copi-
ous stream of irony and sarcasm, reflecting on the Governor's
want of proper early training in liberal knowledge, and
alluding to an infirmity in his pedigree." The Governor was
deposed, denounced as an enemy of the liberties of the people,
and finally shipped off to Connecticut as a prisoner.

On June 28 Richard Stockton, John Witherspoon, Francis
Hopkinson, Abraham Clark, and John Hart were seated as

delegates from New Jersey in the Continental Congress. There Richard is said to have made a short speech in favor of the Independence that was declared six days later; and his young son Richard never forgot the enthusiasm with which, on his return home, he described John Adams as "the Atlas of Independence" who sustained the debate and demonstrated the expediency of the measure. Princeton, town and college, celebrated the event on July 9. "Nassau Hall," the *Philadelphia Evening Post* reported, "was grandly illuminated, and independency proclaimed under a triple volley of musketry, and universal acclamation for the prosperity of the United States . . . with the greatest decorum."

The provincial congress had adopted a constitution for the new-born state, and on August 27, the very day of the Battle of Long Island, the first state legislature met at Princeton and proceeded to elect a governor. The first vote was a tie between Richard Stockton and William Livingston; the second gave Livingston the office by one vote. Richard was elected chief justice but declined, preferring to keep his seat in the Continental Congress instead.

It was no sinecure that he had chosen. He was back at Morven on the 1st of October but deep in the problem of paying for clothes for the army; and soon after, with the military rank of colonel, he set off, accompanied by George Clymer, of Philadelphia, on the arduous task of inspecting the troops that were guarding the Albany frontier against invasion from Canada. At Saratoga, he wrote to Abraham Clark, he found the New Jersey contingent "marching with cheerfulness, but great part of the men barefooted and barelegged"; and there was not a single shoe or stocking to be had in that part of the world "or I would ride a hundred miles through the woods and purchase them with my own money." It was the 10th of November, after a visit to Ticonderoga, before he could write to John Hancock, President of the Congress, that he and his companion had "gone through with their business" and were on the way home.

## "The End of All Perfection"

They left Albany on the 21st. On the 23rd Richard was appointed on a congressional committee of five to see that the Board of War attended at once to the pressing business of sending reenforcements to Washington. But more fundamental responsibilities now claimed his attention. Throughout his travels in the north he must have been haunted by fears for the wife and little children to whom the fighting drew steadily closer. Washington had been defeated on Long Island near the end of August, and early November must have brought Richard the news of White Plains, the capture of Fort Washington, and the evacuation of Fort Lee. As Richard traveled down the Hudson, Washington was retreating across New Jersey with the British close behind him, and Richard can hardly be blamed for making straight for his home to remove his family from the path of the enemy.

The ancient peace of Morven was shattered by preparations for immediate flight. With the British at New Brunswick there was time for little else. The Governor and the legislature had already fled to Trenton, thence to Burlington, and finally to Haddonfield, where they dispersed on the 2nd of December. On November 29, the day of the Stocktons' departure from Princeton, President Witherspoon bade the students of the college an affectionate farewell. But in the midst of packing the family silver and other treasured objects and seeing that they were safely buried in the garden, Annis remembered certain important and dangerous papers that had been deposited in Whig Hall. She fetched them secretly herself and hid them with the family valuables—a feat for which she was made the only woman member of the Whig Society.

Young Richard, now twelve years old, was left at home in the care of a trusted old servant. Why this was done is not clear. Perhaps he was ill. Or, it has been suggested, some sort of legal security may have been given the house by not leaving it entirely deserted by the family. On the other hand, there is a tradition that the old servant hid the boy in the woods. But that seems unlikely, considering the length of the British occupation of the village.

The rest of the family—Richard and Annis; the twin girls, now fifteen; Lucius Horatio, aged eight; and three-year-old Abigail—drove off for refuge in John Cowenhoven's "Federal Hall," thirty miles away in Monmouth County. All the leading patriots were leaving the town. Mrs. Witherspoon went in the "old family chair," with her husband riding his sorrel mare at its side. Doctor Bainbridge routed Mrs. John Dickinson Sergeant out at two o'clock in the morning and sent her away with her sister and her infant child. Her husband was with the Congress, which had retired to Baltimore. These fugitives, and others, sought safety across the Delaware by way of Howell's and McKonkey's ferries. Why Richard Stockton did not do the like is difficult to understand: Monmouth County, to which he fled, was notorious for its tory sentiments. Perhaps he was influenced by the fact that Washington, hard pressed though he was, had detached troops to keep the tories in order there. Or the assurance of Cowenhoven's hospitality at the end of the journey may have decided him. As it turned out he could hardly have made a worse choice of refuge.

In the middle of the second night after his arrival he and his host were dragged from their beds by a band of tories and delivered into the hands of the British at Perth Amboy. As a signer of the Declaration of Independence, Richard was treated with particular brutality, marched through the freezing weather to the common jail and sent thence to the Provost Jail in New York, where he was put in irons, kept without food for twenty-four hours, and then given only the coarsest fare. Reports of his ill-treatment were such that on January 3 of the new year the Congress directed Washington to send a protest against it to General Howe, if he found reason to believe them. But by that time or a few days later Richard was set free.

On November 30 Sir William Howe and his brother,

Admiral Lord Howe, had proclaimed a full pardon, with the assurance of their liberty and the enjoyment of their property, to all who within sixty days would swear to "remain in a peaceful Obedience to His Majesty and not take up arms, nor encourage Others to take up arms, in Opposition to His Authority." Richard, sick, worn out by the hardships of his captivity, and harassed by anxiety for his family, took this oath. Early in January he and his wife and children were back in their beloved Morven—or in what the British occupation had left of it. "God be thanked that it is not worse with us," Annis wrote near the end of February to Elizabeth Graeme, who was now the wife of the tory Henry Hugh Ferguson, "but I assure you that it is quite bad enough." A great comfort must have been the presence of her beloved son-in-law, Benjamin Rush, who was at the house when the family arrived and had doubtless done what he could to make it habitable for them.

Writing on the 7th of January, after three days of caring for the wounded of the battle on the 3rd, Doctor Rush said Princeton looked like "a deserted village" and "as if desolated with plague and earthquake" as well as war. Nassau Hall and the Presbyterian church had been used as barracks during the three weeks in which the British had occupied the place. The soldiers had wrecked the college library and museum and the celebrated orrery and had burned the church pews for firewood. Quartermaster Robert Stockton's Constitution Hill had been stripped of furnishings, produce, and equipment. Mr. Sergeant's fine, new house a few hundred yards from Morven had been burned to the ground, and at Morven Doctor Rush estimated Richard's loss, including horses, cattle, and sheep, to be not less than five thousand pounds.

Morven had been Cornwallis's headquarters for his two brief stays at Princeton, and the headquarters of Colonel William Harcourt, of the Sixteenth Dragoons, the captor of General Charles Lee, for the rest of the time. Although the house itself was unharmed, it had been sacked and pillaged. Furniture, clothes, and pictures were gone, the wine cellar looted. The portraits of the master and mistress of the house had been torn from their frames, slashed, and bayoneted, and thrown outdoors. Most tragic of all, the valuable library of a book-loving family, and their personal papers, had been burned, defaced, or forever lost.

A faithless servant, or perhaps one under duress, had revealed to the enemy soldiers two of the buried chests of valuables, and these had been looted. But one had remained hidden, and in it, together with other silver, was the highly prized tankard bearing the family coat of arms. Annis's two favorite books, her Bible and Young's *Night Thoughts*, were among the few volumes salvaged; but searching among the straw that had made the soldiers' beds, she collected many of the letters her husband had written to her during his various absences.

From the ruin of his home Richard looked out upon what many a man would have regarded as the ruin of his career. To himself, doubtless, the course he had taken to obtain his liberty seemed a reasonable one. He had signed under duress. The alternative was a long imprisonment, liability to execution as a traitor by the barbarous punishment of hanging, drawing, and quartering, and the confiscation of his property, which would have reduced his wife and five young children to penury. And except as a martyr, he could have been of no more service to the American cause than if he were liberated under his promise not to serve it.

At first, however, his action was condemned by the generality of people. From Baltimore, on February 8, Abraham Clark wrote of it drily as Mr. Stockton's "late procedure"; and a month later President Witherspoon wrote to his son David: "I was at Princeton from Saturday s'en night till Wednesday. . . . Judge Stockton is not well in health and is much spoken against for his conduct. He signed Howe's

Declaration and gave his word of Honor that he would not meddle in the least in American affairs during the war. Mrs. Cochran was sent to the ennemies [*sic*] Lines by a Flag of truce, and when Mr. Cochran came out to meet his wife he said to the officers that went with the Flag that Judge Stockton had brought evidence to General Howe to prove that he was on his way to seek a protection when he was taken, this he denies to be true yet many credit it, but Mr. Cochran's known quarrel with him makes it very doubtful to candid persons."

Common report, moreover, may have attributed to him some of the exploits of a distant cousin, Major Richard Witham Stockton, of Courtlandt Skinner's "perfidious corps," a particularly obnoxious tory, who was captured that February and kept in irons until Washington put a stop to it, since he had been taken in arms.

But evidently people were then less inclined to be censorious of the decisions of others than they are in wartime today. Gouverneur Morris, for instance, was only twenty-four years old and perfect officer material both physically and mentally, but one finds no criticism of him for preferring to serve his infant country in the Congress rather than in the army. Discriminating people were not long forgetful of the services Richard Stockton of Morven had rendered to the cause of Independence. Up at Morristown Washington took time out from his struggle to raise a new army to issue a general order on February 3, instructing all officers and soldiers who possessed bonds or other papers belonging to Richard Stockton to deliver them to the adjutant general. After the victory at Princeton the American soldiers had been free to roam about the village and its surroundings for two or three hours, and the thought behind Washington's order was, evidently, that some of them might have picked up in the ruins of Morven valuable documents belonging to Richard.

Richard promptly set about fulfilling his bargain with the enemy. Two days after his capture he had written out his resignation from the Continental Congress, in order, no doubt that the state legislature might fill his place without delay. But the legislature had dissolved before it could be delivered, and on February 10 he sent to the legislature, which was then sitting at Haddonfield, a second resignation, which was accepted.

That his influence with the Continental authorities was still considerable is evidenced by his moving in behalf of Annis's friend, Mrs. Ferguson—something that he would hardly have attempted otherwise. In the midst of his own troubles he remembered those of others. As the wife of a tory who now held a commission in the British army, Mrs. Ferguson was in danger of losing her property; and Richard had been at home only a few weeks when he wrote to her. He had been confined to his room for a week, he told her, and had ridden only as far as a near neighbor's the day before, but as soon as he was well enough he would visit her at Graeme Park. Meanwhile he sent her advice about her estate, and two years later he was striving to get leave for her to pass through the lines to bid farewell to her husband.

In contrast with the old days when the college was in being, when distinguished visitors kept dropping in, and when the "Flying Machine," the swift coach that made it possible to travel from New York to Philadelphia in twenty-four hours, changed horses there, life at Princeton must have been dreary enough this winter. Congressional and state investigations found that the losses inflicted by the British troops on the inhabitants of the village and its vicinity totaled between five and six thousand pounds, although the almost equal amount of damage to Morven was not included in these reports. Scudder's mills had been burned, entailing a loss of twelve hundred pounds. The damage to the Presbyterian church was listed at one hundred and sixty pounds, four shillings, and two pence. From early in January until the middle of June Continental troops under Putnam took over both church and college, and inflicted on them any damage that the British had failed to do, and in the following October the buildings became hospitals, in which Governor Livingston found "unparalleled mismanagement."

The community was continually harassed by the demands of the troops. Teams to haul firewood must be furnished "by impressment or otherwise" or "the soldiers will go out themselves and take them where they can find them." Forty wagons had to be furnished to move the sick and wounded to the base hospital at Bethlehem in Pennsylvania, and five two-horse sleighs to haul Indian meal. And over all, for the next eighteen months, hung the threat of a fresh advance by the British.

A system of alarm guns and beacons was established. When a British officer under a flag of truce spent a night in the village, Putnam had every house lighted and kept his few hundred soldiers moving about so conspicuously that the Britisher estimated their number at about five thousand. But Putnam had orders to retire across the Delaware if the enemy should advance, as Howe threatened to do in February. In the spring Sullivan arrived in the village with his division, and the fortifications that the British had built in the past December were reconstructed. Upon Howe's advance in June, however, Sullivan was ordered back into the Sourland hills, leaving the place practically undefended.

Amid these repeated threats of invasion Richard and Annis must have led a life of continual anxiety. Because he had signed Howe's protection papers, Richard's loyalty was doubted in these parlous times. In December 1777 he was called before the Council of Safety to take the oaths of abjuration and allegiance. The actions of other members of the family must have increased their uneasiness. Another Richard, son of the Signer's uncle, Samuel, was a notorious Tory, major in the New Jersey Volunteers, a Loyalist troop. At war's end he emigrated to St. John's, New Brunswick, becoming the progenitor of the Canadian Stocktons. Closer to home, a jury of twenty-four freeholders voted the confiscation of Springdale, the nearby plantation of Joseph Stockton, who had joined King George's forces.

Nearer relatives, however, Richard's brothers, Philip and Samuel Witham, were strong for Independence; and his cousin Robert Stockton was assistant quartermaster of the Continental army for the district. Robert's home was Constitution Hill, so called, it is believed, because the first constitution of the state was drafted under its roof. Upon his shoulders fell the enormous labor of supplying fuel, food, and transportation to the troops in the district.

With Howe's capture of Philadelphia in the early autumn of 1777, the military pressure on Princeton slackened. Even in the following summer the contending armies passed it by—the American to the north of the village, the British to the south of it—on their march to battle at Monmouth Court House. The place remained a military post until February 1779. But after that, troops used it only in passing, and although they did considerable damage during their brief stays, something closely resembling peace returned to the neighborhood. President Witherspoon had already got hold of a number of prisoners of war belonging to Scottish regiments and kept them hard at work repairing college and church. In the fall of '77 the state legislature returned to Princeton, which remained the seat of the state government for the next eleven years. In the spring of '78 soldiers and citizens illuminated the village at the joyful news of the alliance with France.

At Morven time and hard work went far to repair the ruin wrought by war. Fields, gardens, and orchards had lost none of their old-time productivity. The slashed portraits, skillfully repaired, were restored to their old places; the furnishings were repaired or new pieces purchased to replace those which had been destroyed. By the winter of 1777-1778, the house was fit to receive Doctor Rush and his wife Julia, now a matron of eighteen, who sought refuge there with their baby when the British occupied Philadelphia. In annoyance at what he considered the mismanagement of the army medical department, the doctor had resigned his position as physician general. The following June, Richard's sister Hannah, Elias Boudinot's wife, came on a visit. The Boudinots had prospered rapidly and greatly in the sixteen years since their marriage. But the war had driven them from "the Great House" at Elizabeth Town, which Elias had bought, with his brother-in-law's help, in 1772, to the rather doubtful safety of a farm at Basking Ridge; and Elias had spent the winter of 1777-78 at Valley Forge as commissary of prisoners.

So short-lived appears to have been the public resentment at the course Richard had taken that it is to be doubted that either Governor Livingston or the members of the Legislature hesitated to avail themselves of Morven's hospitality during these years. Of the letters Richard wrote at this time, none of the few still existing contain any evidence that he felt himself to be under a cloud of disapproval. His health improved, and with it came something of his former strength. He resumed his law practice and traveled as far as Philadelphia on legal business. In February 1780 young Robert Troup proposed to equally young Aaron Burr, who had lately resigned from the army, that they study law under Mr. Stockton at Princeton. Actually they became pupils of Richard's former student William Paterson. But the change of plan may well have been owing to circumstances in Richard's life more deadly than any loss of reputation could have been.

One bitter winter's day Richard had ridden home from Somerset Court House, where he had been on legal business, with severely chapped lips and, in the lower one, a deep crack that resisted all efforts to heal it. On November 30, 1778, just two years after his capture by the British, he wrote to his "Dear Emelia" from Philadelphia: "I hoped to have finished at Gloucester last Saturday, but must return this week for a few days; after that I must pay all my attention to my poor lip, it is not worse I think than when I left you, but my mind

47

is in a continued state of uneasiness about it—for your sake and that of the dear children, as well as my own, I trust God that I may be relieved." But he adds: "I have got your muff and tippet, and shall attend to your other memorandums, for all your *requests* within my power, have the effect of *commands*." And anxious though he was, it was at this time that he strove to relieve Mrs. Ferguson's distress about her husband. He concluded casually enough: "I hope to be able to return sometime next week, the day I cannot fix, but perhaps may write you again before that time—love to the children all—Your most affectionate Richard Stockton."

So his next letter must have had the effect of a bombshell when it arrived at Morven.

"Phila, Wed 9th Dec 1778

"My dear Love

"I have carefully concealed from you the state of my lip for some time past, until by the blessing of God I could give you some agreeable tidings. I have now the pleasure to inform you that yesterday, at one o'clock, the malignant part was extracted by Dr Jones, in the presence of several others of the faculty, whom I had consulted. You'll readily conceive the anxiety of mind I have possessed since I left you—for upon my first coming to this town, I found that it must be cut out. Dr. Jones concluded to attend me at home, *at first*; but I well knew the additional distress I should receive from the anxiety which would fill you, and the children—I therefore very speedily concluded to have it done here, and in the meantime to prevent your distress by concealing it from you. I trust God that it is totally extracted, for they have made a large hole in my lip—they say it will grow up again. I thank God for the fortitude and patience he was pleased to grant me *before* and *at the time* of the operation. I did not utter a sigh, or move a muscle. I have also abundant reason to bless God for the ease and comfort I feel now—I have not the least pain, and a comfortable night, the last.—I was uneasy for about two hours after the operation, but the anodine [*sic*] they gave me immediately upon tying up the wound, composed me, and I feel as easy today, as I ever did in my life—as an evidence of it, I have come down from my chamber and am writing this in the parlour.

"I am thus particular as I know how greedily you will catch at everything that gives you any information respecting this interesting [illegible]. I cannot be certain of the day in which I shall return home; but it may be sometime next week —perhaps by the middle. In the midst of my own distresses I have been much concerned to hear, by Polly's letter, that you have had the rheumatism: I hope it has been of short duration—my love to the Girls, and all the lesser children— poor little creatures! I know how much they will feel for me, among the rest. Julia [Mrs. Rush, at whose house he was evidently staying] was remarkably preserved yesterday in a fall of the top of a Chest of drawers, while she was pulling out the bottom drawer—she [illegible] and fainted, but received no considerable hurt, as they went over her head— God be praised for his repeated mercies. Adieu my dearest, and be assured of my unremitting and constant affection."

It was eight o'clock in the evening when Annis received that letter, but whatever the state of her rheumatism, she was well on her way to Philadelphia before the late December dawn of the next day. She arrived to find her husband doing as well as could be expected but his physicians in marked disagreement. Doctor Jones had prescribed a most meagre diet and had forbidden wine. Doctor Rush remonstrated. Such a total change of diet for a man nearly fifty years old, who had always lived well, would probably produce a "scrofulous tumor" in the neck, he contended, which might be more dangerous than the lip would ever have been. But Jones was considered to be the best surgeon in America, and Richard, despite Annis's persuasion, followed Jones's orders. On April 10 of the new year Richard wrote to his sister, Hannah Boudinot, of "an

ugly kernel in my throat, which the Doctor says is an appendage of the complaint in my lip." While he awaited Jones's
return from a three-month trip up the Hudson, it grew
amazingly. A second trip to Philadelphia became necessary.
Dr. Bond operated. But it was too late.

Throughout the next two years Richard was never free
from pain unless under the influence of anodynes, and near
the end of 1780 his agony had become such that Annis wrote
to Elizabeth Ferguson that she was "confined to the chamber
of a dear and dying husband, whose nerves have become so
irritable as not to be able to bear the scraping of a pen . . . or
even the folding of a letter." In her commonplace book she
gave utterance to her grief:

> "While through the silence of the gloomy night
> My aching heart reverb'rates every groan,
> And watching by the glimmering taper's light,
> I make each sigh, each mortal pang my own.
>
> .    .    .    .    .    .    .
>
> Oh! could I take the fate to him assigned,
> And leave the helpless family their head!
> How pleased, how peaceful to my lot resigned,
> I'd quit the nurse's station for the bed."

A few weeks later, in the beginning of 1781, the mutinous
Pennsylvania troops from Washington's army at Morristown,
thirteen hundred of them, with cannon, marched into Princeton. Under the command of their sergeants they maintained
perfect order and discipline, hanged as spies the emissaries
Sir Henry Clinton sent to persuade them to enter the British
service, and, through Wayne and a committee of Congress,
peaceably adjusted their grievances. But little, if any, of all
this can have percolated to the mind of the sufferer in the
bedchamber above the drawing room where he and Annis
had celebrated their daughter's wedding five years before;
and on the last day of February, 1781, death freed him from
his torment.

## "The End of All Perfection"

The grief at his death was general and sincere. The action that had brought upon him the hasty condemnation of many was forgotten in sorrow for the loss of one who had been a great and good friend to all. They crowded to his funeral. The service was held in the college chapel, and the Reverend Doctor Samuel Stanhope Smith, Vice President of the college and son-in-law of President Witherspoon, delivered the eulogy, on a text that Annis chose from Psalm 119, verse 96: "I have seen an end of all perfection, but thy commandment is exceeding broad."

It was one of Richard Stockton's "earliest honors," said Doctor Smith, "to have been a son of this college, and it was one of the first honors of this college to have given birth to such a son. . . . Another of the fathers of learning and eloquence is gone. . . . In council he was wise and firm, but always prudent and moderate. . . . The office of a Judge of the Province was never filled with more integrity and learning than it was by him . . . a man who has long been foremost in his country, for power, for wisdom, and for fortune."

They buried him among his forebears in the old Quaker Meeting House burial ground. But if any monument marked his grave, it is long since gone, and the location of the grave is now unknown.

# CHAPTER IV

## "Ye Stately Elms! And Lofty Cedars! Mourn"

ANNIS'S grief was deep and lasting, but she dealt with it with the wisdom and courage that characterized her throughout her life. She had lost a husband who had been both lover and devoted companion for twenty-six years. But, suffering as he was, she could not wish him to have lived another day; and he had left her with responsibilities that demanded her best efforts to meet them. Each anniversary of his death she commemorated with a poem. Notable among them were "Anniversary Elegiac Ode" in 1782 and "Resignation, An Elegiac Ode" six years later.

The sincerity of her feeling shines through the artificiality of the form of its expression. One senses it even in the anapestic verses which she dashed off to Elizabeth Ferguson in a "Pastoral Elegy, First Day of Harvest, 1781":

> "Can Laura forget that this day
> Brings fresh to my woe-piercéd mind
> The hour that tore me away
> From Lucius, the constant and kind?"

And there is an undeniable dignity in the lines from one of the odes:

> "Ye stately Elms! and lofty Cedars! Mourn,
> How, through your avenues, you saw him borne,
> The friend who reared you, never to return."

But she was as far as possible from what in her day would have been described as repining. Her husband had named her as one of the executors of his will. She had Benjamin Rush and Elias Boudinot to help her, but the burden of managing the large landed estate fell necessarily upon her, although her eldest son, now seventeen, was doubtless able to see to many of the details of the work. She evidently rejoiced in the task and kept on with it even after he had married and become master of Morven in fact as well as in name.

Her twin girls, Mary and Susan, were now nearly twenty years old, Lucius Horatio thirteen, and Abigail eight. To have enclosed their lives in the retirement of widowhood would have been to deny them the advantages to which their wealth and position entitled them. Their mother made visitors welcome and entertained many. Her interest in the world without—her country's cause, and the war—continued unabated. "Though a female, I was born a patriot," she wrote to her brother Elias eight months after the death of her husband. Washington had for some years been her idol.

In a poem after the Battle of Princeton she had written of his "temp'rate zeal" and "saintlike patience" and called him:

> ". . . Thou the basis of this mighty fabric
> Now rising to the view, of arms, of arts,
> The seat of empire in the western world."

Probably she had already met him at that time. Certainly she did so in August 1781, when the French troops bivouacked at Princeton on their march to Yorktown and Washington and Rochambeau dined there, on the 29th. Upon the news of Cornwallis's surrender, the gentlemen of Princeton celebrated with a punch at Beekman's tavern. A salute of thirteen rounds was fired from a fieldpiece. There was an address by a professor of the college faculty. A public dinner was followed by thirteen toasts; and in the illumination of the village, which closed the celebration, one may be sure that Morven's windows shone as brightly as any.

Annis dashed off a letter to her brother Elias on receipt of the joyful tidings, though of late, she told him, she had seldom felt a gleam of joy on her own account. "Pardon this fragment," she went on, "but when the fit is on me I must jingle," and she enclosed a stanza of four rhymed couplets, with an alexandrine line to finish, in praise of Washington.

Expanded, these appeared as "by a Lady of New Jersey" in the *New Jersey Gazette* for the 28th of November that year and later were published in a long pastoral poem that she called "Lucinda and Aminta," for which Washington wrote her a letter of thanks in the following summer.

Among other distinguished visitors to Princeton about this time was the Marquis de Chastellux, a major general in Rochambeau's army. The village consisted of some sixty or eighty houses, he noted, and he was impressed by the "immense" size of Nassau Hall, which he approached through "a large square court surrounded with lofty palisades." President Witherspoon joined him there, and they talked in French, on Witherspoon's initiative, though the Marquis perceived that the reverend doctor's French had evidently come from reading rather than conversation. Morven, too, must have interested De Chastellux, if only by its name, for he was a devotee of Ossian. When he and Jefferson discovered that they both admired that poet, it was, he wrote, "as if a spark of electricity passed between us."

Late in June of 1783 Princeton changed overnight from a quiet country village to the bustling, overgrown capital of the United States. Badgered and threatened by mutinous Pennsylvania troops at Philadelphia and left without proper protection by the Pennsylvania authorities, the Continental Congress followed the suggestion of its president, Elias Boudinot, and adjourned to Princeton. Elisha, Elias's brother, rode in with his troop of horse to ensure their safety there, but his action was superfluous. All Jersey, and especially Princeton, received them with protestations of support and the most cordial welcome. The college gave them its "library room" in Nassau Hall for their meetings, and other rooms for the offices of the War Department and the Paymaster General. The members, usually about twenty-two in number, some of them with their wives and servants, crowded uncomfortably into the various inns and lodgings in private houses. President Boudinot established himself at Morven—later at Mr.

Woodruff's house opposite the college—and entertained so lavishly that his bills from one merchant alone amounted to a thousand dollars a month.

The vaunted republican simplicity of the Founding Fathers is something of a myth. Those people were accustomed to living and dressing well and to paying well for doing so; and the Princeton shopkeepers were prompt in supplying their wishes. Boudinot's first order to Thomas Stockton, the leading merchant, was for a side of lamb and a gallon of wine, which were supplemented next day with two more gallons of wine, seventeen pounds of sugar, and a couple of three-shilling "Juggs"; and his steward forwarded to him fifty lemons and fifty limes.

Undergraduate Ashbel Green wrote home of the constant passing of coaches and chaises in the street and a "crying about of pineapples, lemons, and every luxurious article both foreign and domestic." West Indian fancy goods and haberdashery were to be had at Enos Kelsey's. John Harrisson sold American and foreign cloths, silks, velvets, and calicos. Daniel Van Voorhis, a Philadelphia goldsmith, opened a shop east of the college, where he offered the latest thing in silver knee and shoe buckles, gold beads and chains, punch strainers and soup ladles. A Philadelphia dancing master, Monsieur D'Orssière, started a dancing school that flourished, at least until the college trustees forbade the students to attend it.

The members of congress entertained one another at private dinners and cozy wine parties at the Sign of the New Jersey College, at Jacob Bergen's Inn opposite Nassau Hall, and the Hudibras Tavern on the south side of the street. President Witherspoon's Tusculum attracted more serious gatherings, and Annis Stockton's gracious hospitality made Morven a social center. Under the flattering illumination of the wax candles that lighted the rooms, these assemblages, in which the men followed the fashion of the time in vying with the women in the brilliance of their dress, must have made charming scenes. At a reception at army headquarters up at

Morristown three years before this, Washington had appeared in black velvet, his wife in black lute-string. But his three aides wore plum color, blue, and dark green velvet, with white silk stockings, a profusion of lace at throat and wrists, and their hair in queues and powdered, while Kitty Livingston's yellow dress, it was said, "outshone the candles." As it had been known since the end of March that a general treaty of peace had been signed and the war was over, everybody was in a happy mood; and with such men as Madison, Alexander Hamilton, James McHenry, and the elegant Reverend Doctor Smith among the company, the conversation must have been as brilliant as the scene.

The village was full of officers on leave—the French noblemen De La Rouërie and Duportail, who had been serving in the American army since Brandywine days, and John Paul Jones, the most notable among them—who came seeking adjustment of claims against the United States. The Marquis de La Luzerne, the French ambassador, came up from Philadelphia from time to time and, with two counts, one Italian, the other Polish, and an Englishman on his travels, gave a cosmopolitan flavor to society.

Public and semipublic festivities were frequent. The Fourth of July was celebrated with an oratorical contest between the Cliosophic and American Whig societies and a dinner at Morven, at which President Boudinot entertained Monsieur de La Luzerne and between seventy and eighty other guests. The ceremonial thirteen toasts were drunk, each accompanied by a discharge of artillery, and there were fireworks on the campus later in the evening. Young Ashbel Green, who had spoken for Whig and was therefore among the guests, got back to his room in Nassau Hall just as the nine o'clock curfew was ringing. But it may be inferred that the festivities did not cease at that hour, for the next four days are a blank in the journal of the Congress.

Another high point in that summer was the public reception of Washington by the Congress, which had asked him to come to Princeton to advise it on the subject of a permanent military establishment. On August 23, accompanied by Mrs. Washington, he took up his residence at Rocky Hill, in "Rockingham," the house of the late Judge Berrien, while his modest escort of twelve New England cavalrymen pitched their tents on the lawn. Three days later, with these troopers behind him, he rode into Princeton on his "little, hard-pulling, double-bitted roan gelding," with its old crooked saddle and flowered saddlecloth of buff and blue. Main Street in front of the campus was packed with visitors who had come from as far as Philadelphia for the occasion. The black-gowned collegians, grouped around the door of Nassau Hall, cheered him as he entered. The gallery of the prayer hall was crowded; the floor was reserved for the members of Congress; and on the wall hung the empty frame of the portrait of George II, which Alexander Hamilton's cannon ball had destroyed in the fighting of January 3 six years before. Two members conducted Washington to a chair beside President Boudinot, who remained seated on the platform, with his hat on his head to symbolize the superiority of the civil authority over the military. When the General had seated himself, Boudinot proceeded to read an address of welcome. From the pocket of his close-fitting, skirted coat Washington drew his carefully written reply. He read it, and the simple ceremony was over.

There is no record of any banquet later in the day. But it is unlikely that a thing so customary on such occasions was omitted. If there was none, however, one may be sure that the hospitality of Morven filled its place. In either event this was a great day for Annis Stockton. She expressed her feelings in a poem headed "Morven, August the 26" and sent it out to "Rockingham."

> "Say; can a female voice an audience gain
> And Stop a moment thy triumphal car?
> And wilt thou listen to a peaceful Strain
> Unskilled to paint the horrid Scenes of war?"

she asked, after touching on his glory, his martial fame, and
his country's blessings on his head; and she continued:

> "The Motive only stamps the deed divine.
> But thy last legacy, renownéd Chief,
> Has decked thy brow with honors more Sublime,
> Twined in thy wreath the christian's firm belief."

Knowing that as soon as his work was done at Princeton he
planned to return to his beloved home in Virginia, she added:

> "Thus crown'd, return to Vernon's soft retreat;
> There, with Amanda, taste unmixed joy.
> May flowers Spontaneous rise beneath your feet,
> Nor Sorrow Ever pour her hard alloy."

And she ended on a wistful note:

> "And, oh, if happly in your native Shade
> One thought of Jersey Enters in your mind,
> Forget not *her* on Morven's humble glade,
> Who feels for you a friendship most refin'd."

She signed the poem with her old pen name Emelia.

Washington replied with a lightly humorous touch with
which he is rarely credited. She had sent an apologetic letter
along with the poem. So he began:

> "Rocky Hill, Sept. 2d, 1783

"You apply to me, my dear madam, for absolution, as
though I was your father confessor. . . . You have reason
good, for I find myself strongly disposed to be a very in-
dulgent ghostly adviser on this occasion, and not withstanding
'you are the most offending soul alive,' (that is, if it is a crime
to write elegant poetry,) yet if you will come and dine with
me on Thursday . . . I will strive hard to assist you in expiat-
ing these poetical trespasses on this side of purgatory. . . . I
will not dare to charge you with an intentional breach of the
rules of the decalogue in giving so bright a coloring to the

services I have been able to render my country, though I am
not conscious of deserving anything more at your hands than
what the purest and most disinterested friendship has a right
to claim; actuated by which, you will permit me to thank you,
in the most affectionate manner, for the kind wishes you have
so happily expressed for me and the partner of my domestic
enjoyments. Be assured we can never forget our friend at
Morven, and that I am, my dear madam, with every senti-
ment of friendship and esteem,

"Your most obedient and obliged servant,

"G. Washington."

Washington entertained frequently and lavishly at Rockingham. The dinners were excellent, for he had written to
Fraunces' Tavern in New York for a cook; and it was observed
that the host's geniality and vivacity were in marked contrast
with the "contracted, pensive" expression his face had worn
in wartime.

There was, of course, a return dinner for the General and
his wife at Morven; and to his charge that she had indulged
in fiction in praising him in her poem of August 26, Annis
replied on September 22, the day before the college commencement, begging him:

"Oh, charge me not with fiction in my lays,
For heavenly truth stood by and twin'd the bays,
Then bid me bind them on my heroes [*sic*] brow
And told me fame would every sprig allow."

That commencement was another great occasion. Congress
attended in a body. Washington was the most important guest.
He made the college a gift of fifty guineas, and the trustees
responded by commissioning Charles Willson Peale to paint
the General's portrait and ordering that, "when finished, it
be placed in the hall of the college, in the room of the late
king of Great Britain"; and there it hangs today. But, for
Annis, the central figure of the occasion was doubtless her son

Richard, now nineteen years old, who had been graduated in the class of 1779 and this day received the degree of Master of Arts.

A month later the Dutch minister Peter John Van Berckel, Burgomaster of Rotterdam, arrived and was received with all due ceremony. Again the prayer hall was packed with distinguished visitors—Washington, De La Luzerne, "and a number of ladies of the first character" among them—while a great crowd outside listened to the proceedings through the open doors. A round of banquets followed, President Boudinot giving two of them; and on Sunday afternoon Washington had Van Berckel, most of the Congressmen, and many officers of the army to dinner with him at Rockingham. Evidently the Dutch envoy seized upon such opportunities as there were to return these hospitalities. For although he remained at Princeton only five days, he wrote home stating that he had spent so much there on entertainment for the honor of his country that he would have to have more money.

After this burst of conviviality Princeton's role as capital of the United States drew rapidly to a close. The people were eager to have it continued, at least through the winter. Colonel George Morgan, of Prospect, compiled and delivered to the Congress a list of forty-two householders who were willing to let houses, rooms with fireplaces, and stabling, and would furnish breakfasts, teas, and dinners. Annis offered the whole of Morven, with the stables and coach room. But the New Jersey winter climate did not appeal to the Congressmen. On November 1 the session ended. The new Congress met two days later, elected Thomas Mifflin president, and adjourned to meet at Annapolis on the 26th of the month.

But Princeton was never again to be the rural, scholastic retreat that it had been. Not only did the state legislature continue to meet there until 1788; the battle that was the culmination of the most brilliant campaign of the late war had placed the village on the map of the world. Distinguished visitors, both American and foreign, civilian and military alike, were frequent. It had its own weekly newspaper, the *Princeton Packet and General Advertiser*, publication of which began in 1787. At Jacob Bergen's Tavern, not only the "New York Flying Machine" and other stages, but also the "New Wagons," changed horses while their passengers snatched a hasty breakfast or dinner. On the best of these vehicles that carried passengers between Newark and Phila-delphia, with four changes of horses, in a single day, the fare, including passage by boat from Newark to New York, was forty shillings in gold or silver.

The village still had only about a hundred houses. But the Reverend Manasseh Cutler, who put up at the Sign of the College in 1787, wrote of it that it was "a small town—or rather, has but a small number of houses in the most compact part." He noted a few large buildings but "none very ele-gant," and that the ground "descends considerably to the street from the college yard," which was "walled with stone and lime." Monsieur Moreau de Saint Méry, who visited the place seven years later, wrote of the *avant-cour* in front of Nassau Hall as being filled with the dung of browsing ani-mals and surrounded by a brick wall with pilasters topped by gray wooden urns, some of which had fallen to the ground. But in the same year as that of Cutler's visit Miss Rachel Bradford wrote to young Samuel Bayard: "Princeton . . . Sam, I am fairly enraptured with the place."

Even Moreau, though he thought the students more given to *le jeu* than to study and the masters careless and of the "indolent disposition" he ascribed to most Americans, called Rittenhouse's orrery "justly celebrated"; and Cutler was much impressed by two of the citizens: the Reverend Doctor Smith, the Vice President of the college, whom he described as a young gentleman living in elegant style, and Colonel Morgan, of Prospect, the celebrated agriculturist, whom he found already busy over his books though he called on him at five o'clock of a July morning.

Colonel Morgan, at the age of thirty-seven, had retired from the army after the Battle of Monmouth, and the following year had moved with his family into his house, "Prospect near Princeton," which stood where the official dwelling of the presidents of Princeton University stands today. In the next eight years he made the neighboring two hundred acres one of the finest farms in the United States. He had a garden of three acres and sixty-four swarms of bees. His successful struggle against the wheat pest known as the Hessian fly gave him a wide reputation. In the cultivation of Morven's broad acres in these years Annis Stockton was doubtless one of the many who profited by his advice. For when he was getting his start on the land, her husband, ill and himself not too prosperous, had helped him with a loan.

Hers was a task that many men would have found quite enough to keep them busy, but it failed to absorb the whole of Annis Stockton's energy. In the spring of 1784, her son Richard wrote to his uncle Elias that he "found Mama bravely and in tolerable spirits," though not in completely good health. But her care of the place, the garden as well as the fields and orchards, was such that Monsieur André Michaux, King Louis XVI's botanist, who was engaged in collecting rare plants in America, came to see it, had tea with her, and presented her with the seed of a Persian plum tree. Ten years later, when she was nearly sixty, Richard wrote to his absent wife at harvest time: "Our outdoor family are able, with Mama's directions, (who has devoted her whole time to them) to do very well." The men breakfasted at six, and went off to work in the meadows; the women breakfasted at about seven; Richard and his mother at about eight.

To manage the type of labor at her disposal must have required the nicest blending of firmness and kindness. For, slaves though they were by law, these people enjoyed a status that justified Richard in referring to his farm hands as "family." His uncle Elias was active in a movement to abolish slavery, though its evils were greatly mitigated, at least in

New Jersey, by the humanitarian feelings of the owners. In 1784, for instance, Richard wrote to Elias, who wished to purchase "a black jade" at New Brunswick, that she was too much attached to her husband to be separated from him, even though she would still be only as far away as Newark. And that apparently prevented the sale.

In 1788 Richard married Mary Field, of White Hill in Burlington County. But Morven continued to be home for Annis and her other children even after they married and had homes of their own. There was "a friendly little circle at Morven almost every afternoon and evening," Julia Rush wrote of a visit there in 1790. Three years later she was back again, with her children, a refugee from the yellow fever that was raging in Philadelphia. Her husband remained in the city, as few physicians did, survived an attack of the disease, and made a world-wide reputation by his new treatment of it.

Annis's youngest brother-in-law, Samuel Witham Stockton, dropped in with his wife, Catherine Coxe, from time to time. After spending the war years abroad as secretary of the American commission to the courts of Austria and Russia, he had settled in Trenton, where he practiced law with conspicuous success until he was thrown from his chaise and killed in 1795. His brother, the Reverend Philip, became a neighbor of Morven in 1786, when he bought the Castle Howard property at the opposite end of the village. He married Catherine Cumming; and to him his brother Samuel wrote happily from Trenton that year: "My Kitty desires her love to your Kitty and yourself."

Annis had the joy of seeing all her children happily married. Three weddings brought gaiety to Morven in these years. Of Annis's twin daughters, Susan married Alexander Cuthbert of Canada, thus following the lead of her Aunt Rebecca, her father's youngest sister, who had married James Cuthbert. Mary, the other twin, married the distinguished Revolutionary army chaplain, the Reverend Andrew Hunter, but remained within easy visiting distance in the neighborhood of Trenton. Two years later Annis's youngest, and perhaps her dearest, child, Abigail, became the wife of Robert Field, her brother Richard's brother-in-law, and went to live at White Hill. Lucius Horatio married Elizabeth Milnor and, like his uncle, began the practice of law in Trenton.

With all her girls, when they were not near by, Annis kept up a lively correspondence. She missed them sorely. When Mary went to visit the Cuthberts at Berthier House, Annis wrote that nothing since her husband's death had distressed her so much as her "dear Polly's" departure. Gallant and even gay as was the front she faced the world with, precious memories of her husband were seldom absent from her mind. She wrote to Abigail twelve years after his death: "You could not, my dear Abby, have made a request more mournfully pleasing, than that of copying for you your dear, and ever lamented father's letters. Your tender years when he left us [Abigail was only eight at the time of her father's death] prevented you from forming any adequate idea of your loss in such a parent." And in the conclusion of her "Elegiac Ode" on the seventh anniversary of his death she had written:

> "And what so potent as a lover's tomb?
> And what can preach so earnest as the grave?
> The world shut out, within myself at home,
> All other preachers at a distance leave."

She always kept, as she wrote, "this day, from all the world retired." But her impulse to versify was still stirred by less unhappy occurrences. The ruinous effect of an ice storm at Morven evoked an "Elegy on the Destruction of the Trees by the Isicles [*sic*], Sunday and Monday of February the 17th and 18th, 1788." Six years earlier, when the Marquis de La Luzerne celebrated the birth of the Dauphin of France with magnificent festivities, she sent him "An Ode" on the subject, in which "the Genius of America with two Attendant

Zylphs" enters the gardens of the Marquis with baskets of flowers and, after calling upon Naiads and Tritons to join the celebration, beseeches the newborn heir of the Bourbons:

> "Turn, lovely Infant, turn thy beauteous eyes,
> Nor scorn the rural present that we bring;
> A mighty empire from these woods shall rise,
> And pay to thee the aid they owe thy King."

Her admiration of Washington continued undiminished. To a letter in prose that she sent him at Mount Vernon in the summer of 1787, he replied, touching upon their country's affairs, manners, and fashions with a seriousness that indicated a high opinion of her mentality and judgment. Upon the news of his election to the Presidency she went all out in a long, congratulatory letter. "I bless myself—I bless posterity—but I feel for you." And she reverted to "the ardor that almost censured my delicacy—which impelled me to seize your hand and kiss it, when you did me the honor to call on me in your way to York town." She knows that he will be very busy, but she is confident that she will sometimes see him and "my dear Mrs. Washington, whom I sincerely love."

With this letter went "The Vision, An Ode," from which it is sufficient to quote only:

> "I saw great Fabius come in state,
> I saw the British Lion's fate,
> The Unicorn's despair."

She was one of the group of distinguished persons who watched the President-elect's triumphal entry into Trenton on his way to his inauguration in New York. But Major Richard Howell—not she, to whom it has been attributed—wrote the ode beginning, "Welcome, Mighty Chief," that was sung by the young ladies who lined the bridge over the Assanpink as Washington rode across it. Instead, she sent him on the 1st of May a letter beginning: "Sir, Can the muse, can the friend forbear. . . ?" and enclosing a poem to "The President General," of which the second stanza tells how

"The Muse of Morven's peaceful shade
Gave way to all the gay parade
For transport of her own.
She felt the tears of pleasure flow
And gratitude's delightful glow
Was to her bosom known."

But—due allowance being made for the poetical conventions of her time—it is with strength and dignity that she recalls the memory of the men who had fallen in the fighting around New York:

"For erst on Hudson's whitened plain
Where the blue mists enshroud the slain
And heroes' spirits came,
Anxious to seal thy future fate,
Each in his cloud of awful state
Pronounced thee good as well as great,
And filled thy cup of fame."

Washington evidently appreciated and liked these tributes. There is nothing forced in his prompt acknowledgements of them. The President and Mrs. Washington spent a day at Princeton in 1790, and Annis wrote of it glowingly to her beloved Polly. The distinguished guests arrived about nine in the morning, and Annis, her son Richard, and Doctor and Mrs. Smith "attended" them on a visit to the college. At one there was a "collation" of fruit and cake, wine and sweetmeats at Morven, and Mrs. Washington remained there until the "gentleman in waiting" came to conduct her to the Tavern. Washington meanwhile "gave audience" to all the gentlemen of the neighborhood, and that evening gave a dinner at which the Stockton family was again honored: for he asked only young Richard, Doctor Witherspoon, and Doctor Smith to dine with him.

After a zestful account of the doings of the great ones,

Annis's letter ends on a happy, domestic note. Wagonloads of peaches are coming into town every day now, she tells her daughter; they were never so plentiful; and "Abby is in the piazza clear starching."

Annis was in her middle fifties now, but she had retained her vigor of mind and body, much of her good looks, her dominant position in the society of the neighborhood, and her excellent sense of humor. George Washington Parke Custis, an undergraduate at the College of New Jersey in these years, wrote of her: "She was familiarly called 'the Duchess' from her elegance and dignity of manner." But she cannot have failed to see the fun in the situation when President Witherspoon, widowed in 1789 at the age of sixty-seven, began to pay her attentions that were the joke of the family; and she doubtless shared their amusement when the vigorous old gentleman, who rode in on horseback every day from Tusculum to his collegiate duties, married the twenty-four-year-old widow of Doctor Dill, of Philadelphia.

A New Rochelle friend wrote to Mary Stockton in February 1790: "You say nothing of the venerable Adonis. Has he yet thought it expedient to propose himself? I find the report travels far and wide." She continued in verse:

> "This little God of Love is a roguish elf:
> He makes old age look foolish as himself.
>            'Gainst sixty-two—
>            Oh, luckless lot—
>            His bow he drew
>            And true he shot
>        Twang—went the string
>        Whiz—flew the dart
>            On a *gray* goose quill
>            To an old man's heart."

And even from distant Berthier House Cuthbert wrote to Mary: "I hear that your Mama has lost her young gallant, Dr. Witherspoon."

It was in this same year, 1790, that Richard wrote of his mother's efficient direction of the "outdoor family" at harvest time. But as she passed her sixtieth birthday, six years later, time began to tell upon her. She ceased to live at Morven, perhaps because she felt that she could no longer be useful there; and again the old house was filling with little children —six small boys and girls by the summer of 1799. When Washington paid his last visit to her, she was boarding at a friend's house in the neighborhood. Later she went to live with her youngest daughter, Mrs. Robert Field, at White Hill. Her brother Elias's changed opinion of the President doubtless troubled her. "That once worthy man," Elias wrote to Samuel Bayard in 1795, had made a "puerile" and "violent" speech. And she was saddened by the deaths of her brothers-in-law, Philip in 1792, and Samuel Witham in 1795.

In May of 1799 she wrote regretfully that she was unable to walk and no longer had horses and carriages at her service. In another eighteen months she had failed so greatly that in January 1801 as many of her children as could do so—Julia Rush, Abigail, Richard, and Lucius Horatio Stockton, and her brother's daughter, Susan Bradford—gathered to bid her a last farewell. On the 20th Julia wrote to Mary Hunter that their mother was dying, anxious to depart, and that she blessed them all. "Her mind was perfectly clear and rather joyous," wrote her brother Elias. "Her latter end was happy, full of peace and joy," her beloved son-in-law Benjamin Rush wrote of her in his autobiography. She died on February 6, 1801, having outlived her dearly loved husband almost exactly twenty years.

# CHAPTER V

## "The Old Duke"

ANNIS could die happy in the knowledge that Morven was again lively and gay with a brood of boys and girls, her grandchildren; that the place was again the possession of a young master and mistress who lavished upon it their loving care, as she and her Lucius had done; and that her son, its owner, had become such a man as his father would have had him be.

Though his mother had done her best to conserve and restore the family fortunes, young Richard, on coming of age in 1785, had found them sadly reduced from what they had been in his father's best days; and even before his majority he had set himself to the task of their restoration with that seriousness that comes to a thoughtful boy who is left at the age of seventeen the eldest son of the widowed mother of a large family.

Prepared for college by private tutors, he had been graduated from the College of New Jersey at the age of fifteen and upon the advice of his brother-in-law Benjamin Rush had begun the study of law in the office of his uncle Elias Boudinot. At nineteen he wrote to a friend in an otherwise gaily humorous letter that he had "renounced the world, the flesh and the Devil," and he evidently meant it. He was admitted to the bar a year later, began to practice at Princeton, and by the time he was twenty-five his eloquence and knowledge of the common law had placed him among the leaders of his profession—a position that he continued to hold until his death.

His chaise, with its "gentle and steady" young man driving it, became a familiar sight on the roads from one New Jersey court house to another. He frequently represented clients in New York and Philadelphia, and before the Supreme Court of the United States; and in 1801 President John Adams wrote to him about the abilities of another lawyer, whom

Richard had recommended for an office: "I doubt, however, of his being literally at the head of his profession at the bar while Mr. Richard Stockton is there."

He was an untiring worker. When he was well past fifty, one of his daughters wrote of him from Morven: "Papa is as usual from home attending court." The numerous and growing family that kept Morven's nursery occupied during the first two decades of his married life gave him good cause for industry. The first child, named Mary Field after her mother, was born in 1790, the second year after his marriage; his son Richard the following year; and after that, at two-year intervals, came Julia (1793), Robert Field (1795), Horatio (1797), Caroline (1799), Samuel Witham (1801); and in 1802 and 1804 respectively, William Bradford and Annis brought the number of his hostages to fortune up to nine.

As early as the birth of Robert Field, however, Richard had found time for those avocations public and semipublic that come naturally to a man of his position and ability. He was made a trustee of the College of New Jersey in 1791 and was active in that position until his death. In 1805, though not a communicant, he became a trustee of the Presbyterian church. Politics had always interested him greatly. When he was eleven, on a visit to the Rushes in Philadelphia, his father had written of him: "As Dick is so great a polititian [sic]...." He was chosen a Presidential elector in 1792 and 1801, and in 1796, when he was thirty-two, the New Jersey legislature elected him United States senator to fill the unexpired term of Frederick Frelinghuysen, who had resigned.

But in spite of his many private cares and public duties, thoughts of his wife, his children, and his home were seldom absent from his mind. A boyhood and youth that had been darkened by the war and the misfortunes and death of his father, and his determination to make for himself a professional position that was beyond his years, though no higher than his abilities justified, had given his tall and commanding presence a reserve and dignity that his enemies found "haughty and imperious." In his profession his manner was such that the younger lawyers called him "the Old Duke" years before his age justified that appellation. He was generally admired for his high character, ability, and stern integrity. But he lacked the ready courtesy and affability to high and low that had made his father universally popular. Those, however, who saw only the side he showed to the world would have been amazed if they could have read the letters he wrote to wife and children.

"Separation from my dear Mary and my sweet babe is becoming irksome to me. . . . God bless you, my love," he writes to his wife from Philadelphia in the earliest years of their marriage; and again: "My dearest Mary . . . Oh! you bad girl for not writing"; and when they have been married for six years, he concludes a letter: "Don't forget but continue to love Yr affectionate husband, R.S."

To his daughter Mary, twelve years old and away at school, he writes with humorous resignation that all the children—there were six at home at that time—have measles, or have had them, or are going to have them. Wherever he went he was mindful of presents for them, even on occasions when, in some celebration or other, "the bottle was pushed," and he had failed to write his usual letter. Julia, at school in Philadelphia, was "almost ready to jump out of her skin" when he made an unexpected appearance there. He took her and a friend to the play, and she "diverted" him "more than the actors" did, her "big eyes rolling every which way."

He would have their mother remind Mary and Richard, who were visiting in Lancaster with her, that since they are strangers there, "the eyes of many will be upon them." But he was his children's ardent champion, if he thought they had been treated unjustly. When ten-year-old Caroline's teacher, Mr. Whittlesee, set her to sweeping the schoolroom and she and her grandmother Field became greatly "ruffled" about it, he wrote Mr. Whittlesee that Caroline was too much of a child for that work and that he would consult the school trustees about it, if Whittlesee did not agree with him.

When, at fifteen, Mary got herself expelled from boarding school, her father's indignant support carried him beyond the bounds of common sense. In December 1805 he was writing to Joseph Hopkinson, counsellor at law, to engage his services in the prosecution of a "miscreant" who had attacked his daughter's reputation, making use of certain letters "abominably." The "miscreant," Hopkins by name, was the husband of the mistress of the school and had been accused of entering the room of two of the girls at night. Mary had written a lampoon on the subject; and Hopkins, to get even, had circulated a silly tale which Mary, in pure impishness, on her return from the holidays, had told the other girls—that she had been secretly married and was pregnant.

The case dragged on for a couple of years without coming to trial. Hopkins and his wife put what Richard called a "scandalous" advertisement in the *Gazette*, charging him with persecuting them. Richard included Doctor Rush in his counsels and, after another year, wrote Joseph Hopkinson, wisely if belatedly, that he had decided to "consign the infamous authors to silence and oblivion," since he saw no honorable way to deal with them. "In the innocent joys of the table and the field," he concluded his letter, "there can be no alloy," and he hoped the Hopkinsons would visit him at Morven by the Fourth of July at latest.

In the midst of politics and business he thought of Morven longingly, as the place where he could find the best blessing of life: "leisure with dignity." Busy in court at Trenton the year after his marriage, he yearned to be gardening at home, feeding the chickens and searching for eggs with his "dearest Molly." At Philadelphia, eight years later, senator from New Jersey and with cases before the Supreme Court, he is involved in a round of dinners, dances, plays, and tea parties; he has lately dined at Uncle Benjamin and Aunt Julia Rush's in company with the President and Mrs. Washington and the

British minister and his lady; but he yearns for his "dear little girl and boy" and "to be after the ducks and chickens." In 1804, though he was to be a candidate for governor that year, he wrote to his wife, who was in Philadelphia on a visit, that he was concerned entirely with his children's happiness and the management of Morven and its farm.

In circumstances that, by Morven standards, were somewhat straitened in the earlier years of his married life, he kept the smallest details of the management of the place in mind, especially at harvest time. He might sit up late, preparing a speech on a point of constitutional law that was to be delivered before the Senate next morning; but he took time to write his wife directions about the hay. Jack must take the yellow flowers out of the wheat, he wrote home from one of his many trips; the threshed wheat must be put into hogsheads; the window of the meat cellar must be opened or the meat would spoil; and the barn and stable doors must be locked every night.

When he was at home and she was off on a visit, he wrote her, "Your domestics do middling well," and that, since candles were nineteen pence a pound, he was using up her "mold candles." "The poor little orphan colt," he went on, had the distemper, but not dangerously, and "the gray mare's colt is the finest in the state." When the first baby was but a few weeks old, it was he who did the Christmas shopping for the house. Andirons, he reported from Philadelphia, were twenty-one shillings and sixpence a pair, and a solid silver cream jug would cost four pounds, ten shillings. Cases of knives and forks were very scarce. In fact, the newly imported plated ware was preferred by the best people in the city, and a set of it for the tea table could be bought for forty dollars.

But except when her maternal duties monopolized her time, his wife took her full share in the management and improvement of the place. The dairy and hennery were her particular charge. According to tradition, her husband returned from a prolonged court session at Somerville to find that she had used the profits from those sources to give the house a new portico, although this may merely have been some improvement to the piazza, or perhaps the elaborate doorway, which appears to date from the 1800s. They continued to improve the garden, and Mary Hunter sent her brother three fine English walnut trees for its further beautification.

Through the early years of the new century Morven continued to be a center of gay and generous hospitality. It became also one of the centers of Federalist party politics. A bitter opponent of Thomas Jefferson and the policy of the Democrats, Richard Stockton would doubtless have endorsed his uncle Elias's characterization of some of Jefferson's supporters as the "whisky boys." In 1801 and the three years following he ran for governor of New Jersey on the Federalist ticket and was each time defeated. But in 1812 he was elected to Congress and served through the terrible years from 1813 to 1815. He considered the War of 1812—"Mr. Madison's war," the Federalists called it—"political insanity," wrote of his country as "gone to the dogs" ten months before a British army reduced its capitol to ashes, and at the end of that year confessed to a sort of sympathy with "the doings at Hartford," meaning thereby the Hartford Convention.

To his wife and his eldest daughter he sent amusing accounts of his life at the capital. His sister Mary and her husband had been living in Washington for some years. The Reverend Mr. Hunter, having become a naval chaplain, was engaged in the education of midshipmen; he had found the city greatly to his liking, Pennsylvania Avenue very fine, and "a drawing room" at the executive mansion full of elegance, splendor, dignity, and beauty, with a hostess, the brilliant Dolly Madison, who "exceeded all the rest." Mr. Hunter noted also—perhaps as a sign of the changing times—that rye whisky appeared on every table where he was entertained and that "Some say, sir, we use no brandy."

Bad roads kept Richard in Washington for Christmas in

1813. "The gulf between this and Baltimore," he wrote home, was almost as "bad as that in our neighborhood." The next year a press of matters in the Senate and numerous admiralty "causes," with which he divided his time when the court was in session, kept him too busy to leave. For diversion he played whist at a shilling a game, two rubbers at a sitting, and attended the President's reception on New Year's Day. He was "received *most formally* by the Queen," he reported; but he had evidently gone there, like most of the other Federalists, to enjoy the confusion of the party in power, which was "much upset" by the bad news from Europe, where Great Britain and her allies had finally vanquished Napoleon.

He hoped for peace—at almost any price that was not dishonorable, one gathers—and with good reason. His second son, Robert Field, who had entered the College of New Jersey at thirteen, had been a midshipman in the navy for the past three years, serving on board the frigate *President* under Commodore Rodgers, and Richard was looking forward anxiously to an opportunity to observe the effect of the "new life" upon the appearance, manners, and character of the young man, now nineteen years old.

To Morven, in September of 1814, had come frightening news from Washington. A long letter from Mary Hunter told how she had remained in her house, trusting in the discipline and chivalry of the British army, when the enemy entered the city, while her husband, like most of the official male population, took children and servants to the safety of Virginia. The British officers, Mary Hunter wrote, had been most courteous, and the soldiers perfectly orderly. But there must have been anxious weeks for Mary Field Stockton until she heard of the safety of her sons. Robert won commendation in dispatches for his conduct in the defense of Baltimore. Seventeen-year-old Horatio was evidently in the navy also by this time, though his warrant as midshipman was not sent him until the beginning of 1815. For when news of the Treaty of Ghent finally arrived in Washington in February, Richard wrote home thankfully of the end of their fears for their "poor boys."

That year was not over, however, before young Horatio died of injuries received in the line of duty. He arrived at New York in the frigate *Guerriere*, with a leg sorely bruised by a fall from one of the decks of the ship when she was at Naples. He was taken to the house of his married sister Mary, Mrs. William Harrison, for nursing. But mortification set in, and a fatal fever followed. His body was brought home to Morven for burial. "Poor Mrs. Stockton," Abigail Field wrote to her sister Mary Hunter: her nerves were weak, but she was resigned to the will of God.

Perhaps it was because he wished to remain at home to comfort his wife in her sorrow that Richard declined to run for reelection to Congress. He had expected, moreover, that the country would know whom to blame for the disastrous war. But it had not, and disappointment at the prospect of Monroe as the next President may have made him unwilling to go on taking an active part in the struggles of the waning Federalist party. And there was plenty to keep him active in private life.

There had been a good many changes in the Princeton neighborhood in the past few years. Improvement in communications had done much to enliven the village. The Raritan had been bridged at New Brunswick in 1795, the Delaware at Trenton eleven years later. By that time a turnpike ran from Trenton to New Brunswick via Penns Neck; three years later, local merchants, fearing loss of trade, opened a competing Turnpike, following Main Street from Kingston to Princeton, and laying out the present Mercer Street to carry traffic to Trenton.

These roads were busy, especially during the war years, when the British blockade made seagoing traffic impossible. On them plied the great Conestoga and Jersey freight wagons that went by names, and whose drivers were known as "captains" and were supposed to sing:

## "The Old Duke"

"Our march is on the turnpike road,
Our home is at the inn."

On these roads rolled also the carriages of the wealthy with a new smoothness, and the stage coaches raced each other. It was not long before the quiet of the Princeton nights was broken by the spinning wheels and flashing lamps of the "night mail" coaches. But all this was only when bad weather had not combined with the heavy traffic to produce such "hopeless ruts and quagmires" as had kept Richard from his home that Christmas of 1813. For the directors of the turnpike companies were more interested in locating tollgates at ten-mile, and even five-mile, intervals than in substantial foundations and a weatherproof surface. The Princeton-Kingston Turnpike dividends were often six or seven per cent. But during the busy days of the war the road had been strewn with wrecked and bogged-down vehicles; and now companies were being formed for the building of canals that would obviate these difficulties.

In such enterprises Richard Stockton had taken an active and often a leading part from their beginnings. Other calls, both on his time and on his purse, were frequent. Like other wealthy residents of the neighborhood, he bore his share of the cost when, in 1812, the Presbyterian Theological Seminary was established in a building that even the critical New Yorker John Pintard said "would do credit to New York." When, early on a February Sunday morning in the following year, the Presbyterian church burned to the ground, Richard, as one of the trustees, must contribute liberally to its rebuilding. His relation to the college also cost him time and money.

There was a new spirit abroad among the youth of the land. They felt it up at Harvard and at Yale. At Princeton, back in the days of the French Revolution, Richard had helped to deal with what President Smith called an effort among the students to "jacobinize" the college. In 1802 a fire, which Richard's investigation caused him to believe the students had started, gutted Nassau Hall. Five years later

77

came the Great Rebellion, which began with the burning of the steward's fence and "the new cloascenia" and ended with the expulsion of eleven boys and the dismissal of five others.

The possession of swords and sword-canes by the students was forbidden; the steward was instructed to serve small beer instead of "cyder"; and the state legislature was persuaded to prohibit the local tavern keepers from selling liquor to the students. But the disorders kept on year after year. In the sleighing season liquor could be bought in the neighboring towns. There were nights when the college bell clanged all night long and the corridors of Nassau Hall resounded with pistol shots, yells, and the explosion of firecrackers. Registration, which had risen to two hundred, was reduced by expulsions to little more than half that number and remained there for many years.

At their wit's end, Richard, Elias Boudinot, and the rest of the trustees began to blame the President and faculty. The courtly and elegant Samuel Stanhope Smith was gently eased out of office and replaced by the sour and uncompromising Ashbel Green, brother-in-law of Doctor Ebenezer Stockton, of Constitution Hill. But a bomb, made of a hollow log and stuffed with gunpowder, blew out the doors and windows of Nassau Hall and hurled its fragments through the door of the prayer hall, and the students barricaded themselves in the building. In an attempt to quell a fresh riot the Vice President had to dodge a heavy glass decanter that was aimed at his head, and a shower of lumps of ice drove President Green to the shelter of the side door of his house, where he could only stand shaking his cane in impotent rage. In 1823 the Reverend James Carnahan succeeded Green as president. The explosion of a great firecracker signalized the beginning of the new administration, but under Carnahan conditions gradually improved.

Richard, who was sometimes the only resident trustee and was bound to become involved in these troubles whenever he was at home, took his responsibilities with more seriousness than good judgment. In handwriting that betrayed his haste and agitation he wrote to President Carnahan in 1823 about "the late atrocious and midnight attack upon your House and Family" and proposed as the only adequate remedy an investigation by "the most imposing and solemn process" before the justices of the supreme court of the state. For "unless these midnight Depredators can be brought to condign punishment," he concluded, "we might as well close the college doors."

With the improvement of the roads and the addition of the numerous divinity students, the village had grown. It had been chartered as a borough in 1813. Its business had increased and prospered. But its character and atmosphere, both social and material, appear to have changed but little from what they had been twenty years before, when a tutor at the college had written of it: "I think it has the most complete separation of rank of any place of its size in the United States." One who was described as a "coach painter" might be a ruling elder of the church and marry the daughter of a member of the college faculty, but such a case was exceptional.

In appearance there was little, except Nassau Hall, to keep Main Street from looking a good deal like the thoroughfare of an English village, with Morven as the manor house just around the turn in the road, and five or six other fine places a little farther away. In 1806 Mr. Samuel Bayard had bought forty acres of land and improved a fine house on the lane that ran northward a couple of hundred yards east of Morven and still bears his name. A member of the college class of 1784, he had spent four years in London, prosecuting the claims of American citizens before the British admiralty courts. After he settled in Princeton he became judge of the Court of Common Pleas of Somerset County and the county's representative in the state legislature. His wife was Martha, daughter of Lewis and Susannah Stockton Pintard and so a cousin of the family at Morven. His house, which he called Clermont, became, like Morven, famous for its hospitality.

Later much enlarged and altered in the fashion of its day, it became Henry Van Dyke's Avalon. It stood where the YM-YWCA stands today.

John Pintard, another Stockton cousin, wrote that "the sun appearing over Mr. Stockton's elegant grove" was a sight that repaid him for the long and tiresome journey from New York. But he was less favorably impressed by its owner, who was his cousin by adoption, and whom the young lawyers were by this time referring to as "the Old Duke." After the old man's death he described him as "very selfish . . . not benevolent." But he might have modified his opinion had he known more of Richard's dealings with his relatives.

To all who were connected with him by blood or marriage Richard was a tower of strength, "an ever present help in time of trouble," though it is possible that he was not always very gracious about it. Fragmentary records of loans, sales, and leases involving the property at White Hill indicate his frequent relief of the financial difficulties of his sister Abigail's husband, his wife's brother, Robert Field. After Robert's death he gave Abigail a home, which she described as a "sweet little cottage," across the road from Morven and built an addition to it for her greater comfort.

Later this cottage was occupied by Richard's sister Mary Hunter, whose husband died in 1823. But life at Washington had accustomed Mary to living on a more liberal scale: in 1816 the Reverend Andrew had bought on Capitol Hill a house costing five thousand dollars, a large sum for the time and place. At Princeton Mary soon built a spacious house on Main Street, where she lived until she died in 1846 at the age of eighty-five. Another widowed sister, Susan Cuthbert, returned from Canada in 1813 and liked the old home surroundings so much that she bought a house, took two divinity students as boarders, and lived there until her death in 1821.

Richard's brother, Lucius Horatio, four years younger than he, must also have caused him much anxiety from time to time, judging from the various documents that have withstood the attrition of the years. Eminent as a lawyer, he at one time held the office of district attorney of New Jersey. John Adams nominated him to be secretary of war, but the succession of Jefferson prevented the nomination from being confirmed. As a businessman, however, he appears to have been less successful. Over a period of twenty years Richard was endorsing his notes and otherwise supporting his credit. In 1826, in return for old loans and a cash balance, he deeded to Richard two tracts west of the Princeton–Red Hill road, and other land—about five hundred acres in all—that had been bequeathed to Lucius Horatio by their father; and the following year he did the like with the Red Hill property.

During these years Morven kept its atmosphere of gay hospitality despite its owner's repellent manner. There was a continual come and go of guests, both relatives and others. Daniel Webster and his wife and the Marquis de Lafayette were among the latter. Mary Field, the eldest of the daughters of the house, had been married before the war to William Harrison, of New York, but the other three girls were still at home, except for excursions into Philadelphia and Washington society. When Cousin John Pintard made his visit to Morven in 1817, he thought Julia, the second daughter, "very handsome . . . a perfect sylph," and Caroline "a little fat but one of the smartest in conversation." Julia had lately returned, with Mr. Webster as her escort, from a gay winter in Washington with Uncle and Aunt Hunter and told amusingly of her journey home: how she had beaten General Brown at chess on the steamboat and enjoyed a "cotillion party" at Philadelphia and a dinner given there by Mr. Hopkinson, who had been on the boat with her.

The social event of the winter of 1820 at Morven was the celebration of the return of Lieutenant Robert Field Stockton, United States Navy, Richard's second son, who had been on a four-year cruise on the U.S.S. *Washington* and had distinguished himself by fighting three duels, two of them with

British officers, at Naples and Gibraltar. Cousin Robert Hunter, who was at Morven on a visit, wrote to his brother Lewis that the whole clan, uncles, aunts, and cousins, and "all of the great people of Princeton" gathered for "a great teaing" and the girls kept the young men busy sleigh-riding while their elders spent their time eating and drinking.

The following July Caroline was married to William R. Rotch, of New Bedford, Massachusetts. The Rotch family were in the whaling business; and Cousin John Pintard, who now thought Caroline the beauty of the family, considered it "a rich and promising marriage." In Annis's marriage, which took place six years later, there were elements of drama. Until almost the day of the wedding, the match had appeared to be as brilliant as those of her sisters. The bridegroom, John Renshaw Thomson, was the son of a great Philadelphia tea merchant and had made a handsome fortune of his own as supercargo in numerous voyages to Canton. The bride's father had given her a tract of land across the road from Morven, and the young couple were planning to build a handsome house upon it after spending a gay winter in Washington.

But the senior Thomson fell into such grave financial difficulties that he attempted to leave the country. He was arrested on shipboard and brought back from New Castle; and his son's fortune was involved in his ruin. The wedding was, nevertheless, a brilliant affair. The house (demolished in 1973, and known for the many years it housed the Borough's offices as Thomson Hall) was completed in due time, and Annis and her husband came to live in it after a period in which he acted as agent and overseer of the lands in which his father-in-law had invested in Georgia.

Julia, with all her beauty and wit, seems to have been harder to please than her sisters. She was still at home and her father's frequent companion, when he made his will in 1826. Later she married Doctor John Rhinelander, of New York, where they had a house on upper Broadway.

Meanwhile Morven had opened wide its doors, probably

not for the first time, to one of the most notable of its guests. In 1824 Lafayette and his son arrived at Princeton. The college entertained him at a sumptuous breakfast in its refectory. Near the central gate of the campus, a "Temple of Science" enshrined, under a circular canopy supported by white columns, Peale's portrait of Washington; and there, before a great crowd, President Carnahan presented to Lafayette the diploma of Doctor of Laws, signed by President Witherspoon, that had been conferred upon him *in absentia* in 1790.

The Old Duke had been chosen by the reception committee to make the address of welcome, but when, in rehearsing it before them, he began, "Marquis de Lafayette," Judge Bayard ventured to suggest that Lafayette would prefer to be called "General," since he had renounced his title of nobility. "Once a marquis, always a marquis," Mr. Stockton retorted. "I shall address him by what was his title before the infamous French Revolution." And so he did.

Interludes of misfortune and sorrow darkened Morven at times. In March 1821 a room in the second story of the main house took fire. Although the blaze was eventually contained, the roof was destroyed. The fire was a shock, but the damage, as John Pintard noted, was not so severe as that from a fire about fifty years earlier, in the Signer's day, when the house burned to the ground. In 1813 Uncle Benjamin Rush died, after bitter quarrels with his nephew Lucius Horatio and Elias Boudinot.

Over at Burlington old Uncle Elias, full of years, great wealth, and still greater piety, had been spending most of his time since 1810 either in bed or on a reclining chair. In 1815, on one of the frequent visits that his Princeton relatives made to him, one of them thought that he seemed "to have nothing to do but die." But two years later, John Pintard, who drove over with the Bayards in their carriage, found him "cheerful and keen" and thought he was "like Saint John on Patmos" when he said family prayers. When in 1821 he finally died, "the good old saint," as Pintard called him, left ten thousand dollars to each of his nieces and nephews, who were fifteen in number, and sixty thousand dollars to various public causes.

There were family troubles also. In 1825 John Pintard heard that Mary Harrison had broken up housekeeping and returned to her father from "a venal match . . . soon ended in indifference and misery" and a husband without mind or education, "an inflated bladder in prosperity," who had taken to drink when adversity came. Pintard called Caroline's husband "a wet Quaker" now, "a *bon vivant* and debauchee." And tragedy itself darkened Morven in the Old Duke's last days.

Richard, his eldest son, was charming in manner, an able lawyer, when he chose to work, but more given to enjoying the advantages of his position than to accepting its responsibilities. Gambling appears to have been his besetting weakness. In his early twenties his father was writing to him as "My dear son," telling him of the difficulties of financing certain canal projects, of his speeches in the Senate, and other bits of Washington news and gossip, and signing himself "your affectionate father." But a few years later the young man's bad habits led to a bitter quarrel between the two, and young Richard left Morven, vowing, according to the gossip that reached John Pintard, never to return until his father had died or he had made a fortune of his own by the practice of his profession.

By 1823, however, there had been a reconciliation. From Greenville, Mississippi, that January the young man wrote of his "delight" at being once more allowed to address his father. "The name I bear," he promised, "shall never again be tarnished in my person." He now had "the friendship of some of the best gentlemen in the state" and was "on circuit." Things continued to go well with him. The lawyers in that part of the country were so ignorant, he explained modestly in another letter, that his attainments were "superior" to theirs. He had three thousand dollars owing to him for professional services. But nobody ever paid a circuit rider:

only in Natchez was it possible to build up a lucrative practice. So he had accepted a position on the supreme court of the state. Later he became attorney general.

So the blow must have been a crushing one when the news came in February 1827 that Richard Stockton, Jr., had been killed in a duel with John P. Parson, of New Orleans. Moreover, according to the particulars that John Pintard had from Judge Bayard, he had been "grossly in the wrong" in the quarrel. The one consolation for his bereaved parents was that he had not fired his pistol and had left a letter stating that he did not intend to do so. His mother, now grown very deaf, strove bravely, his sister Julia wrote, "to preserve her equanimity." Someone, probably his sister Mary Harrison, mourned for him in verses that recall her grandmother Annis's:

> "A foreign turf was on thy breast, and hands
>     Of strangers scoop'd thy final resting place;
> The hearts that yearn for thee were in far lands;
>     Nor knew when death clasped thee in cold embrace;
>
> .     .     .     .     .     .
>
> Yet in that fatal hour thy thoughts did turn
>     To them—to boyhood's home and native shore,
> And stronger in thy heart the love did burn
>     Of those enshrined within its inmost core,—
> The far-off faithful few who in their home
> A thousand leagues, still looked for thee to come."

Mr. Pintard's rather unfeeling comment was that the young man took after his mother's family, the Fields: that her brother had dissipated a comfortable estate.

A source of strength and comfort to the aging but still indomitably industrious father at this time must have been the presence of his brilliant and successful second son. While on duty in Southern waters Robert Field Stockton had met Harriet Maria Potter, a beautiful and wealthy girl of Charleston, and in 1823 brought her home to Morven as his bride.

On "prolonged leave" he built, in 1825, the stately house that still stands on the northeast corner of Nassau Street and Bayard Lane, on land given him by his father. Meanwhile, the Old Duke had the pleasure of seeing the first two grandchildren of his to bear the family name: another Richard, born in 1824; and John Potter, named after his other grandfather, born in the following year.

Now in his early sixties, the old man continued to work at the law with undiminished energy. In 1827 he found time to serve on the commission that settled the dispute with New York over the eastern boundary of his state. But at the beginning of April in the next year he came home from a busy term of court at Somerville and died suddenly—as Cousin John said that a man of his corpulent habit of body was bound to do—of a stroke of apoplexy, on the 7th of April, aged sixty-four years.

At the time of his death he was still one of the leading lawyers of the country. More than a decade earlier Queen's College, now Rutgers University, and Union College had honored his attainments by making him a Doctor of Laws. But with an irony not unique in the records of eminent lawyers the will that he left behind him was so intricate that fifty years after it was written it had to be submitted to the highest courts of the state for judicial construction.

By the terms of this instrument Morven went to his widow "during the term of her natural life in full compensation of dower," then to his eldest surviving son, Robert Field. With the house went also to his wife "all my silver plate, also the carriage and horses in use at the time, one common wagon and gears, three cows and four hogs to be chosen by her, all liquors, meat, and other provisions in the house, all grain either in the ground or to be gathered, all hay in the barn or stacks or barracks to be used by her for the maintenance of the stock until it be sold, all household and kitchen furniture which she may choose to keep, all my books except my law library and encyclopedia." And included with the house were "the ground in front, with the garden together with the adjoining lots of land . . . to the east of the Mansion house" and with boundaries at "the corner of the old Orchard near the quarry . . . , the young orchard used as a hog pasture . . . , the old Trenton road . . . [and] the road to Mr. Bayard's," a total of two hundred and seventy acres. His "servants"— like most owners of slaves, he evidently shrank from using the word—were also bequeathed to his widow.

To Robert Field Stockton, in addition to the reversion of the Morven property, went one fourth of the sixty-five thousand acres of lands in North Carolina; in Oneida County, New York, on the route of the Erie Canal; and elsewhere in the west. Samuel Witham received the Tusculum farm, which his father had brought back into the family by purchase in 1815. And to William Bradford, the other surviving son, went the Springdale farm, which had been confiscated from Richard the Signer's tory uncle Joseph. The residue of the estate, estimated at between sixty and eighty thousand dollars, was left in trust to Robert Field Stockton and Samuel Bayard, the interest to be paid to the widow and the four daughters during their lifetimes. "I think the daughters have hard measure," commented John Pintard, and added that he expected no better from "Mr. Stockton's aristocratic notions."

# CHAPTER VI

## Robert the Magnificent

"A VERY correct, high-spirited officer," wrote Cousin John Pintard of the new master of Morven; and again, "a fine, good hearted seaman, partaking of his mother's side of the house." But that told only half of the character of Robert Field Stockton. He was greatly changed from the enterprising young midshipman of nineteen, in straw hat, blue jacket, and white linen trousers, of the summer of 1814. But the change wrought by the years between that time and his establishing his own home at Princeton was one of degree rather than kind.

Robert Field Stockton's career had been a brilliant one, though he had proved to be, as a recent biographer has called him, "the navy's problem child." With many other junior officers he had signed a round robin of protest against the outrageous tyranny of their captains. In later years he would advise young officers about dueling: "Remember, gentlemen, there is always time enough to fight; keep cool; never get into a passion under the grossest provocation." But he had, nevertheless, fought those three famous duels on the Mediterranean station.

He was bitterly opposed to the punishment of the enlisted men by flogging. He was free-spoken to a fault, and his readiness to accept responsibility in the interpretation and execution of orders had more than once landed him in hot water with the highest departmental authorities, and even in the civil courts. But he was liked and trusted by his superior officers, and where a task requiring courage, resolution, and sound judgment based on a knowledge of the regulations and the law was to be undertaken, he was frequently chosen to accomplish it.

As a midshipman in the War of 1812 he had earned the name of "Fighting Bob" among the sailors. Promoted to lieu-

tenant for gallantry in the defense of Baltimore, he had distinguished himself under Decatur in the war with Algiers,
and had been selected to bring home on the *Erie* a number
of captains whom Commodore Stewart, commanding the
Mediterranean squadron, had placed under arrest. When he
arrived at Morven that winter of 1820, he was on the first
leave he had taken in his ten years of service.

Off again in command of the twelve-gun schooner *Alligator* for the coast of Africa in suppression of the slave trade,
he proceeded to put into practice his hatred of flogging.
Mustering his entire ship's company on deck, he solemnly
"buried the cat" by throwing the cat-o'-nine-tails overboard,
and proceeded to maintain perfect discipline without it.

He was the first United States naval officer, says Samuel
John Bayard, his contemporary and biographer, to act on
fundamental principles against the slave trade. He captured
four slave ships on this voyage, and thereby got a reprimand
from the Secretary of the Navy, because all four had flown
the French flag. But when the case came to court, no less an
authority than Justice Story held that his action had been
correct, since France had outlawed the slave trade. So Robert
was not without reason in feeling that the reprimand had
been unjust.

In the following November he sailed for Africa once more,
and once more in command of the *Alligator*. He was accompanied by Doctor Ayers, of the lately organized American
Colonization Society. Their mission was to find a more healthy
location than Sherbro, the existing one, for the colony of
liberated American Negro slaves whom it was the purpose
of the society to return and establish on the continent of their
origin. The Cape Masurado country, about two hundred and
fifty miles south of Freetown in the British colony of Sierra
Leone, seemed most suitable. But the natives were ferocious
by nature, and King Peter, their chieftain, made doubly hostile by a mulatto slave dealer who told him that Stockton had
captured slave ships, slipped quietly away up the river.

Robert and Doctor Ayers, accompanied only by a single seaman and a Croo interpreter, followed him. They found him sullen and dangerous, his people armed and threatening. The mulatto shook his fist in Robert's face and denounced him as an enemy of the slave trade. Drawing a couple of pistols from his belt, Robert handed one of them to Doctor Ayers. "Shoot that villain if he opens his mouth again," he ordered. The other pistol he pointed at the head of the king and held it there while he repeated his explanations and persuasions. The upshot was that King Peter deeded the desired land to Robert and Doctor Ayers personally, and in due course it became the territory of what is now the Republic of Liberia.

On the voyage home the *Alligator* exchanged shots with the Portuguese *Marianna Flora*, which carried twenty-two guns, and brought her into port as a "pirate." Again Lieutenant Stockton was called into court. The capture was declared to have been illegal and damages were assessed at $19,675. But upon appeal to the circuit court, with Robert's father's old friend Daniel Webster as lawyer for the defendant, the decision was reversed, and the reversal was sustained by the Supreme Court. Robert and Webster became fast friends; Webster continued to be a frequent guest at Morven after the Old Duke's death and wrote one of his famous speeches there.

In March 1822, still in command of the *Alligator*, Robert joined Commodore Biddle's squadron, which was engaged in the extirpation of the long-standing nuisance of piracy in the Caribbean. The pirates had a frustrating way of taking refuge in the bays and inlets of the coast of Cuba, and the captain general of that island refused to permit the Americans to follow them there. Biddle accordingly forbade his ships to do so. But Lieutenant Stockton, regardless of captain general and commodore alike, pursued his quarry even onto the shore, with the result that on June 11 he was relieved of his command. Returning home, he asked and was granted a "prolonged leave."

It was four years later when, at his own request, he returned to duty. But his assignment for the next two years was the surveying of the harbors of Charleston, Savannah, and Brunswick, Georgia—a task that he described with characteristic frankness to the Navy Department as "truly tedious." Upon its completion in 1828 he returned to Princeton, and ten years were to pass before he again sailed salt water in the line of duty. He was promoted to commander in 1830 and was known thenceforth, even among his near relatives, as "Captain Stockton." But he declined when opportunities to return to active duty were offered him. In doing this he was not shirking. The navy had more officers than it knew what to do with, and there were many "awaiting orders," as the phrase went, and longing for employment, who were not blessed, like Robert, with an independent income.

Upon his first return home he had busied himself in his father's various projects. In 1828 he at once took a hand in a convention that was being held at Princeton for "the internal improvement of New Jersey," and threw himself into the other activities of civil life with all the self-confidence, enterprise, and steadfastness of purpose that characterized his naval service. None of his forebears had been wanting in these qualities, but Robert was dynamic. In business, politics, religion, philanthropy, and sport he became a leader in the community and in the state.

His father-in-law, John Potter, had moved to Princeton soon after his daughter's marriage, and had made his home at Prospect, Colonel Morgan's old place. Mr. Potter had made a large fortune from a fleet of vessels plying between Charleston and England and now, with his sons, James and Thomas, joined his energetic and venturesome son-in-law in an enterprise of great financial magnitude for the time, and of still greater risk.

This was the project for a canal to connect the Delaware and Raritan rivers. It had been in the air for some years. In

1826 the Old Duke, though he owned none of the scrip of the company, had been on the list of managers to be elected as one who would not be influenced by "the great New York stock brokers" and would serve only with Jersey men. Opposition by Philadelphia financiers, who feared that the canal would draw business from their city, caused the stock subscription to be a failure. There was local opposition too—which the shrewd Old Duke suspected to be the same as the old objection to turnpikes: that the travelers went through the towns so fast that they left no money behind them.

A similar failure threatened the new enterprise. But Captain Stockton, who had been in the South, making experiments in the manufacture of sugar, returned in time to subscribe for enough stock to ensure the granting of a charter to the Delaware and Raritan Canal Company. His cousin Mary Hunter, Aunt Mary Hunter's daughter, wrote to her brother that the Captain had put five hundred thousand dollars into the venture and that he and Mr. Potter held one half of the stock. Cousin John Pintard heard that they cleared one hundred thousand dollars in the transaction and retained control of the company.

It was touch and go, however, for several months. Capitalists in New York and Philadelphia held aloof, objecting that the canal would be too short to pay. Robert met that difficulty by going to England and raising the money there. But Robert Stevens and his brother John feared the canal as a prospective competitor of their projected Camden and Amboy Railroad, and did their utmost to prevent the granting of a franchise to the canal company by the New Jersey legislature. They also were seeking a franchise, and neither party could obtain a majority in the legislature, although, as Mrs. Hunter noted, "the gentlemen of the family have lived some time at Trenton, trying to get a charter from the Legislature."

A chance meeting between Robert and the Stevens brothers at the Park Theater in New York led to a compromise.

The rival projects were united by what was popularly known as the "Marriage Act," of which a local balladist wrote:

"The peerless pair their jealousies forego,
Unite their stocks, and thus their wisdom show."

Robert became president of the canal company at a salary of twenty-five hundred dollars a year, Potter a director, and John R. Thomson, sister Annis's husband, secretary. His yearly salary was fifteen hundred dollars, which, Cousin John Pintard observed, would enable him and his wife to "live comfortably in his handsome new house." In its essence the "Marriage Act" gave the joint companies a monopoly. It made the state a sharer in their profits to the tune of thirty thousand dollars a year. But by its critics, who were many and bitter in those parts that were not benefited by either the canal or the railroad, New Jersey was dubbed "the State of the Camden and Amboy."

In November 1830 work was begun on the stretch of the canal between Rocky Hill and Trenton, and gangs of Irish laborers made the New Brunswick nights hideous with their drunken brawls. In less than a year the company's stock was selling at fifty-two dollars for every fifteen-dollar installment paid on it; the subscription books were closed; and Mr. Bayard, who had refused to subscribe, tried in vain to invest five thousand dollars in it. In June 1834 the canal was opened with a splendid celebration. The Governor, on a barge with thirty other guests, was received at New Brunswick with a military display and a salute of twenty-four guns, and champagne relieved the tedium of the leisurely progress of their vessel.

The enterprise had its less edifying side, to be sure. Politics of a rather low order had a large part in it, but those engaged in it must be judged by the standards of their time. In the business of obtaining the franchise Robert Stockton proved himself an expert lobbyist. Headquarters for the companies were established at Trenton, in Snowden's hotel, and Apartment 10 became notorious as a place where tired legislators could refresh themselves with champagne and terrapin free of charge. Under Robert's leadership a political machine was created.

He was not without experience in politics. Back in 1824 he had started the *Princeton Courier* newspaper, written many of its editorials, and made many speeches in support of John Quincy Adams for President of the United States. He had been the center of a stormy scene at the convention at Trenton in 1826, when a drunken partisan of Jackson had demanded: "What right has this damned rascal here with the Government's commission in his pocket? Turn him out!"

Robert knocked the man down, sprang upon a table and, in a voice trained to be heard above the roar of a hurricane, went on with his interrupted speech. In the ensuing riot—for the crowd in the lobby rushed into the hall, and fists began to fly—he refused a dirk that somebody offered him. "It's brains, not arms, that are required now," he said. But when President Adams, "proscribing the old Federalists," as it was charged, passed over the Old Duke and appointed another to the office of United States judge, Robert had declared for Jackson and had come out on the winning side in 1828.

Now it was his brain that directed the course of the joint companies, and his experience stood him in good stead. In the election of 1836 he and his associates wrote what the Whigs vainly denounced as the "Van Buren Monopoly Ticket" and won the local offices that were important to them, though their candidates were a director of the joint companies, three of its lawyers, and two members of the legislature, and New Jersey cast its vote for William Henry Harrison for President. They celebrated their victory at Princeton, and Morven was the scene of the occasion.

But where "brains" proved unsuitable, Captain Stockton did not hesitate to use other means. When a rival steamboat attempted to carry passengers from Philadelphia to the railroad's terminal at Trenton and a gang of "bullies" was assembled on the Trenton waterfront to support its right to do so, he headed a similar force and knocked down the leader of his opponents with what the newspapers described as "a large stick."

But business and politics combined were not enough to absorb the Captain's energy. In 1824 he had been active in organizing the New Jersey Colonization Society and had become its first president. Soon after his marriage, if not earlier, he had left the church to which he belonged by birth and family tradition for that of his wife and her family, the Episcopalian. In 1827 he was out with Samuel Bayard, soliciting subscriptions for a church building for that denomination. Cousin John Pintard, good Episcopalian though he was, regarded the project as a forlorn hope in Princeton, that stronghold of Presbyterianism. But in 1833 Trinity Church, "a handsome Grecian building," was consecrated by Bishop George Washington Doane. Robert became a vestryman, and in the next few years was in frequent correspondence with the Bishop about suitable preachers for its pulpit.

This decade of the 1830's brought many other changes to the community. Princeton Township was created, and Mercer County was formed of parts of the counties of Middlesex, Burlington, Hunterdon, and Somerset, with Trenton as the county seat. Formerly Princeton north of Nassau Street lay in Somerset County, south of Nassau Street in Middlesex. The prospect of the canal accelerated business and enterprise. "Jugtown," the area at the eastern end of the village, and more properly known as Queenston, had a hotel, a chapel, factories, a number of new houses, and a large trade in pork, hay, and produce. In Princeton proper, where most of the dwellings had been only on Nassau and Witherspoon streets, new houses sprang up on new streets, with the good fortune to have Charles Steadman as their architect and builder. "Morven near Princeton" had been the address of the Stockton family for almost a century. But Morven was *in* Princeton now.

To connect the town with "the Basin," the local stopping place of the canal boats, the Captain opened Canal Street (now Alexander Street) across the Springdale farm. It, too, was soon lined with Steadman houses, and down its dusty length plied the hacks of passengers who at first had to go as far as Hightstown to take "the cars" of the Camden and Amboy Railroad. In 1839, however, the Trenton–New Brunswick branch was built along the canal bank, and the station for Princeton was established at the Basin.

The Mansion House hotel had already reared its three-story brick walls next door to Joline's Tavern and opposite the new Presbyterian church, which had lately replaced one set on fire by a Fourth of July rocket. On the campus East College, West College, and Whig and Clio halls were built. The College of New Jersey was prospering under the presidency of Doctor Carnahan. The Seminary had a hundred and ten students. In 1830 Cousin Mary Hunter wrote that many strangers had been in town that summer, her friends' houses filled with guests, and commencement the gayest ever, with two balls, and tea parties every night. Five years later, when she had become the wife of Samuel Witham Stockton and lived at Tusculum, she reported that "our little town is filled with strangers and much increased since you were here."

It may well have been at this time, when the population of the community was swelled by laborers on canal and railroad, that a bloody town and gown riot was narrowly averted by Captain Stockton's promptness and dominating personality. When both civil authorities and faculty had failed to quell the tumult, he was sent for. Down some eighty yards of the turnpike he found the two parties, both armed with pistols, clubs, and dirks, and ready to fly at each other. Over six feet in height and of a build notably muscular, he walked slowly between them and in that magnificent voice of his demanded silence. The yelling stopped. The two sides stated their grievances. They listened quietly to his proposal for settling the quarrel, and as quietly dispersed.

Riotous conduct was not restricted to the students and those who, in the still-persisting social atmosphere, may be described as the commonality. In November 1837 the Captain's young son Richard wrote in his diary of how "a party of gentlemen full of champagne" attacked the office of Mr. Robert Horner, editor of the *Princeton Whig*, and wrecked the place. Presumably the Captain was out of town that day, for although he was an ardent Democrat at the time, he was a stickler for decency and order and would doubtless have interfered in defense of even his political opponents had he been at home.

He was frequently away in these years, either on business or for amusement. For the latter he had turned to horse racing and, with his large inherited fortune and his wife's expectations from her father, had done so with an extravagance that amounted to prodigality. All the Stocktons, notably those of Burlington, had long been distinguished for their fine horses. But the Captain could be satisfied with nothing less than blooded stock imported from England from which to breed his racers. His Langford, Diana, and Trustee became famous. When he traveled with them from one race meeting to another, he was accompanied by two covered vehicles rather like the trailers of the present day, one of which was fitted up as his bedroom, the other as dining room and office.

He gave the training of his racers his personal supervision. When Langford was entered for the "Produce Stake" on the Washington course and his trainer fell ill, Robert took the man's place. Gravel in the animal's hoof gave it a temporary lameness. President Jackson's horse became the favorite, and most of the jockeys and knowing ones put their money on it. But the lameness disappeared when the stone was removed, and Langford romped home, the winner of the ten-thousand-dollar stake. Its owner, however, was seldom so successful. According to family tradition his losses on the turf were very heavy in the long run.

In the midst of these various activities the Captain was not forgetful of his ancestral home, particularly after he assumed possession following his mother's death in 1837. Undoubtedly he made minor improvements over the years, and in January 1848 he informed his daughter-in-law, Sara, of his decision to "build upon" Morven. For assistance in carrying out this scheme, he probably turned to Architect John Notman of Philadelphia. Then at the height of his fame, Notman had already designed a house for John Potter and Sara and had also drawn plans for the magnificent estate of Cousin Richard Stockton Field.

Robert attacked the improvements to his own dwelling with characteristic verve. To encompass his expansive style of living, he added the east wing and raised the height of the west wing to two full stories. The facade was unified by redesigning the main portico and adding small porticos to the wings. The outbuilding known as the slave quarters was enlarged and covered with stucco scored to simulate stone. In the main house new heavily molded doorways gave access to the parlor and dining room, and more modern sash was hung in the windows. At the rear, two small rooms were built. One held the new bathroom—one of the first in Princeton—with paneled walls of carved mahogany of a fairly baronial dignity. It was reached by a special staircase, the "secret staircase" of legend.

The gardens and grounds also were altered in accord with the fashion of the times. True, the great chestnut tree still spread its limbs across the entire length of the west wing. The chestnut walk, with the tan bark silencing its gravel surface, still stretched from Mr. Bayard's lane westward along the old post road for nearly a quarter of a mile, with its border brightened by spring bulbs and flowering shrubs.

Annis and Richard the Signer's plan for a replica of Pope's garden was outmoded now. The delicate romanticism they had aimed at was replaced by a more robust picturesqueness. With Notman's aid, Robert laid out a varied landscape that extended along the road as far as Constitution Hill. Old features were joined by favorites of the Victorian era; copper beeches, weeping evergreens, and brilliant beds of perennials, in the care of which he had the expert services of Mr. Petrey, who had been a gardener at Chatsworth, the Duke of Devonshire's estate.

Morven tended to become chiefly a summer home for Robert and his wife in these years. He established a winter residence in Philadelphia at Walnut and 13th streets. One winter those whom Cousin Mary described as the "Morven family" spent with the Thomsons, and iron shutters went up to protect the Morven windows against burglers. Another winter only Mary Harrison and Robert's mother remained at the house. At least twice Robert took his family south for the winter, and Mr. Potter and two others did likewise, so that "four of our largest and gayest houses" were shut up.

But when Robert was at home, and generally when he was not, Morven remained, as it always had been, a second home for visiting relatives and a center of cordial hospitality. There had been what Cousin Mary described as "differences" between Robert and various members of the family. But these were now "made up all around"; and all was done with a lavishness that was notable even for Morven, where things had never been stinted. In that commencement week of 1830 Cousin Mary wrote that Captain Stockton gave "one of the grandest dinners ever seen here." He was not yet living at Morven, however, but was still in the house he had built for his bride at the corner of Mr. Bayard's lane. The table was set "from one end of those large parlors to the other." There were sixty guests, and a fine band from Philadelphia played on the front portico. It was six o'clock of a September evening, and in the candlelight the ladies in their ball dresses made a beautiful scene.

Harriet Maria had brought with her her own Negro servants, including the Mammy of her childhood, who still called her "little Miss." But whereas most of the children's clothes had formerly been made at home and their shoes fashioned by the village shoemaker out of leather from the hides of Morven cattle, such things were now ordered from the shops in Philadelphia. As in previous generations, the nursery was fast filling up. Another Richard had been born in 1824, John Potter the next year, Catherine Elizabeth at Charleston two years later, and in Princeton Mary (1830), Robert Field (1832), Harriet Maria (1834), Julia (1837), Caroline (1839), and Annis in 1843. Nine in all, they must have been an expensive brood at best. One bill from the family doctor amounted to a thousand dollars, although in rendering it he expressed gratitude for past kindnesses. He was Doctor William Forman, and the bill must have covered a good many visits, for when the Captain's cousin Doctor Ebenezer Stockton made a visit and supplied a remedy, his charge was only twenty-five cents for each service.

Busy though he was, Robert evidently had, like his father and grandfather, the gift of winning the affectionate admiration of his children. He expected much of them but appears to have been not only just but kind and friendly. In 1838, when his sons Richard and John Potter were fourteen and thirteen respectively, and their father was returning to active duty in the navy, he placed Richard in charge of the Springdale and Morven farms and John Potter in charge of Tusculum and another farm, Tusculum having been left masterless by the untimely death of the Captain's brother Samuel Witham two years before.

It was no merely formal commission for the boys. A thousand dollars was placed to their credit for necessary expenses; they lived on the places for which they were responsible; they had the difficult job of ousting a troublesome tenant from Tusculum; and they were expected at the same time to keep up their studies. Richard was the private pupil of Professor the Reverend Joseph Addison Alexander, D.D., who some years later published his *Earlier Prophecies of Isaiah*, among other works. For the improvement of the boy's mind and spirit he and Richard exchanged letters in the form of diaries;

and Richard's presents a vivid picture of his life and surroundings from 1838 to 1841.

It was the sort of life that a man who had begun his own life as a midshipman would think proper for his son. In Richard's room in the Springdale farmhouse were two high desks, book-shelves, a furnace register, but also saddles, bridles, and barrels of chicken feed. There, even on a bleak mid-March morning, he was up before six, studied for two hours, and fed the chickens before he had his breakfast. Next came an inspection of the stables, in which he was attended by his three dogs, Dan, Bess, and Dash, and after that, study again until "the bell rang for twelve."

Then he was on his horse, on which he "floundered through the slough" to Morven and down the lane to the Morven stables. There he stroked the colt until it took him by the leg and lifted him off the ground. The deep mud kept him from riding "down the town." He had dinner, recitations until half-past four, made a trip by wagon to the blacksmith's, and so back to Springdale, where he rubbed spirits on the neck of one of the dogs. After supper came more study—Cicero, algebra, a Racine tragedy in French, and Tasso in Italian—followed by an examination of the departed tenant's bills, the writing of a letter to his father, a reading from the Bible, and bed at nine.

But there were many and interesting relaxations from this strenuous· life: Washington Irving's *Sketch Book*, for example, and *Pickwick Papers*, which Professor Alexander read aloud. Among public entertainments were The Russells' Concert, a lecture by Mr. Parker on his recent tour beyond the Rocky Mountains, and a speech by Doctor Skinner, formerly governor of Liberia. There was shooting in the Morven woods, and farther afield with a team and wagon: reed birds, cedar birds, and hopes of woodcock, one of which brother John actually brought down.

There were drives to the Basin in the carriage with his mother. One could skate on the canal, and when the ground was frozen hard, it was stirring to ride Boxer down Mr. Bayard's lane to "the commencement of our woods" and thence through woods and fields, jumping fences and ditches, until one came to "the Morven house" and so home. But best of all were a couple of trips to New York. For these one took "the green wagon" to Hightstown and was lucky if one was not held up for the passage of canal boats through the drawbridge at the Basin; and one was pleasantly thrilled as the boat from Amboy to New York met with quite a swell on the bay.

On Washington's Birthday there were speeches in the Seminary Chapel both morning and afternoon, and "the Blues," the local militia company, paraded. But the most exciting event of these years was undoubtedly the fire in Mr. Passage's house on Nassau Street, which was extinguished by the Resolution Fire Company only after the roof fell in. Mr. Horner's neighboring printing office and reading room were protected from the flames by a covering of wet carpets, and Mr. Philips saved his house by standing on the roof and wetting it with buckets of water that were passed up to him. The engine was kept supplied with water by a bucket line, in which the elegant Craig Biddle leaned on his cane with one hand and passed buckets with the other: "a magnificent picture of indolence and effeminacy" in the opinion of young Richard Stockton. The second floor tenants, maiden ladies, had to move to Doctor Forman's former house at the corner of Canal Street. Major John Perrine, the postmaster, organized the students into a procession to transport their possessions, each one carrying the first thing that came to his hand, while one of them marched at their head, waving an old sword he had found in the rubbish.

All in all these were fine years for young Richard. He hated to see them pass, wished on his fifteenth birthday that it was only his twelfth or, better still, his ninth, but resolved to "try to improve the time that is yet left to me in this world."

On Tuesday, March 12, 1839, he wrote: "Nothing particular happened except that I had a little sister born this morning." This was Caroline, the eighth of his mother's children, and Richard may be excused for his blasé attitude toward the event: he must have had a pretty clear memory of four of these biennial occurrences in the family. To him the really important events were those in his father's career. In 1838 Captain Stockton returned to duty in the navy in command of Commodore Hull's flagship, the line-of-battle ship *Ohio*. Richard had the honor of packing the things his father wished to take with him, went up to New York to see him sail, stayed at the Astor House, and dined on board the vessel. Before dinner the *Ohio* was visited by the Mayor and Corporation Council of the city, and the Mayor made a "poor speech" in Richard's opinion, "about Rome and Athens and all the other old places."

Going home he traveled on Sunday "for the first time in my life." He could have gone on Saturday, he confessed, but his father said he would go with him if he waited. When the *Ohio* finally sailed, he felt for the next few days considerable anxiety as to how his father had managed in taking such a great vessel down the harbor and out through the Lower Bay after his many years on land. "Mr. Buchanan"—probably the commander of the *Merrimac* at Hampton Roads twenty-four years later—had been humorously skeptical about his ability to do so properly. But on December 6 a friend who had remained on board the *Ohio* until she passed Sandy Hook reported that the Captain was not at all "rusty" but "with speaking trumpet in hand piloted the ship the whole way." Neither the mysterious disappearance of a check from Uncle Thomson for $950.82 nor a sound rebuke from Doctor Alexander for traveling on Sunday diminished Richard's satisfaction in this, and he settled back into his routine, while awaiting a letter from his father by the steamship *Great Western*.

The next year he became a student at the College of New

Jersey, where he was impressed by the prevalence of "stomping" in the classrooms. He lived at Morven, though his mother spent that winter at the Philadelphia house; and again he was rebuked by Doctor Alexander for traveling on Sunday when he returned from visiting her there, although it was done at her direction. Also to his pious mentor's horror, he gave his brother John a black eye. He was impressed, evidently observing it for the first time, by the name of Elias Boudinot "written on a pane of glass in our parlor window, dated 1805." In August 1841, when he was sixteen, the single word "Καθαρίνε" (Catharine) brings this record of boyhood, understandably, to a close.

Captain Stockton's service on the *Ohio* was of short duration. After a brief term on the Mediterranean station he went to England, where he spent several months in the study of British naval architecture and the manufacture of heavy ordnance. There he met John Ericsson, the Swedish engineer and inventor, whose screw propeller had lately been rejected by the British Admiralty on the ground that it would interfere with the steering of vessels. Stockton had Ericsson build him an iron tow-boat equipped with a screw propeller, named her, with a characteristic lack of false modesty, the *Robert F. Stockton*, and ran her up and down the Thames to demonstrate the practicability of Ericsson's invention. In the spring of 1839 the little vessel, only seventy feet by ten, crossed the Atlantic under sail, with a crew of four men and a boy. The canal company bought her, and she did excellent service between New Brunswick and Trenton, being able to break her way through ice that rendered paddle-wheel steamers powerless.

Home again after an absence of only about ten months, Robert was in time to arrange for the continuance of a loan of five hundred thousand dollars to the joint companies by the United States Bank of Philadelphia, for which he promised payment of fifty thousand dollars every six months, the deposit of all the companies' monies in that bank, and the maintenance of a monthly balance of between fifty thousand and ninety thousand dollars. He was assigned to duty at the Brooklyn Navy Yard and promoted to post captain. But when his best efforts failed to persuade the Navy Department to build a screw-propeller frigate, he asked for a two-year leave, which was granted him, and turned once more to politics. He had formerly supported Van Buren. But he was never one to feel bound to any party when he saw what he thought to be good reason to make a change. He now threw himself, with his usual energy and impetuosity, into the "Log Cabin and Hard Cider" campaign of William Henry Harrison.

He toured the state, making speeches for "Tippecanoe and Tyler Too" in almost every town. A log cabin was built in the center of Princeton for local headquarters. Harrison paid a brief visit to the borough, was a guest at Morven, and made a speech from the steps of the college library. Upon his untimely death the following spring, after only a month in office, Captain Stockton found a warm friend in his successor. According to family tradition, President Tyler offered to appoint him secretary of the navy, and he declined.

Two years later Morven once more had the honor of entertaining a President of the United States. President Tyler spent a June Saturday-to-Monday there with his suite, which included, among others, the secretaries of War and the Treasury, his son Robert, who was his secretary, and his official hostess, his charming daughter-in-law, Priscilla Cooper Tyler, the Sophie Sparkle of Washington Irving's *Salmagundi*. On the Saturday he was "visited by the populace," Mary Harrison wrote in her diary. On Sunday the whole party, twenty-three in number, sat down to "a handsome dinner that went off well," and on Monday they departed to the strains of a band, with a great cortege following them.

As they passed the house of Mr. J. S. Green, the Reverend Ashbel Green, D.D., came out of the front door. At sight of him, President Tyler stopped his chariot and four, got out, and "made obeisance," hat in hand, to the old man, now eighty-one, who had borne arms in the Revolution and been president of the College of New Jersey for ten stormy years. It was "the only impressive scene in the melodrama," in the opinion of the Reverend J. W. Alexander, D.D., Professor of Rhetoric and Belles Lettres at the college.

But the whole occasion was doubtless a delight to Captain Robert Field Stockton. Tyler's administration had given him the opportunity to undertake an enterprise dear to his heart, and the President's visit enabled him to make a demonstration of his gratitude.

# CHAPTER VII

## "A Very Correct, High-Spirited Officer"

BY THE time of Tyler's visit to Morven Captain Stockton had cut short his leave and been back on active duty for a year or more. His project for building a propeller-driven warship had found favor with the new administration, and in 1841 he had been ordered to the navy yard at Philadelphia to superintend the construction of a sloop-of-war that was to embody his ideas of what a modern war vessel ought to be.

"With one gun aboard," he boasted, she would "be able to defy all the steamships built, or that were now building, for the navy." In addition to his ideas and supervision, he made, with his usual munificence, a large financial contribution out of his own pocket for refinements not covered by the appropriation of government funds. So it was not inappropriate that the vessel should be named the *Princeton,* after his native town.

The first propeller-driven warship in the world, she was also unique in having her engine below the waterline, where, in contrast with the side-wheelers, it would be comparatively invulnerable to enemy fire. She was the first also to burn anthracite coal and thus avoid betraying her presence at a distance by her smoke, as the soft-coal-burning steamers did; and her funnel—"smoke-stack" they called it in those days— was collapsible so as not to interfere with her spars and canvas when she was under sail.

Her armament, too, embodied the advanced ideas of her sponsor. Her main battery consisted of two twelve-inch guns weighing ten tons each, which Stockton had named defiantly— considering how hot the Oregon Question was at that time— the Peacemaker and the Oregon. Mr. Philip Hone, of New York, believed that the Peacemaker was intended to "hurl defiance" at Great Britain and regarded Stockton as "the firebrand which was to ignite the whole." The Oregon had been made in England out of wrought iron, a new material for ordnance. Stockton had caused it to be shipped to the United States, and there he had personally supervised the construction of the Peacemaker, its mate.

In his enthusiasm for this brain child of his, Robert evidently transgressed the bounds of official decorum. For on the 9th of May, 1843, he was writing, presumably to the commander of the navy yard at Philadelphia:

"Dear Sir:—

"I regret that anything should have caused you to think that your proper authority had been overlooked. . . . I have never presumed to give *an order in the yard*. My *wishes* are all that I have ever thought of expressing. I hope hereafter to avoid all cause of complaint.

"Yours truly,

"R. F. Stockton."

The authority he was able to arrogate to himself in civil life was better suited to his temperament. There he could write, as he did in 1851: ". . . I must have my own way in the matter. I cannot be bothered with the interference of others."

The *Princeton* proved to have all the excellent qualities that he and Ericsson had claimed for her. She overtook and passed the crack liner *Great Western*, holder of the trans-Atlantic record, in a race from the Battery to Sandy Hook. Late in February 1844, she smashed her way through the ice of the frozen Potomac and dropped anchor off the Washington Navy Yard; and on February 28, she steamed off down the river to demonstrate her powers to a company of notables whom her commander had invited on board. It promised to be the great day in the life of Captain Stockton. Among the four hundred guests were the President, the secretaries of State and the Navy and other members of the Cabinet, many senators, and some two hundred distinguished ladies, among whom was seventy-seven-year-old "Dolly" Madison, who had snubbed the Old Duke at her reception a generation before.

The *Princeton* sped swiftly and smoothly down the river, passed Fort Washington and Mount Vernon. The great guns hurled their two-hundred-and-twelve-pound shot a distance of three miles with a charge of thirty-five pounds of powder. A "splendid collation" was served below decks and followed by a toast to "the Oregon, the Peacemaker, and Captain Stockton." It was about four o'clock, and the ship had turned homeward, when Secretary of the Navy Gilmer requested that the Peacemaker be fired once more. Only twenty-five pounds of powder were used this time, but the great gun burst at the breach, blowing away twenty feet of the bulwark.

Fortunately most of the guests had remained below, but even so the casualties were awful. Secretary of State Upshur and Secretary of the Navy Gilmer, a servant, and two sailors were killed. Only the chance that somebody detained him in the companionway had kept the President out of danger. Captain Stockton, who was standing close to the breach of the gun, was hurled to the deck, scorched, burned, and half blinded. When Mr. Henry Alexander Wise visited the ruined deck of the ship next morning, he saw the dead bodies bound up and laid out decently in their clothes, and talked with poor Stockton. The Captain had staggered to his feet after the explosion and directed the rescue work and the care of the wounded until he had fainted. Mr. Wise found him in his cabin, his eyes bandaged, a prey to grief and mortification that were sharper than the pain of his burns.

But a searching official investigation, which was made at his request, exonerated him from all blame for the accident. The gun had been thoroughly and repeatedly tested under his own eyes before being put on board the ship, and there had been no departure from the regular routine in loading and firing the fatal charge. The Captain made a quick recovery from his injuries. The *Princeton* went on to demonstrate her excellence in the Mexican War both in the blockade and in the landing of General Scott's expedition at Vera Cruz, where she towed the sixty-five whale-boats of the first wave of invasion to within easy rowing distance of the beach.

As the prospect of war with Mexico grew more menacing and troops began to assemble at New Orleans for General Zachary Taylor's advance to the Rio Grande, Stockton, with the rank of commodore, was sent to the mouth of the Sabine in command of a squadron that was composed of the *Princeton*, the sloop-of-war *St. Mary's*, and several smaller vessels. But his relations with the Texans were distinguished by more energy than tact. He was relieved and placed in command of the frigate *Congress*, with orders to sail for the Hawaiian Islands and thence to the coast of California, where he was to relieve Commodore Sloat as commander of the United States naval forces in the Pacific.

The weeks of his preparation for his departure were busy ones. The *Congress* was at Norfolk. But he snatched time from making her ready for sea to settle, so far as possible, his affairs at Morven and elsewhere. His stud was broken up, his racers sold. The letter book of his agent, William Gatzmer, of Philadelphia, reflects the complicated state of his finances that had to be dealt with in view of his prolonged absence on the other side of the continent. But by the end of July things seem to have been straightened out, at least for the time being. On the 26th Gatzmer acknowledged to the Commodore, that being his new status, the receipt of $115 in American gold, $5,057.01 in British sovereigns, and $70 in guineas.

For personal expenses on his voyage he drew five hundred dollars in American gold and, moderate drinker that he was for his time, included in his personal stores five dozen bottles of old whisky that cost him fifty dollars. He presented to the crew of the *Congress* a "Seamen's Friends Library" of between three hundred and four hundred volumes, made "a short and pertinent address" to his officers and crew, and set sail in October 1845 on the expedition that was to place his name with Zachary Taylor's and Winfield Scott's in the record of the war that carried the boundaries of the United States to the Rio Grande and the Pacific.

For those left at Morven there followed two years of anxiety, punctuated now and again by joy and pride, as news of the well-loved husband, father, and generous friend filtered through from Monterey and from Yerba Buena, on the Bay of San Francisco. Once it came by courtesy of the British minister at Washington, who had it from his opposite number at Mexico City; later it came in letters that Kit Carson and other Western scouts had borne across mountains and plains in official dispatch bags. Always the news was good; always, too, it implied further dangers to be faced, fresh risks to be run.

But there had seldom been a time in the past seventy years when such anxiety and a similar pride in brave deeds in faraway lands and on distant seas had not been felt at Morven. The Revolution, the War of 1812, Algiers, and the bloody fighting against the West Indian picaroons all had a place on Morven's flag. If the master of the house was not involved, there were nephews and cousins to be prayed for. One of Aunt Mary Hunter's boys had been for many years serving in the dragoons as far west as Fort Leavenworth. Another, a medical officer in the navy, would bring home a quarter cask of Canary from his Mediterranean service and straw hats that cost eighteen or twenty dollars at Leghorn, where they were made. Still another son, Richard Stockton Hunter, had come home from the navy to die at Princeton in 1825.

The ladies of the family had also been great travelers. Aunt Mary, at seventy-eight, had braved the fatigues of stage coach, canal boat, and the primitive steamers of the Great Lakes to spend a winter with her son David at Fort Dearborn, under whose stockaded walls Chicago had lately shot up to be a city. About the same time Aunt Julia Rush, two years her senior, had made the arduous trip to Canada. The eldest and last surviving children of Richard the Signer, these two old ladies could remember clearly the dangers and glories of the Revolution. This year, 1846, both died, aged eighty-seven and eighty-five respectively: Julia at her home at Sydenham, Mary in the house she had built for herself at Princeton.

But no doubt the great event in the Morven family circle that year was the beginning of a new nursery. With the Commodore and Harriet Maria's youngest child, Annis, not yet three years old, their first grandchild made his appearance. Early in 1845 young John Potter Stockton, their second son, who was not yet quite twenty years old, had met in Philadelphia society the beautiful, accomplished, and highly intelligent Miss Sara Marks, of New Orleans, aged seventeen. Their attraction to each other was spontaneous and so powerful that when their youth and the fact that she was a Jewess were urged against their marriage, they made a runaway match of it on the 15th of May of that year.

Relations, friends, and all Princeton, says family tradition, were scandalized by the unsuitability of the marriage. The bride was an Episcopalian, her family held an excellent position in New Orleans society, but Princeton gossip had it that her father was a caterer. Henry Green gibed that the Stockton coat of arms ought thenceforth to be charged with an oyster impaled on an oyster fork. Morven, however, had opened wide its doors to the young couple, and there on the 4th of March, 1846, a new Richard Stockton came into the world.

From the baby's grandfather, nine months later, came the first letters, telling of his splendid achievements in California.

The Commodore had arrived at Monterey on July 15 to find Commodore Sloat, the commander of the Pacific squadron, eagerly awaiting official notice of his retirement. Ill and hampered by orders to take no action until he received information of a formal declaration of war, the old man had shrunk from making any decision lest he blot his record. But on hearing of Taylor's victories on the Rio Grande, he had screwed up his resolution so far as to land his marines and occupy the forts and the town. He was hardly a day too soon. The powerful British man-of-war *Collingwood* dropped in shortly after, and her commander, Admiral Seymour, remarked: "Sloat, if your flag was not already on shore, I should have hoisted mine there."

No such hesitancy marked Stockton's course upon succeeding to the command, as he shortly did. The marines, with their customary versatility, had collected horses from the neighboring ranches and extemporized a company of dragoons composed of some men of their own, some civilian volunteers, and sailors who knew enough about a horse to board it on the larboard side. This force Stockton augmented by landing as many seamen as could be spared from his ships, arming as many of them as possible with muskets, the rest with carbines, pistols, cutlasses, and boarding pikes.

Frémont and the hundred and sixty tough frontiersmen who had marched to Monterey from the Mission of San Juan Stockton promptly mustered into the service of the United States and shipped off by sea to San Diego, of which they made an easy conquest. He hoisted the American flag over Santa Barbara and, anchoring off San Pedro, where Los Angeles was only an eighteen-mile march away, he demanded of Castro, the Comandante General, that he accept independence under that flag. Castro retired in haste toward Sonoma; and on August 12, though positive information of a declaration of war was still lacking, Commodore Stockton led his marines and sailors into Los Angeles, with a brass band blaring at their head. It was exactly four weeks since his arrival at Monterey.

Five days later came positive news that war had been declared. The Commodore immediately proclaimed California to be a part of the United States. In another month he had caused a school to be opened and a newspaper started, each the first of its kind that the country had ever known. Municipal elections were held with excellent results, alcaldes were appointed, and Kit Carson was dispatched overland to carry the good news to Washington.

With his customary audacity, Stockton now entertained the fantastic scheme of invading Mexico from the Pacific coast. But upon a report that a thousand Indians were about to attack the settlements in the Sacramento Valley, he set sail for San Francisco Bay; and during his absence a complete reversal of fortune befell his forces in the south. A popular rising compelled the little American garrison at Los Angeles to capitulate; Santa Barbara had to be evacuated; San Diego was closely besieged; an attempt to retake Los Angeles failed. The California legislature declared martial law and made the leader of the insurrection provisional governor and comandante general. General Stephen W. Kearny, marching westward from the easy conquest of New Mexico, had to fight his way to San Diego, though Stockton reenforced him with the troops he could spare.

But the insurrectionists lacked money, ammunition, and, above all, popular support. By the 1st of December the Commodore had reoccupied San Pedro and relieved San Diego, and on the 29th, with his four hundred sailors and marines and Kearny's dragoons, he advanced up the hundred and forty miles of sandy road that led to Los Angeles. About five hundred and fifty poorly armed Californians tried to stop him at the San Gabriel River on January 8. But the Americans charged with the cry "New Orleans"—it was the anniversary of Jackson's defeat of the British in 1815—and two days later the same flag that they had been forced to haul down was hoisted once more over the City of the Angels.

There were no further hostilities. The Californians, disgusted by the Mexican government's failure to support them, felt that they had satisfied their honor by the resistance they had made, and they appreciated the magnanimity of the terms of peace that were offered them. By midsummer their relations with their conquerors had become so friendly that

Señora Pico, wife of the late governor of the city, was among the many Californian ladies who attended the ball that the officers of the American forces gave at Los Angeles on the Fourth of July.

By that time the Commodore was almost a week on his way homeward, at the head of a party that numbered forty-nine. His biographer, who wrote some seven or eight years later, credits him with killing forty-five buffalo on the way; and the journey was not otherwise uneventful—such journeys seldom were. Stockton had ordered that the Indians, who dogged the party persistently, were not to be molested. But when he was shot through both thighs by an Indian arrow, he reversed his orders and, as soon as he could travel, acted with his habitual energy, ambushing the ambuscaders.

The party did not reach the frontier town of St. Joseph's in Missouri until early in November, having been a little more than four months on the trail. The Commodore arrived in Washington on December 1, 1847. There was, however, no conqueror's welcome awaiting him at the capital, nor could he expect one. President Polk could see nothing but probable political opponents in the generals who had won for him what his enemies called in derision "Mr. Polk's war." A stickler for implicit obedience, he was unable to understand how changing conditions at the seat of war must modify decisions made in the Cabinet. General Kearny had arrived in California with an order appointing him governor of the country. Stockton and Frémont, who had conquered the country while Kearny was on the way, refused to recognize its authority, holding that the situation had completely changed since the order was issued. Frémont had assumed the governorship and Stockton had backed him in doing so, with the result that Stockton had been relieved of his command by order of the Secretary of the Navy, and Frémont, ordered to Washington to face a court-martial, was sentenced to dismissal from the service. Polk approved the sentence but had the decency to remit the penalty, and Frémont promptly resigned from the army.

There was no obscuring, however, the brilliance of Stockton's and Frémont's achievements, let the attitude of the administration be what it might. Stockton was Frémont's eloquent champion at the court-martial, and the powerful Senator Benton, Frémont's father-in-law, made a forceful speech discrediting the attacks upon the Commodore. Even Secretary Mason, by whose order the Commodore was relieved, praised him. His home-coming was celebrated at Princeton by a public meeting that passed resolutions of admiration. The New Jersey legislature thanked him for his services to the nation. Philadelphia gave him a banquet, at the Musical Fund Hall, and New York did likewise. Back in California grateful settlers gave his name to a city and to one of the principal streets in San Francisco. His previous exploits had already placed it on an African river and a bay in the Isla de Caja de Muertos south of Puerto Rico.

Clearing up his official business with all possible dispatch, the Commodore had lost no time in setting out for Morven, where his grandson, now nearly sixteen months old, awaited him. Whatever he may have thought of the fitness of his son's marriage, his joy and pride in the child were such that in the next five months he made the father a present of Tusculum, "stock and all," which had been John's boyhood care six years before, and he proposed almost at once to build a fine house for the young couple at the west end of the Morven property: he had the plans ready for it by the 1st of February. On the 14th of March, Sara's twentieth birthday, he presented her with what even that highly discriminating young lady described in her diary as "a beautiful dress."

"The Commodore was particularly agreeable this morning," Sara wrote in her diary near the end of this year and added, "not that he is not always so, but this morning he was particularly so." It was much to his credit—or it would have been to a man not blessed by his buoyant temperament. For he had found many problems awaiting him on his return.

During his absence Mr. Gatzmer's business letters to him had been brightened with news of the doings of family, relatives, and friends. Brother-in-law James Potter, whom Mr. Gatzmer thought "very smart," had taken his wife on a trip to Europe. Brother-in-law Thomson and Mr. Stevens had given a brilliant party to the "chief officers"—the governors and others—of Pennsylvania and New Jersey on board the *John Stevens*, the joint companies' new iron steamboat on the Delaware. Mr. Stevens had built a fine, new, sloop-rigged yacht that was believed to be the fastest craft of her type afloat. Son Richard, now twenty-one, had repaid through Gatzmer the hundred dollars he had borrowed from his mother. Mrs. Stockton and the family were now back at Princeton after a month in Philadelphia.

But the situation that the prudent and sagacious Gatzmer had been forced to deal with while his principal was absent was a serious one. Railroad and canal, to be sure, were doing well. Even in the panic year of 1837 a steady stream of sloops, schooners, barges loaded with Pennsylvania anthracite, and some ships of five hundred tons had plowed the narrow waters between Trenton and New Brunswick; and the Basin at Princeton had continued to present a scene of unceasing activity ever since. There were years in which the tonnage exceeded that of the Erie Canal; and if the earnings were small, those of the railroad were sufficient to pay handsome dividends to the stockholders of the joint companies. "Our stock," wrote Gatzmer in March of 1846, was selling at 120, the bonds at par. But, three months earlier, he had been at his wit's end to raise twenty thousand dollars to meet the Commodore's liabilities: interest rates ran as high as twelve per cent, owing to the fear of war with Great Britain over the Oregon boundary.

The Commodore's notes, totaling forty-five thousand dollars, had to be met a few months later. His investments in

Arkansas land, Mexican certificates of debt, and the New Brunswick Manufacturing Company made poor collateral for a loan to meet these obligations. There remained large loans, long past due, which the Commodore had made to friends, often borrowing himself in order to do so. But Mr. Reverdy Johnson, who could pay the painter Sully his top price of a thousand dollars for the portrait of Mrs. Johnson that now hangs in the Princeton University Library, was appealed to for the repayment of his loan in vain; so was Mr. James Bayard.

"It is a very pleasant and easy thing to lend," Mr. Gatzmer wrote to his principal in plaintive expostulation on July 28, 1846, "but to collect from borrowers is most difficult. I must persuade you to send such borrowers hereafter to your agent, for I can say no."

The advice fell on deaf ears. The Commodore continued to be incorrigible in his generosity. But somehow each recurring crisis had been met, and he had not long been home again before he engaged in fresh financial ventures.

He was not without good reason in believing in his financial judgment and ability. In the panic of 1837, after his father-in-law had invested close to half a million in the railroad and canal project and he had done the like with almost the whole of his family's fortune, the joint companies had spent their entire available funds on railroad construction and were in a bad way for money to go on with. The fortunes of many a businessman of far greater experience than the Commodore's were shaken and even shattered. But, undaunted, Commodore Stockton had gone to England and so impressed the London bankers that he had been able to float a six-per-cent bond issue secured by a mortgage on the canal for two hundred and twenty-five thousand pounds at 95—and this although American securities had earned a bad name in the London market.

A letter that he addressed to the Governor and Directors of the Bank of England was republished in the American newspapers and won the admiration of so competent a judge of such matters as Mr. Philip Hone, of New York, who wrote in his diary that while Lieutenant Stockton "is not of the timid sort and does not often find his modesty crossing the path of his undertakings . . . there is a great deal of excellent sense in his letter, and it is said to have had a salutary effect upon the decisions of the bank and done more to enlighten the public mind in London than anything that has been 'said or sung' on the subject of American affairs."

But the same love of long chances that had lured his unfortunate elder brother to the gaming table led him into speculations that were to bring sorrow to his family in the end. Wild land, especially if it was supposed to contain minerals, had an irresistible fascination for him. He already held land in Georgia and 1,280 acres in the state of Arkansas, which had lately been admitted to the Union. The Fluvanna Mining Company had sold him some in Virginia. He bought more of it the year after his return, and although warned that Virginia copper lands were no good, he increased his holdings in Fluvanna and Goochland counties and appears to have had a hand in organizing the Northeast Gold Mining Company. At the family dinner, next New Year's Day, 1849, he gave his grandson a gold piece and his daughter-in-law a piece of Virginia gold, out of which she planned to have the jeweler make her a brooch.

He plunged again into politics. The interests of the joint companies had suffered during his absence in the service. Back in 1844, when the building of the *Princeton* had kept him too busy to take a hand in the campaign, his Thomson brother-in-law had run for governor of the state and had been defeated, being regarded as too obviously the tool of the "Barons of Apartment Number 10" in Snowden's hotel. Even some Democrats had become disgusted with the machinations of the Camden and Amboy machine, and the antimonopolists had captured control of the party from the Stevenses and the aging John Potter.

Antimonopolist meetings were held in many parts of the state. The companies lost the wise counsel of Mr. Potter, who died at Morven at the age of eighty-six in October 1849; and the Commodore's task was not lightened by a wreck on the railroad, in which eighteen passengers were killed, and for which, Sara wrote, Princeton people blamed the railroad bitterly. Henry C. Carey, of Burlington, a financial authority, demanded that the joint companies' agreement with the state be abolished: a proposal that caused such excitement at Morven that Sara became keenly aware of it.

But the Commodore defended the companies' actions and his own in a series of articles in the *Princeton Whig* that were moderate and sincere in tone. Commissioners appointed to examine the companies' books found certain transactions by which the state had been the loser, but on the whole their report was favorable; and people in general were placated by a reduction in railroad fares. The better to attend to his business matters, the Commodore resigned from the navy in 1850, after thirty-nine years of service. Now, moreover, a career in national politics began to open before him. In November the Democrats, who were in control of the New Jersey legislature, began to talk of him as a candidate for the United States Senate, and in December 1851 he took his seat in the Senate chamber at Washington.

Meanwhile life at Morven went on in its usual, prosperous, and generally harmonious way. Young Mrs. John Potter Stockton left a record of it from 1848 through 1854 in a spasmodic but vivid diary that fairly pulsates with her mercurial temperament. It was by no means the life of luxurious indolence that might be imagined of a household in which there was no want of servants. There were plenty of amusements, much entertaining. There were winters in Philadelphia, summer weeks at the seaside, excursions to the Delaware Water Gap, and brief visits to New York. But there were household duties that are now almost unknown. When ice cream was to be made for dessert, the ladies made it. The summer of 1848 Sara pickled peaches, helped her sisters-in-law in making marmalade and quince preserves, and sighed with relief when her sixteen pounds of plum preserve, her first attempt at that dainty, turned out to be a success.

Arduous shopping trips to Trenton, Philadelphia, and New York left plenty of sewing to be done at home: hemming towels, marking sheets, making the children's shirts and slips, and flannel sacks for the ladies themselves. For quiet evenings, when one did not feel like reading *Tales of the Alhambra* or *Ferdinand and Isabella* or *The Queens of England,* there were tidies or a silk purse to be knitted, or a tablecloth or a screen to embroider with flowers, while they "talked the Rotch crowd over [the family into which Aunt Caroline had married] with little mercy." The semiannual house-cleaning was done under the personal supervision of "Mother," who was Harriet Maria. But at those times Sara, at least, took refuge in her room with a book.

But she, like the rest of the family, was always at church on Sunday morning. Once, having overslept, she went without her breakfast in order to be there. When he was at home, the Commodore martialed the whole family across the road to the little "Grecian" Trinity Church of those days, and there came a time when his assembled children and grandchildren filled three pews. By 1854 Richard, his eldest son, had married Caroline Bayard Dod and had three children. Robert Field, his youngest son, had married Anna Marguerita of the Philadelphia Potter family, whom Sara regarded as "very peculiar people." Their children also numbered three by this time, and Sara had given little Richard a brother and sister—a second John Potter Stockton, born in 1852, and little Sara, born a year later.

In 1850 the Commodore's eldest daughter, Catherine Elizabeth, had become the wife of the Reverend William Armstrong Dod, D.D., later the pastor of the Second Presbyterian Church at Princeton. Later still, having taken Episcopalian orders, he became rector of Trinity Church, and Catherine Elizabeth became the mistress of the spacious rectory that her maternal grandfather had given to the parish.

At commencement time in 1854—it had been changed to June ten years earlier—the wedding of her next younger sister, Mary, to John C. Howell, of the United States navy, was celebrated at Morven with lavishness and splendor. When the bridal couple took their departure, a special train on the Camden and Amboy Railroad conveyed them and the rest of the bridal party, Mr. Edward Stevens, of Hoboken, and other distinguished guests as far as Bordentown.

The Stocktons and their relations must have gone far toward filling the nave of the little church in these years. There were James and Thomas Fuller Potter and their families, the Bayards, and the Richard Stockton Fields. Upon his father's death, Thomas Potter had torn down the old house at Prospect and built the present mansion. His brother James had bought the house at the head of Bayard Lane, which the Commodore had built for his bride. Richard Stockton Field, son of Aunt Abigail and Robert Field, of White Hill, had built Fieldwood, which he later called Woodlawn, and which has since been known as Guernsey Hall, about half a mile out on the old road to Trenton. Before building, he had spent ten years in beautifying the thirty-acre estate that surrounded the house, importing rare trees from Europe and, with the advice and assistance of his architect, John Notman, laying out romantic vistas of lawns, woods, and winding drives.

With his customary prodigality, the Commodore saw to it that his children should be suitably established when they married. The "gothic cottage" on Mercer Street, now the residence of the president of the Theological Seminary, he built for Richard. According to tradition its elaborate design cost him half again as much as the Reverend Doctor Hodge spent in building a dignified and equally commodious house almost next door. For "Betty," Catherine Elizabeth, he built a house near the lower end of Bayard Lane. The house he built for Sara and her husband—since known as Allison House —was "the finest house in Princeton, and one of the finest in New Jersey." Or with such words did Sara comfort herself when other matters sent her spirits down to zero, as they often did.

The relations between these various establishments were generally friendly, frequently cordial. But close as were the ties of blood and marriage, a social protocol prevailed among them that seems strangely rigid in our careless days. The failure to return a call within the prescribed limit of time was taken as an intentional slight and was intended to be one.

Of such things young Sara kept a record in her diary and she was probably not alone in doing so. But her life at Morven, and in her own house, must have been a singularly happy one, all things considered. She seems to have been on the best of terms with the three of her sisters-in-law who were of about her own age. They walked to Pretty Brook together, and went on fishing parties. On June 15, 1849, she records an especially merry time with "the girls." It ended with poundcake and ale and much laughter after a stroll around the Morven place from the chestnut walk to the stables.

The building of her house was a continual delight to her. And there was the shopping in Philadelphia for linen and china, the arranging of the parlors and the hanging of the pictures. For June 5, 1849, she wrote that she and her husband had "our first tea" there. They slept there that night, and next morning she noted: "It is perfectly delightful." A month later they had the Commodore and old Mr. Potter to dinner and, the following week, "my little soiree." In August Sully, the painter, came to dine. He had been painting the Potter children, and in September she took her little son to be painted by him. Later, things seem to have gone less happily. She found old Mr. Potter "as disagreeable as ever." Her mother-in-law teased her about growing fat; and after an evening at Morven during which she felt neglected, she "quietly came home and won't go there again soon."

Through these years the Commodore came and went, generally too busy to spend more than a night or two at home. A stickler for correctness in everything, he insisted upon his engaged daughters and their fiancés' confining their endearments to the privacy of the chestnut walk, and he was a stern critic of the dress of his daughters-in-law. But on these visits he came as a dispenser of high spirits and good gifts. He had fireworks at Morven on the Fourth of July, gave delightful dinners, to General Belknap and other distinguished guests, took a family party on an excursion to Philadelphia, and found time for long rides on horseback.

In breaking up his racing stable he had not deprived himself of fine saddlehorses. To each of his children he had given an excellent horse, and he loved to ride out at the head of a cavalcade of sons and daughters. The girls were all accomplished horsewomen, and if Sara's performance can be accepted as typical, they were indefatigable. It had taken her some years to persuade her husband to allow her to ride. But in the summer of 1849 he consented, gave her her own horse, Mayflower; and she proceeded to make up for lost time. During the following winter she would ride fourteen and even twenty miles in an afternoon or early morning, though the mud might be deep. And once she rode ten miles, though it was "snowing terribly" and the weather was so cold that she "nearly froze" two days later in driving to Trenton in a sleigh.

The family, married sons and daughters and their children included, spent some weeks at Long Branch in the summers. Since there was no railway, the journey of some fifty miles had to be made by road. To avoid the heat they started at three in the morning; and one may easily imagine the lantern-lit departure, the convoy of carriages filled with cross and drowsy elders and children asleep in their nurses' arms, and the baggage wagon bringing up the rear as they rolled away from the Morven portico. At Freehold they halted for some hours to rest and escape the midday heat and reached their destination in time for supper. In the following days the ladies bathed, if the sea was not too cold or rough, bought baskets of the basket man, and rehearsed songs. Sara took a modeling lesson and "made three spares" in the bowling alley one morning.

Of winters the Commodore had his married children and their families to visit him at the Walnut Street house in Philadelphia. On one of these occasions Sara went shopping with "the White House ladies," who were evidently preparing their wardrobes for Zachary Taylor's inauguration the following month, and among whom was Mrs. Bliss, the President-elect's daughter, soon to become known as "our Betty" in Washington society. But Christmases and New Year's Days were generally celebrated at Morven, with many presents, much gaiety, and ices, poundcake, and eggnog for callers.

One February Sara and her husband gave a grand party, at which she noted that "the gentlemen were very fashionable." The guests arrived between eight and nine in the evening; supper was served at midnight; and they departed about half past one. Trips to New York brightened the early spring. There one stayed at the Astor House, shopped at Stewart's store, visited the Dusseldorf gallery, and walked on Broadway. In midsummer one made a few days' excursion by carriage to the Delaware Water Gap, stopping for the night at the hotel in Somerville, where one was bitten by the same sort of "unmentionable insects" that one had lately been horrified to discover in one's own house.

One May there were "tableaux" by some of the Princeton ladies. Sara thought them "no great shakes," but she wore her "India dress, looked quite grand, had a magnificent bo-

quet[*sic*]." Some of the ladies wore their costumes to the
dance that followed, and she "blushed for her sex," the conduct of one of its number being "most vulgar and horrid to
be conceived of." Commencement brought its annual round
of festivities. One June evening Sara attended what she described as "the speaking," at which she and her husband had
"miserable seats among the rabble of Princeton." But the
crowning social event in Princeton in these years was the marriage of Martha Dod, young Richard's wife's sister, to the
rich and influential Edwin Augustus Stevens, of Hoboken,
in 1854.

The announcement of the engagement "set Princeton by
the ears," wrote Sara, and she added cattishly, "May and December," but perhaps "M.D." was only "May with a little
muddy snow scattered about." Sara wore her "camels hair
dress and diamonds etc." to the wedding, which was attended
by "a host of Stevens, Hodges, Conovers, Dods etc." She
admitted that the presents were "really very pretty, diamonds,
pearls, etc., etc." and was sufficiently impressed by other details to record them: the special train that took the bridal
party to Hoboken, with a band to play them on their way and
another to meet them on their landing there; the bridal
chamber done in pink and white satin; and the bridegroom's
yellow nightcap.

But she thought the bride, in elaborate white veil and
wreath, looked "very commonplace," and she evidently had
to hide a grin at "Mrs. Dod in her element, trying to look
sad" over losing her daughter. But perhaps Sara may be excused for the bitterness of her comments: these long-estab-
lished Princeton families had doubtless made the beautiful
young Jewess well aware that in their opinion John Potter
Stockton had married beneath him. Until Martha's engagement was announced she had not called on Sara for nearly
two years; and Sara was feeling hurt this summer anyhow.
Her mother-in-law had not asked her and her husband and

children to visit them at the shore, though the Commodore had invited them on his own account.

His wife did finally send them an invitation in August. He brought it on one of his frequent brief returns to Princeton. On this occasion he spent a whole week there, "full of business," Sara noted. He had reason to be, for by this time he had a Presidential bee buzzing in his bonnet.

# CHAPTER VIII

## "The Commodore Is Irresistible"

THE Commodore had not yet taken his seat in the Senate when certain people began to talk about him as a Presidential possibility, and he himself had already begun to plot a course to that end. In a letter of Christmas greetings in 1851 the editor of *The Truth*, a New York publication, expressed the wish that Senator Stockton might be elected President. That same month a correspondent in the *Richmond Inquirer* hailed him as "a distinguished advocate of . . . our glorious union," and a job-seeker wrote to him of his Presidential aspirations. He began to dicker for the purchase of the *New Jersey Eagle*. Combined with the *Newark Mercury*, it would, he believed, become "the most efficient party organ in the state," with Judge Bayard as "its principal head."

His career in the Senate, though brief, was a distinguished one. He was an eloquent, skillful, and persuasive speaker, and with his forthright character and impetuous temperament, he was little likely to be troubled by the convention that fledgeling senators were to be seen more often than heard. Ardent and frequently passionate in debate, he was at the same time "generous and chivalric . . . ever ready to make amends for any hasty expression." "The Commodore is irresistible," a fellow senator said of him.

Incensed by the fact that the *Princeton*, his pet brain child, had for some unknown reason been scrapped in spite of her efficient service during the late war, he brought about the building of a new ship that bore her name and contained some of her timbers and her main engine. By his efforts the punishment of flogging, which he had so deeply hated throughout his service, was abolished in the navy. His scheme for a reorganization of the navy on a departmental basis was adopted, and he worked hard for the strengthening of the country's harbor defenses. In the field of foreign affairs he went so far as to urge that the United States support the Hungarians in their revolt against their Austrian ruler.

For a short time the prospects of his Presidential nomination seemed to brighten. As the campaign summer of 1852 drew near, he was queried as to his probable course if he should become President. But with the sound political instinct that had made him so successful in New Jersey politics, he refused to allow his name to be submitted to the convention. Even among the Democrats of his own state he sensed that he lacked the strength that would be necessary for his success. Many were still growling about the dictation of the joint companies' political machine—"the Princeton Junto," they called it—and the dominance of the "Earls of Bordentown, Marquises of Hoboken, and Dukes of Princeton." They quoted the Commodore as having said that he had the state in his breeches pocket and meant to keep it there; and it had required a deal with the Whigs to win him his seat in the Senate.

Franklin Pierce won the Democratic nomination and was duly elected; and that December the Commodore resigned to make way for his brother-in-law John R. Thomson, whom the Governor appointed to fill the unexpired term. It is probable that the Commodore expected Pierce to appoint him secretary of the navy. But if so, Pierce's failure to fulfill his expectations aroused no resentment. For Pierce became yet another President who distinguished Morven by being a guest there.

Back in private life the Commodore resumed his duties as president of the canal company. His policy in that position did nothing to strengthen him politically. People complained, and with justice, that he considered public utilities "sacrosanct." In the New Jersey legislature the joint companies had been able to defeat a bill authorizing the construction of a railroad from Keyport to Delaware Bay, and local indignation had reached the point where Commodore Stockton was burned in effigy. When the state's investigating committee submitted their report on the companies, it was said that its lenient tone was owing to the members' having been taken on several pleasant yachting trips.

In his "Appeal to the People of New Jersey" in the *Princeton Whig* he had called Carey and his fellow antimonopolists "socialists, speculators, and demagogues," and had quoted Marshall and Story to support his thesis. As the criticism of the companies continued to grow, he announced that they would sell their stock to the state at the average price at which the last thousand shares had sold in the market. A fair proposition on the face of it, it was anything but an ingenuous one, for he well knew that the state could not assume the large bonded indebtedness of the companies. But he had the effrontery to add that if the offer were not accepted, then it was only just that the charter of the Camden and Amboy should be extended for twenty years. In return the railroad would double-track much of its line and also promote a railroad, the West Jersey, for the benefit of the southern part of the state. He won at least a partial victory. After months of politics and intrigue the charter was extended for thirteen years, and he became president of the West Jersey Railroad, which was chartered in 1853.

It was fortunate that the matter was settled when it was. Two years later an event occurred that still further increased the public feeling against the Camden and Amboy. A collision of two trains, far worse than the accident near the Basin in 1849, killed a number of passengers and injured many more. The company refused to pay compensation for the casualties and the destruction of baggage. The Commodore was blamed for this decision and felt deeply hurt by the resulting criticism.

He had never been generally popular, as his grandfather the Signer had been. He had not, on the other hand, repelled people by a dignified reserve that verged upon pomposity, as the Old Duke had done. The "imperious temper" that was attributed to him was mitigated by a courtly politeness.

"Proud, impetuous, headstrong, frank, brave, and sincere" made up a characterization of him that even his enemies would have had to accept. But many disliked what they called his "self-righteous" manner. Others enjoyed the somewhat condescending geniality that seems to be acquired along with high military and naval rank and which he had in full measure. He was either loved or hated by all who knew him, and those who loved him would have added to his other excellencies that generosity of his, which bordered upon the fantastic.

Increasing age—he was sixty in 1855—and the remonstrances of his agent had made no change in this respect from the man of forty who had written to a friend in trouble: "I desire that you make use of my name or house or means to do what may be most agreeable to [your family] in their future arrangements"; and again: "Call on me with the freedom of a brother—my house, servants, means are all yours."

Yet from 1850 to 1854 Mr. Gatzmer was writing of "the Commodore's necessities" and of "our wants," which were "very pressing." There was a continual borrowing and renewing of notes. Once his son John Potter's stock had to be borrowed to secure one of them. On the other hand, a friend's note, with the Commodore's endorsement, went to protest; The Honorable John Y. Mason had not paid interest on a loan from the Commodore for more than seven years; and New Orleans property, on which the Commodore had loaned a widow lady twelve thousand dollars, turned out to be worth only two thousand, five hundred dollars.

Like most men who have a talent for salesmanship, Robert Field Stockton was an easy victim of that art when it was practiced upon him by others. The letters addressed to him by promoters of land and mining companies read very much like similar letters written today: it seems as if the spuriousness of their contents must have been obvious to a reader of his business experience. But enormous fortunes had been made in land in his lifetime: Pennsylvania lands, for instance, that had sold for sixty-five cents an acre in 1814 brought more than four hundred dollars an acre a dozen years later. In 1853 the Commodore added nine hundred acres to his "gold-bearing lands" in Goochland County. The next year found him buying machinery for a gold mine in South Carolina, and the late spring and early summer of 1855 he spent in inspecting this and his other southern properties.

Amid these various and numerous business activities, however, he did not relinquish his Presidential aspirations. Nor can these be fairly ascribed to mere personal ambition. Between the Abolitionists of the North and the slaveholders of the South the country was evidently headed for disruption, if the ideal of the preservation of the Union were not put first in the minds of the people. The Democrats were becoming more and more divided on the slavery question; the Whig party, likewise divided, was rapidly disintegrating after its defeat in 1852; and the newly formed Republican party was organized on an antislavery basis. This left the almost equally new "Know Nothing" or American party, whose principles were national: support of the constitution, with its compromises; preservation of the Union at all hazards; naturalization laws to be abolished or essentially modified; and only native-born Americans to govern America. To these principles, every one of which had his entire approval, the Commodore, though he had favored the Compromise of 1850, added a plan for restoring the Missouri Compromise, and proceeded to join the party.

He had never allowed a sense of party loyalty to restrict his freedom of action. He had already been a Federalist, at least in sympathy, a Whig, and a Democrat. He could count on support of his candidacy by the joint companies's machine in New Jersey. A rump convention of the American party placed his name in nomination. To further his cause his friend and neighbor Samuel John Bayard wrote and published a highly laudatory *Sketch of the Life of Commodore Robert F. Stockton*. But the response from the country at large was so unsatisfactory that he soon withdrew his name. He was back in the Democratic party by 1860, and remained in it, a power in New Jersey politics, until his retirement from public life two years later, at the age of sixty-seven.

Princeton had continued to change in the decade of the 1850's. Carriages and wagons bound for the railroad station thundered over a plank road that had been laid on Canal Street. The town had a Gas Light Company; and at Morven its dreary illumination replaced the warm light of wax candles. The old house now also had, for the first time in its history, an adequate water supply, through a pipeline that was served by a hydraulic ram on the Springdale farm. On a cold March morning of high wind in 1855 fire once more gutted Nassau Hall, melting the college bell and leaving only the sturdy old stone walls standing. But the students had saved the portraits and the furniture. The building had been rebuilt, with embellishments according to the taste of the time and Mr. John Notman, the architect of Prospect; and Princeton took pride in the fact that no assistance from the state had been accepted for its reconstruction.

But the influence of the Morven clan remained as potent as it had ever been. The Commodore's three sons, Richard, John Potter, and Robert, had all become lawyers and all evidently inherited the legal talent for which their forebears had been conspicuous. Richard, to whom his father had given the Springdale farm, found time to act as treasurer of the gas company and was secretary and treasurer of the Camden and Amboy Railroad. John, whose first case, at the age of twenty-three, Sara recorded in her diary as "quite an unexpected thing," was not long in establishing himself in a lucrative practice, with the Camden and Amboy as a principal client. In 1858 President Buchanan appointed him United States minister to the Papal States. It was to finance this mission, one infers, that he sold his fine house to his father, who had built it for him, for five thousand dollars and two thousand dollars a year, which was to come out of his share of the late John

Potter's estate, when that was settled. John and Sara departed for Rome, and he kept his position at the Papal court until 1861, when he returned with such marks of the Pope's favor as two gold-filigree tables with tops of marble mosaic, and a ring with a Biblical quotation in Hebrew cut in the stone with which it was set. Robert became adjutant general of the state in 1858 and upon his father's death, president of the canal company.

Of the Commodore's brothers-in-law, Thomas Potter died early in the decade, but his widow continued to make Prospect a place of brilliant hospitality. James, though he kept up his Southern connections, went on living in Princeton, at least in the summers. The Commodore's sister Annis had died in 1842. But her husband, John Renfrew Thomson, continued to live at Thomson Hall, and looked after the joint companies' interests in the United States Senate.

Out at Woodlawn Cousin Richard Stockton Field's generosity had made his estate something like a public park, and he entertained there brilliantly. He had long ago discredited Cousin John Pintard's reflections on the Field strain in the Stockton blood. Having made a marked success in the practice of law, he had built in 1847, facing the upper end of Canal Street, the small stone building later known as Ivy Hall, and established in it the Princeton Law School, which was affiliated with the college and flourished until 1855, when it was discontinued and the building became the office of the canal company.

Himself a law student under the Old Duke, Richard Field became a member of the state legislature in 1837, attorney general the following year, and held that office until 1841, but was not thereby prevented from being a director of the joint companies. As president of the Princeton Bank, he brought that institution safely through the panic of 1837. He had been associated with the Commodore in the canal company from its beginnings and continued to be one of his most able coadjutors.

## "The Commodore Is Irresistible"

Morven, with four of its daughters still unmarried, continued to be gay. Sometime prior to 1857 young Robert Stockton and his wife made their home there, and their children gave it its customary happy atmosphere. Still in vigorous health and with his zest for life undiminished, the Commodore rode out on horseback with some of the young people every afternoon when he was at home. He had laid a waxed and polished floor around the huge trunk of the magnificent chestnut tree and still enjoyed giving dances there on moonlit summer nights when the air was sweet with its blossoms. Distinguished guests continued to be a matter of course. President Pierce's visit has already been mentioned. Later, in spite of the Commodore's affiliation with the American party, came President Buchanan. The summer visits to the shore grew longer, however, in these years. The Commodore had bought a farm in Monmouth County, not far from the sea, and had built at Sea Girt what the family called "the Beach House"; and there he spent what were perhaps the happiest days of his later life.

As the slavery issue became more and more acute and he saw the country he loved and had repeatedly risked his life for drifting toward disintegration, things grew increasingly difficult for Commodore Robert Field Stockton. Married to a Southern woman, and with aristocratic tastes and inherited prejudices that made him strongly sympathetic with the South, he maintained that the Negroes were not worth fighting about; that they had been benefited by slavery, since it had resulted in their conversion to Christianity; and that God intended that they should be returned to their African home through the American Colonization Society. In the state Democratic convention of 1860 the committee of which he was chairman put forward resolutions urging the North to yield and the South to be patient. If both sides would wait until spring, he believed the Union would be saved. As a delegate from New Jersey, he went to the Peace Conference at Washington in the following January. But when he returned, he could only report to Governor Olden that war was inevitable.

When it came, he was not alone among the people of light and leading in Princeton in doubting the justice and wisdom of using force to bring the seceding states back into the Union. A great many of the students came from the South, and the college authorities took no decided stand on the question at first. But not so the generality of the people. Back in 1843 the community had experienced a sample of the working of the fugitive slave laws. A runaway slave from Maryland, who had found a refuge in the town, had been recognized by a Southern student and had been arrested. A jury had voted, according to the law, that the man must be turned over to the United States Marshal from Baltimore, who was on hand to receive him. But popular indignation had run high. There were five hundred free Negroes in the community, and fear that a mob would rescue the prisoner by force had grown so great that he had been confined in an upper room of the Nassau Hotel until he had been purchased from his owner for five hundred and fifty dollars by Miss Theodosia Prevost—a descendant of President Witherspoon—who immediately set him free.

With the spring of 1861 public feeling for the Union boiled over in Princeton. The *Standard*, the only newspaper, came out strongly for the cause and hoisted the national flag above its office. The flag went up over Nassau Hall, but without the sanction of the faculty. It was hauled down, its hoisting officially disapproved, and the College of New Jersey did not fly it again until the spirit of the community had become unmistakable.

It had been hoisted at once, however, over the Theological Seminary and over the houses of a number of private citizens. A procession headed by the local militia company, the Governor's Guard, marched with fife and drum to Senator Thomson's house, to Governor Olden's, and to Mr. Field's. Both Governor and Senator assured the marchers of their intention to do all in their power to restore the Union. Mr. Field, who was an ardent Republican, "warmed up," wrote John Frelinghuysen Hageman, the local historian, "and made an earnest appeal in behalf of the Union." "Morven," Hageman continues, "did not escape a visit from the procession. Adjutant General Robert F. Stockton was then its occupant, the Commodore being absent. The General was unwell but finally came out, and declared sentiments that were satisfactory to his visitors."

A public meeting at Mercer Hall on Nassau Street appointed a committee to obtain volunteers in answer to the call of the President. At its close a choir of ladies on the porch of the City Hotel across the street sang "The Star-Spangled Banner." But a good many prominent citizens were conspicuous by their absence, Commodore Stockton among them. A leader in the community, however, for almost forty years, he could not now avoid stating his position, and he did so in a letter to Governor Olden written at Princeton on the 20th of April.

Since war was already upon them, he wrote, he would take the liberty to suggest that, after the requisition of the national government for troops had been complied with, the Governor consider the best means to preserve their own state from aggression. He would remember that only the Delaware separated New Jersey from the slave states. If the Governor should see fit to call upon him for any aid that he could render, it would be freely tendered. "This is no time," he went on, "to potter about past differences of opinion or to criticise the administration of public affairs. . . . I will hoist the star spangled banner at Morven, the former residence of one of the signers of the Declaration of Independence,— that flag, which, when a boy, I nailed to the Frigate President. . . ."

It was something, but not what might have been expected from Morven and the son of a man who had sent two of his sons to fight for their country in a war that he detested, as

the Old Duke, his father, had done. But like his grandfather
the Signer's decision to place his duty to his family before
adherence to the cause of his infant country, it was a bold expression of his convictions in the face of a general condemnation, which it was bound to bring upon him.

He kept silent and inactive in politics during the war. When
his brother-in-law Thomson died in 1862, Governor Olden appointed Republican Robert Field to fill Thomson's unexpired
term in the Senate, and the Commodore retired from public
life two years later. Like most men of his imperious and dic-
tatorial nature, he had wanted to have his own way and the
high opinion of his fellow citizens as well. He wrote regretfully that however harsh their judgments of him might be,
a time would come when his memory would be cherished as
one who chiefly desired the prosperity, happiness, and glory
of their state.

It was the fifth time that the clouds of war had lowered
over Morven. But never before had the family followed their
country's fortunes with such divided hearts: the father strong
for the Union but deploring the means by which it was being restored; their mother a daughter of the state that had
led in secession. Her brother James Potter had gone to his
home in Savannah and died there before the war was over.
On the other hand, Stockton and Hunter cousins were dis-
tinguishing themselves in the Federal army and navy. When
President Lincoln suspended the Act of Habeas Corpus,
Cousin Robert Field made a speech in the Senate, justifying
his doing so, and the next year the President appointed him
judge of the United States Court for the District of New
Jersey.

The flag had gone up again over Nassau Hall amid the
cheers of the student body. When college reopened in the
fall of 1861, no Southern students returned, and Northern
boys who expressed sympathy with the South received rough
treatment. One of them was held under the college pump by

students loyal to the Union, and when three of these were suspended for this action, they were drawn to the station "in a barouche imbedded in the national colors, by students in long procession, preceded by martial music, and exciting on the way to the depot the wildest enthusiasm," the *Standard* reported.

In July 1863, while the Draft Riots were raging in New York, the peace of the town was threatened by a backwash from those disorders. The Irish laborers on a section of the railroad at Penns Neck quit work for a day or two and sauntered about the town in groups, muttering threats against Republicans and Negroes. The Negroes retorted with threats to burn the house of every Irish family in town, if they were molested. The situation became tense. But fortunately the nights were very rainy, discouraging to gatherings in the streets; and on the following Sunday Father O'Donnell of the Roman Catholic mission came out with a sermon denouncing the New York rioters and telling his congregation that the draft was legal and right.

A torchlight procession, fireworks, and a great bonfire around the cannon on the campus celebrated the fall of Richmond, and ten days later the walls of the First Presbyterian Church were hung with black in mourning for murdered Lincoln. Did the windows of Morven shine with lights, like almost all the other windows in Princeton, in celebration of the end of the Confederacy? It seems most probable that they did, for its owner must have rejoiced that the agony of the South, hopeless for the past two years, was over.

Certainly he must have approved of the closing sentence of the speech that the Reverend Doctor Hodge made from the steps of Nassau Hall that evening: "We have conquered our enemies, it remains for us to conquer ourselves." And however strongly the Commodore had objected to Lincoln's policy, he deeply deplored his assassination, not only as every decent citizen did, but because he was doubtless able to fore-

see something of the dreadful consequences it would have
for the conquered South.

During the years of the war he had kept himself busy
with the affairs of the joint companies. The antimonopoly
people had not ceased their criticism. Of late years, moreover, the transportation situation in New Jersey had been
attracting unfavorable comment outside the state as well as
within its borders. Shippers in both New York and Philadelphia had grown indignant over the Camden and Amboy's
high charges. The New York newspapers, notably Horace
Greeley's *Tribune*, had taken up their quarrel. With many
competing lines between New York and Albany, they pointed
out, the tariff was less than one fourth of that between New
York and Philadelphia, though the distance was considerably
greater.

William Cullen Bryant renewed the attack in the *New
York Evening Post* in 1864, and the Commodore answered
it in two letters that were reprinted, bound, and circulated as
a pamphlet entitled "Defense of the System of Internal Improvements of the State of New Jersey." Characteristically
enough, their tone appealed more strongly to the emotions
than to the reason. "Still there she stands," the author concluded (by "she" meaning New Jersey), "this day, as of old,
heart and hand, with her treasure and her resources, and her
blood, pledged to the Union of the States."

Conscious of his advancing years, though still hale and
hearty, the Commodore appears at this time to have set about
putting his personal financial house in order. It was more than
high time that he did so. He had gradually acquired some
eighteen hundred acres in the neighborhood of his Sea Girt
estate, and in 1857 he had found it necessary to give a bond
and mortgage on them to secure a loan of forty thousand dollars from James Potter and Richard Field. Mr. Gatzmer
was still having the same old trouble in collecting loans
"made some years since." The war wiped out such value as
there was in the Commodore's lands in the South. In 1863

he sold the ranch he had bought in California, and bonds of the West Jersey Railroad amounting to seventeen thousand dollars, and cleared his Philadelphia Walnut Street property of builders' liens.

He, who had been in the habit of dealing with money by tens and hundreds of thousands, now felt the necessity of saving a few hundreds where he could. In a long and detailed agreement with his farmer in 1862 he arranged for the management of the Morven farm on a strictly business basis. It was to be run absolutely separately from the Morven mansion. It was to be highly departmentalized. The plan goes into much detail and smacks strongly of the naval past of its author. The farmhands were to breakfast before daylight, summer and winter, and were to have two hours off at noon, if the morning's work had gone well.

But he still indulged himself in the princely gestures that he loved. Catching an old colored woman in the act of stealing apples from the Morven orchard, he picked up the bag she had dropped and spilled in escaping over the fence, called her back, filled the bag to the brim while she stood quaking, and presented it to her with a friendly word and a smile. When a young lady admired the Chinese Lowestoft on his dinner table, with the American eagle and the coat of arms of the United States navy on each plate, he sent her the entire set as a present. And the Reverend Doctor Baker, the rector of Trinity Church, never forgot how, one Sunday morning, the Commodore was so deeply moved by an appeal for missions that he placed his pocketbook, filled with bank notes, on the plate at the offertory.

The comparative straitening of his circumstances made little difference, if any, in his way of living. But he appears to have grown more and more content with a leisurely enjoyment of life, at the shore in summer and in the winter at his Morven fireside. In November 1861 the gloom of the war was brightened in the old house by the wedding of Julia, his fourth daughter, to Edward McAlister Hopkins, of Philadelphia. In the following year his devoted wife, Harriet Maria, died; and three years later Caroline and Annis, the two youngest girls, were married at Morven: Caroline to Captain William Rawle Brown, U.S.N., of Torresdale, Pennsylvania; Annis to Franklin Davenport Howell, of Philadelphia, a brother of her sister Mary's husband.

Of his six girls there was now left at home only Harriet Maria, who never married. But by 1864 there were five of young Robert's children in the Morven nursery. Their grandfather both disciplined and spoiled them. They adored him, and years later the older ones loved to recall how they would cluster around his chair before the blazing logs in the Morven study and listen to his stories of his adventurous youth and young manhood.

The best of them, perhaps, was of his encounter with the African king, which has already been told. But excellent, too, was the one about the time in the War of 1812 when the United States frigate *President* cleared for action with the British frigate *Plantagenet* and Commodore Rodgers called up to Midshipman Stockton, who was in command of the maintop: "Mr. Stockton, we expect great things of you today, sir." And there was also the one about the time when the Commodore, pausing at Valparaiso in the *Congress* on his way to California, found that the Chileans had unjustly imprisoned an American merchant captain. The Commodore had simply moored his ship opposite the jail and threatened to blow in the door with his guns if the man was not released forthwith.

Then there were the stories of the duels. The War of 1812 had left much hard feeling between the British and American navies. The British sneered at the "gridiron flag," as they called the Stars and Stripes. In a visitors' book at Naples a British naval officer had written and signed, for all to read, an insult to the United States navy. Lieutenant Stockton demanded a written apology and, when the officer refused, challenged him and shot him in the leg.

142

## "The Commodore Is Irresistible"

In answer to an affront to his service at Gibraltar, Stockton, as the only unmarried officer on board the *Erie*, fought two duels, of which the second had an extraordinary sequel. The Governor of the Rock had threatened to hang any Yankee who came ashore for the purpose of fighting; and lest the American should be arrested, the British parties involved had pledged themselves to keep the meeting a secret. The meeting place was near the top of the Rock. But when Stockton reached it with his second and the ship's surgeon, the British raised so many objections to the recognized code of dueling that he grew suspicious of the resulting delay, waived his rights, and severely wounded his opponent in the ensuing exchange of shots.

The wretched man then confessed that treachery had been practiced and that Stockton must flee at once if he would escape arrest. He started at a run down the passage in the face of the Rock only to find himself blocked halfway by a file of armed soldiers and an officer, who stood upon the parapet, chuckling at his quarry's predicament. Stockton sprang upon him, got the man's head under his arm, and leaped with him from the parapet. Down the steep slope they rolled together until the jolting descent caused Stockton to release his hold and he went one way, the Englishman another. From a low cliff Stockton dropped to the beach, battered and bloody, his clothes ripped and torn by the jagged ledges over which he had rolled. In this state he confronted a gentleman who happened to be passing on horseback and asked for the immediate loan of his mount, a request that was, not unnaturally, refused. But now soldiers were tearing down the road to cut off his escape. He seized the rider by the leg, flung him from the saddle, mounted, and galloped madly for his boat. He reached it, sprang into it, gave orders to pull for the *Erie*, and fainted.

They were good stories, and he told them well. Back in 1826, when, a young lieutenant, he had been ordered to Washington to answer for his capture of the *Marianna Flora*, he had told some of them to still younger Josiah Quincy. Quincy liked them so well that he wrote them down and published them in his *Figures of the Past* nearly sixty years later, with the comment that "no mariner of thirty ever had adventures more remarkable, or told them more modestly and agreeably."

At Sea Girt he had reminders of former pleasures and successes all around him. In our day Crescent Park owes its contours to having been a part of the track on which the Commodore trained his racers. His gardener's house was such that after his death it was for many years the summer residence of the governors of New Jersey. About a half-mile inland stood "the ladies' house," at which his female guests might stay, their crinolines, complexions, and coiffeurs unspoiled by the wind and sun of the beach.

He himself lived at "the Beach House," built of eighteen-by-twenty-four-inch beams hewn out of logs of cypress that had been floated up in rafts and landed by the surf. Its sea front was built like the deck of a ship. There he loved to pace on warm summer afternoons, watch the passing ships through his spyglass, and comment upon them to his guests, while his West Indian mulatto servant mixed iced drinks for the company. After his wife's death he gave frequent stag dinners, and on those occasions he mixed his celebrated Fish House punch with his own hands.

At the close of one of these pleasant summers, in September 1866, he returned to Morven and, after a brief illness, died on the 7th of October, in the seventy-second year of his age.

# CHAPTER IX

## "The Old Order Changeth"

ON November 19, 1866, appropriate resolutions on the death of Commodore Stockton were adopted by the Joint Board of Directors of the Delaware and Raritan Canal and the Camden and Amboy Railroad and Transportation Companies. Similar action, deploring the death of their president, who had been for thirty-five years "the ever zealous and untiring friend" of the joint companies, was taken by the directors of the canal company that same day. Their praise of him was well deserved. But there was another side to the picture.

His private affairs were found to be in such confusion as might have been expected to result from his extravagance, his speculations, and his excursions into politics and upon the turf. The rustling of the branches of the famous chestnut tree against the roof of Morven on windy nights gave rise to the legend that the house was haunted by the ghost of the Commodore looking for his "lost will." Actually his will, dated September 30, 1855, was duly proved on October 20, 1866.

By its provisions "all that certain farm, plantation, and Homestead property known as 'Morven'" passed to his children, his wife being dead; and on January 20, 1869, they and their spouses joined in conveying it to their cousin Samuel Witham Stockton, son of the Commodore's brother of that name. The property was described as bounded on the southeast by Stockton Street; on the west by a road recently opened, leading from Stockton Street to the Princeton-Blawenburg road; on the north by that road; and on the northeast by Bayard Lane. From this area, however, the deed excepted forty-one acres conveyed by the Commodore to Paul Tulane in 1860, evidently the place formerly owned by John Potter Stockton; and the transfer was made subject to a mortgage of thirty-five thousand dollars given to James Potter, Richard Stockton, John P. Stockton, and Robert Stockton, Jr., trustees.

Thus was broken the direct succession of Morven from father to son, which had endured for five generations, a hundred and sixty years. Reason for the break may be found in the changed conditions of the times. The day of the "gentlemen farmers" of a century before had long gone by. The Commodore's sons were all prosperous gentlemen: both Richard and John Potter officers of the joint companies, and John Potter United States senator from New Jersey this year; but none of them was so situated as to be willing to assume the burden of maintaining the ancestral home in the old manorial style. Another reason for the transfer to their cousin may be inferred from the following document, dated January 12, 1869, eight days before the execution of the deed:

"It is agreed between John P. Stockton, executor and agent for the heirs of Robert F. Stockton deceased and Samuel W. Stockton that the said Samuel may and will take possession of Morven on the 13th day of January, 1869—that he accepts the same in his capacity of executor of Mrs. Mary Harrison and individually as full payment and satisfaction of all claims against the estate of Robert F. Stockton deceased and agrees to execute formal releases when a proper deed is prepared and tendered. Samuel agrees to permit Mrs. Catherine E. Dod to occupy her present house and courtelage until April 1st, 1869, without paying any rent. And that after that time he will give to her the preference over any other either to sell or rent. Samuel is to pay the taxes and interest on mortgage from January 1st, 1869, as he takes the place subject to the mortgage of $35,000 to H. M. Stockton.

"(signed) John P. Stockton.
"S. W. Stockton."

H. M. Stockton, who is mentioned in the foregoing agreement, was evidently Harriet Maria, the Commodore's unmarried daughter; Mary Harrison his eldest sister.

## "The Old Order Changeth"

Samuel Witham Stockton was a child of two years when his father died at the age of thirty-five in 1836, leaving also an infant daughter and his widow, who married the Reverend Charles Hodge, D.D., LL.D., of the Princeton Seminary. The senior Samuel Witham was the third of the Old Duke's sons to serve in the navy. But he was a home-loving man. A year before his death he wrote from New York to his wife, Mary Hunter, that they were "losing lots of valuable time at Tusculum," and that his brother Robert was seeing the Secretary of the Navy about getting him released from his ship.

Samuel Witham, his son, entered the army. He distinguished himself in the Civil War as a captain in the Fourth Cavalry at First Bull Run and later as aide to his uncle David Hunter, who was colonel of the Sixth Cavalry in 1861 and that same year became a brigadier general of volunteers. At the end of the war Samuel had retired from the army with the rank of major. He returned to Princeton and in 1866, just a week before the death of the Commodore, married Sarah, Doctor Hodge's daughter by his first wife, Sarah Bache.

With a rapidly increasing family of children, and lacking both the great inherited wealth and the rewards of a highly paid profession which the three masters of Morven before him had enjoyed, "Major Sam," as he became affectionately known to his many friends, ran the place quite simply as a farm. It ran down in appearance accordingly. One who visited it when he had been its owner for six years wrote of it in the Christmas number of *Appleton's Journal* in 1875 an article entitled "The Stockton Mansion at Princeton."

Gravity had pervaded all things in Princeton the previous summer, according to this writer. There was more greenery than color in its aspect. House fronts were sleepily closed against the sunlight. Children, "moved by civic pride and a *pour boire*," left off playing in the mud to guide the visitor to the Stockton house. A white fence of three rails in the style of 1830, with square posts topped by ornaments like college caps, leaned here and there as it crossed the front of the place. There was "a stagger of the gates" through which one entered, and moss was noticeable on the roof. But withindoors the parlors, "though not grand, were of an immense dignity," and the number of patriotic paintings was impressive.

But straitened in circumstances though he was, by Morven standards, Major Sam and his wife kept up the reputation of the house for hospitality. He called it "Liberty Hall," and Liberty Hall it was in fact for all who entered its doors. With his erect and wiry figure, handsome features, and drooping mustache that turned white as the years went by, he looked every inch the veteran cavalry officer; and his courteous and kindly manners of the old school combined with his hospitality and that of his witty and good-humored wife to keep Morven what it had always been, the center of life in Princeton.

He was an ardent sportsman, and what is more rare, a generous one. His children and their friends had the run of house, farm, and stables. The young Scott boys, Turners, Winans, Pardees, Browns, Poes, and Sloanes of his time were free to ride his horses, thrilled by the brazen "U.S." on bits and bridles. They skated on Morven Pond, coasted down the long hill inside the fence on Elm Road, and found space for baseball and football in the great Morven orchard that bordered Bayard Lane and covered the property now traversed by Hodge Road, Morven Place, and Boudinot Street; and if a fight got going among them, Major Sam was apt to appear and settle it with a humorous appeal to reason.

For twenty years this happy way of life continued. But at the age of fifty-six the Major found himself no longer able to struggle with the burden of debt that he had assumed with the ownership of the old place. His two sons and three daughters were now grown up or nearly so; and in 1890 he deeded the estate, subject to certain mortgages and small judgments, to Casper Wistar Hodge, Richard S. Hunter, and John F. Hageman, Jr., apparently as trustees, for the sum of two thousand dollars. He lived on until 1899, when he died of a heart attack five days after receiving news of the death of his son Charles, a civil engineer in the employ of the Nicaragua Canal Company.

From Samuel Witham Stockton's trustees, Morven passed in 1891 to the Reverend Charles Woodruff Shields, D.D., of Torresdale, Pennsylvania, who had been since 1866 professor of the harmony of science and religion at the College of New Jersey. The consideration was thirty thousand dollars, but the landed estate, whose area had once been computed in hundreds of acres, had been so reduced by bequests and sales that it was now described by boundaries of some seven hun-.dred to nine hundred feet. This comparatively small tract, however, and the house itself, their new owner at once set about restoring to their old-time beauty and order.

In 1882 Doctor Shields's elder daughter, Charlotte Julia, had married Bayard Stockton, son of the Commodore's son Richard. She died the year her father bought Morven, but not before she had deeply impressed him with her love of the place and her wish that her two boys, Bayard, Jr., and Richard 3rd, should become the possessors of the home of their ancestors. Two years later her bereaved husband married her half sister, Helen Hamilton Shields, who shared to the full her enthusiasm for the place. Bayard Stockton was president of the New Jersey Railroad and Canal Company, the successor of the old joint companies; he was prosecutor of the pleas of Mercer County, held other public offices, and was chancellor of the Episcopalian Diocese of New Jersey. A Master of Arts of the College of New Jersey, he had written the article on Morven that was published in *The Princeton Book* in 1879. The house became his home and that of his children from the time that his father-in-law purchased it.

The work of restoration and rehabilitation went steadily forward in Doctor Shields's time. As he stated in a codicil to his will, he made "many sacrifices of other property" for this purpose, and his daughter Helen devoted herself to the task with the energy and intelligence that may be inferred from the accounts she wrote of it in *A Quest for a Garden* and *The Trees of Morven.*

Inside the house her aim was evidently to re-create the atmosphere of the great days of Annis and the Signer. This she did, according to the tastes and knowledge of the time. Bits of molding were added to the walls to create the effect of paneling. Two of the nineteenth-century gray marble mantelpieces were cast out, and a search was made for what were thought to be the originals. Two, actually early nineteenth-century in style, were purchased—one from the home of the family laundress, one from a bootblack shop—and fitted over the iron fireplace liners installed after the fire of 1821. Old pieces of furniture cast out in the Commodore's day were traced, brought back, and put in their old places. A hand-woven counterpane signed "A. B. and S. S." for Annis Boudinot and Susannah Stockton again draped one of the beds. In the drawing room old gold curtains were hung at the windows; the furniture was black and gold and was said to have once belonged to Citizen Genêt, the first minister of the French Republic to the United States.

Out of doors a similar work was undertaken. The Signer's plan of Pope's garden had long since disappeared, probably destroyed by the British, like most of his other papers. But during a visit to England a motor trip to Twickenham revealed that the old garden was "still there." A copy of the original plan was obtained from the British Museum and, with the guidance of an aged Scotch-Irish gardener who had seen four generations of Stocktons at Morven, was followed so far as was practicable in the changed conditions.

Most of the cedars, cypresses, Spanish chestnuts, elms, and yews of Annis and the Signer's planting had survived. Search revealed many bulbous roots: grape hyacinths, golden daffodils, narcissuses, and "a wilderness of tawny-orange day lilies." New shrubs and flowers were planted in old places, brought from such historic spots as Abbotsford, Kew Gardens, the site of the Manoir Richelieu, the Van Rensselaer Manor on the Hudson, the Chew place in Germantown, and Sandringham. When a wall was needed to carry out the original scheme, no brick of contemporary manufacture was used. Fortunately the former University Hotel, which had become University Hall, was demolished about this time, and soft old bricks, which had been used in its inner construction, became available and were utilized for the wall at Morven.

When what was thought to be the two-hundredth birthday of the house came around in 1901, it was celebrated by placing in the center of the old garden a sundial, around whose gnomon were carved the lines by Doctor Henry Van Dyke:

> "Two hundred years of Morven I record,
> Of Morven's house protected by the Lord:
> And now I stand among old-fashioned flowers
> To mark for Morven many sun-lit hours."

In further celebration of this bicentennial there was a ball on Christmas night that year. A quadrille was danced: the ladies in ancestral gowns, jewelry, and laces; the men in the gay colored coats and "small clothes" of the Signer's time, with powdered wigs and queues. Notable historical figures associated with the house were represented by their namesakes and descendants: Annis Boudinot, Julia Rush, Susan Livingston, Lady Stirling, the Signer, Washington, and Lafayette. The quadrille was opened by a triumphal march composed for a ball in honor of Lafayette in Philadelphia, and in the final figure the gentlemen made an arch of their drawn swords above their partners in the dance.

A Dutch fire dance followed. The Yule log, which had been sawn from a huge tree on the Morven grounds, was drawn in and kindled. By the light of its flames each couple in turn drank to the toast, "May the hearthstone of Morven never grow cold"; and when the lovingcup grew empty, it was refilled from the massive silver tankard, with its motto *Omnia Deo Pendent*, which great-great-grandmother Annis had hidden from the British that dreadful winter night a hundred and twenty-five years before. Then supper was served, and a Sir Roger de Coverly, in which danced old Doctor Shields, his daughter, son-in-law, and grandsons, brought the evening to a close.

Three more names were added to Morven's list of Presidential guests in Bayard Stockton's time. In 1896 the College of New Jersey celebrated its Sesquicentennial and became Princeton University. President Cleveland reviewed the torchlight procession of students and alumni from the steps of Nassau Hall, and at commencement the following June he was honored with the degree of Doctor of Laws. Since his term of office expired in March of that year, he and Mrs. Cleveland had for some time been searching for a permanent home. They had found it at Princeton in the previous autumn. It was a Stockton house that they bought, the one that the Commodore had built for his daughter Catherine Elizabeth Dod, down Bayard Lane, across from Henry Van Dyke's Avalon, which had been Judge Bayard's Clermont. Morven welcomed them in the spring of 1897 with a series of dinners at which other distinguished guests gave them special greetings and messages. In 1902 Professor Woodrow Wilson was elected president of the university and was entertained in his new capacity at the Morven dinner table, where he had already often been a guest. And just twenty years later President Warren Harding sat at Mrs. Stockton's right hand at luncheon on the occasion of the dedication of the Princeton Battle Monument.

Mr. Cleveland had not been a year in residence before he played a minor part in a less pleasant episode, in which Bayard Stockton and especially Doctor Shields were made to suffer for the principles of tolerance and personal freedom that had been a tradition of Morven for generations. In July 1897 the *New York Voice*, virulent advocate of the Temperance Movement, came out with the statement that Princeton University had "taken to the bottle in its old age." Several of its professors, Doctors of Divinity, and Doctors of Laws, the paper asserted, had "asked for a saloon license for a duly authorized university rum shop."

The fact was that a number of the faculty and other prominent citizens, owners of nearby property, Bayard Stockton, Doctor Shields, and ex-President Cleveland among them, had signed such an application, so that the Princeton Inn, which stood on what had lately been Morven property, might serve wine and beer in its dining room and grillroom in "an honest experiment in temperance" with the hope of lessening the temptations of the real saloon and keeping the students' drinking within the bounds of moderation.

But at the news of it, the strictest sect of the pharisees rose up in their wrath. The Reform Committee of the Presbyterian Synod of New York condemned it and its authors. The Synod Convention at Plainfield, New Jersey, urged the New Brunswick Presbytery to discipline those of its members who had signed the application. President Patton retorted that he was "going to fight" in defense of his professors, though he should "have to fight the whole Presbyterian Church." He "would not," he stated, "have the law of the church, as such, imposed upon Princeton University." Grover Cleveland said he was "glad" he had signed the application. But in the face of impending charges, Doctor Shields, disgusted and angry, resigned from the ministry of which he had been a member for nearly forty years and took orders in the Episcopal Church.

Seven years later, in 1904, he died, leaving "the estate known as 'Morven' with the land and premises attached to and forming a part of the property as a whole" to his daughter, Helen Hamilton Shields Stockton, and his grandsons, Bayard and Richard, "to be jointly possessed, occupied and enjoyed by them as the ancestral seat of the Stockton family. . . ."

"The Old Order Changeth"

## OLD LANDMARK IN ALIEN HANDS

For the First Time in Two Centuries Morven Is
Not Tenanted by a Stockton

Thus the *New York Sun* headlined an article on April 24,
1929. Almost thirty years had passed since Bayard Stockton
and his wife and Doctor Shields had celebrated Morven's
two-hundredth birthday. The President of Princeton University had become President of the United States. The United
States had taken a vital part in a world war. Major Samuel
Witham Stockton's son, "Big Dick" to the many who loved
and admired him, had come home to die of a wound received
on the battlefield in France, thus fulfilling his great-great-
grandmother Annis's prophecy to the infant Dauphin:

> "A mighty empire from these woods shall rise
> And pay to thee the aid they owe thy King."

King, Dauphin, and the kingdom had long been dead, but
their country remained to receive the payment of the debt.

Late in the spring of 1922 the monument by Frederick
MacMonnies commemorating the Battle of Princeton had
been completed. On the northwest corner of Stockton Street
and Bayard Lane, it was erected on land that had been for
two centuries Morven land; and its dedication by President
Harding on June 6 recalled the glories and the sorrows of
Morven's past. A salute of twenty-one guns by the Princeton
Field Artillery unit greeted his arrival at the borough line.
United States Senators Frelinghuysen and Edge, of New
Jersey, accompanied him, and detachments of the First Cavalry Troop of Philadelphia and the Fifth Infantry of the
Maryland National Guard—both organizations descendants
of organizations that had fought in the battle of 1777—
formed his escort, wearing their historic dress uniforms.

At the monument, at one o'clock that afternoon, the Right
Reverend Paul Matthews, D.D., Bishop of the Episcopal
Diocese of New Jersey, offered Washington's prayer for his

154

country as an invocation. The Honorable Bayard Stockton, as president of the Monument Commission, made the presentation, and his grandson, Bayard Stockton, Jr., lifted the great flag that covered the face of the monument, revealing the sculptured group of Washington on horseback led by Liberty and supported by soldiers of his army, among whom appeared the mortally wounded Mercer. Bayard and Helen entertained the President and Mrs. Harding and their party at luncheon; and at three o'clock the President passed between the serried ranks of his escort through the great gate of the campus and mounted the steps of Nassau Hall to receive the degree of Doctor of Laws. He was the twelfth President of the United States to be so honored by the university, the eighth to be a guest at Morven while in office.

Bayard Stockton had died six years later, and Morven was rented to Robert W. Johnson, of New Brunswick. Hence the headline in the *New York Sun*. But if the new occupants of the place were alien in blood, they were far from being so in spirit. In Helen Hamilton's later years time and change had exacted a toll from house and garden that she had not been able to pay. A considerable amount of repairs and rehabilitation by the tenant had been made one of the considerations of the lease, and he proceeded to comply with it during the next eight years with a sympathetic understanding of the past, both indoors and out. Plumbing and electric wiring were overhauled, floors and plaster brought again to a state of perfection. The old slave quarters were made habitable once more: and all was done with care that no modern materials should be used that would be out of keeping with the old fabric. Trees and garden received the same scrupulous attention. Drives were rebuilt, the original brick walks and courts relaid.

For seventeen years (1928-45) the old-time spirit of hospitality reigned in dinners and dances. A tennis court and a swimming pool were built. There were hunters once more in the Morven stables, and the shade of old John Stockton, the eighteenth-century Nimrod, must have rejoiced when the trustees of the Stony Brook Hounds gathered in their scarlet dress coats around the Morven table for their annual dinner. The house continued to be a center of public affairs. The forces of the Clean Government Movement gathered there. There the Princeton Surveys were launched, meetings were held for the cause of better architecture and landscape gardening, and there were early conferences in support of good state and national wage-hour legislation.

But a fundamental change was in store for the house. On February 4, 1945, Helen Hamilton Stockton and the other heirs of her father joined in deeding Morven to Walter E. Edge and Camilla, his wife. Again, however, it passed into appreciative hands. Deeply imbued with a sense of its historical significance and essential loveliness, the new owners lavished upon it an affectionate care equal to that bestowed upon it by the old. House, garden, and grounds were renovated afresh. At the far end of the entrance hall the porch, which was probably part of the Commodore's "building upon" Morven and which General Johnson had enclosed in glass, was enlarged. The area of the garden was increased along traditional lines.

On the front lawn one spring morning a party assembled to celebrate the planting of a white-flowering Benjamin Franklin tree, the gift of Doctor Julian Boyd, Librarian of the University. To the Edges' disappointment the tree failed to arrive in time for the ceremony. But in ignorance of this fact the guests departed quite satisfied with the planting of an ordinary maple sapling that was substituted and was later surreptitiously replaced by the genuine article.

Again hospitality was joined with statecraft under Morven's roof. Governor of New Jersey at this time, Walter Edge made the house the executive mansion. Garden parties for Robert A. Taft, Thomas E. Dewey, and Harold Stassen in turn gave those aspirants to the Presidency of the United States the opportunity to meet the New Jersey delegates to the National Convention. From Morven Mr. Taft went to speak at Alexander Hall on the campus. When there was a vacancy in the office of chancellor of the state, Governor Edge entertained all twenty-one of the State Senators at a dinner at Morven, and at its close presented to them Judge A. Dayton Oliphant, whom he had chosen for the office.

In less happy circumstances, in December 1946, the Governor, the Secretary of Labor, and others gathered in the old study, where the Signer had wrestled with the supply problems of Washington's army, to face the threat of a strike by the public utilities employees throughout the state. It was Christmas Eve; the date of the strike had been set; it would deprive the people of New Jersey of light, power, and in many cases heat as well. The men gathered in Morven's study proceeded to draft a law by which, in the event of a strike in the intrastate public utilities, the state would take them over, and a strike against the state was forbidden. The Governor issued a statement from Morven that night that he would act accordingly. No strike took place. The law was the first of its kind in the United States and has been widely copied since its passage.

Governor Edge's term expired on the following 21st of January. During 1946 Morven had seen several meetings held for the purpose of choosing a Republican candidate to be his successor. Their choice, Alfred E. Driscoll, had been elected that November. On January 18 of the new year Morven had opened its doors to some three hundred guests at a reception in his honor; and as if to add luster to the day, Governor Edge's first grandson, E. Brooke Lee 3rd, was born in the Princeton Hospital that morning.

Six years later, the room where so many Morven brides had been married was the scene of the wedding of Mary Esther Edge to John H. MacFadyen, Princeton '46, on the 24th of May, 1953. The occasion formed a happy climax to her parents' years in the house. For their time in it was now drawing to a close. The place was about to pass into the ownership of the state by an act of munificence in the best Morven tradition.

It is described in the following letters:

"Sunny Hill Plantation
Thomasville, Georgia
December 11, 1950

"Hon. Alfred E. Driscoll
State House
Trenton 7, New Jersey

"My dear Governor Driscoll:

"In 1945 when I purchased the property known as Morven at Princeton, I did so with the definite intent of preserving this historic mansion and ultimately having it become the property of the State of New Jersey as a gift from Mrs. Edge and myself for use either as a gubernatorial mansion or a State museum.

"As you know, this property has an extraordinary historical background. It has been the home of one of the signers of the Declaration of Independence, a President of the Council of the Colony before the Revolution, a number of Presidents of the United States have visited and been entertained there. . . .

"When I purchased the property, I voluntarily insisted that there be included in the deed a provision that at a time not later than two years following my death, it would become the property of the State, free and unencumbered, for either of the uses referred to above and, as is well known, I at that time made public announcement of my intention.

"Due to the fact that I was occupying the Governor's office at the time the purchase was made, it did not seem becoming that I recommend legislative action looking toward the acceptance of our gift and as a result, of course, no action has ever been taken by the State in this regard. Both Mrs. Edge and myself are, however, desirous of having this action taken so that the State may have assurances of its future ownership of the property.

"The year 1951 marks the 250th anniversary of the beginning of the construction of this historic edifice and it seems to us that this would be an appropriate time to ask the State to take formal action and, therefore, on behalf of Mrs. Edge and myself, I hereby formally extend to you an offer of a deed to the State of New Jersey for the property known as Morven, free of all encumbrances.

"This conveyance, so far as we are concerned, is to be subject only to the proviso that the property when taken over by the State shall be used for either of the purposes enumerated in the first paragraph hereof.

"Regardless of the provisions in the deed to me (as above referred to) concerning the time when Morven should become the property of the State, we are now offering it to the State with the desire that it will be accepted subject to, of course, whatever terms and conditions the State may impose as to the method and time of acceptance.

"Appreciating the considerate interest you have indicated and with kindest personal regards, I am,

"Sincerely,

"Walter E. Edge"

"State of New Jersey
Office of the Governor
Trenton

December 29, 1950

"Alfred E. Driscoll
Governor

"My dear Governor Edge:

"Your formal offer of a deed, free of all encumbrances, to the State of New Jersey for the historic property known as Morven, in the Borough of Princeton, will be submitted by me in an appropriate Special Message to the Legislature after it convenes on January 9th, 1951.

"Morven has been closely and intimately associated with the history of New Jersey from Colonial days to the present time. This fact makes the generous offer of Mrs. Edge and yourself one that should be appreciated by all thoughtful-minded citizens of our State.

"With every good wish for you and yours for the New Year, I am

"Sincerely,

"Alfred E. Driscoll<br>Governor.

"Honorable Walter E. Edge
Sunny Hill Plantation
Thomasville, Georgia"

On the 12th of February, 1951, Governor Driscoll sent the following:

"SPECIAL MESSAGE

"To the Senate and General Assembly
of the State of New Jersey:

"In 1945 Governor Walter E. Edge, desiring to preserve the historic Princeton property known as Morven for uses in keeping with its rich traditions, purchased the estate with the announced intention of ultimately having it become the property of the State of New Jersey as a gift from Mrs. Edge and himself. So far as it was possible for him to do so at that time, Governor Edge carried out this intention by entering into an agreement of purchase under which he accepted a deed to the property which gave him a life interest and conveyed the fee to the State of New Jersey. This conveyance to the State is expressly declared to be 'for the exclusively public use of maintaining the said property as an executive mansion for the use of successive governors of the State of New Jersey, or if its use as such an executive mansion should for any reason become inappropriate or be abandoned; then for the uses of a State museum or an historic site; and if both of the defined uses should be abandoned, the said property is to revert,' according to the deed, to Governor Edge, his heirs and assigns forever. While the deed was recorded on February 28, 1945, the State has not yet taken formal action to accept the gift.

"The year 1951 marks the 250th anniversary of the beginning of construction of Morven, and it is therefore particularly appropriate that we consider its ultimate disposition at this time. Moreover, I have recently received a formal offer from Governor and Mrs. Edge to deed the property to the State immediately, free and clear of all encumbrances and subject only to the use restrictions which the original deed to Governor Edge contained. By their original offer of this generous gift to the State of New Jersey, as well as by their recent renewal of the offer, the Edges have demonstrated an enduring interest in the great traditions of our State, as well as a notable recognition of the need to preserve for future generations those historic sites which help to etch into the records of history the values for which Americans have long fought and died. I know I speak for all the people of New Jersey when, as Governor, I express our deep appreciation to Walter E. Edge and Mrs. Edge for this most gracious offer of public benefit.

"Morven is one of those few places which has an extraordinary historical background significant in the life of our State as well as Nation. It was originally built in 1701 on land purchased from William Penn by Richard Stockton, grandfather of the signer of the Declaration of Independence. Some sixty years later, the charming Annis Boudinot gave Morven its name inspired by a popular romantic poem of the time. The property, located in one of the most attractive areas of present day Princeton, is full of the traditions befitting its origin. . . .

"The Stockton family continued to reside at the estate

until the late Bayard Stockton died in 1932. Prior to its acquisition by the Edges, the estate was occupied by Brigadier General Robert W. Johnson, who made a number of improvements to modernize the residence in keeping with the distinguished tradition of Morven. The environment, condition and history of the property make it eminently fitted for dedication to public use.

"Conscious as we are of this generous gift, the State of New Jersey would be lacking in appreciation were it to permit the generosity of its benefactors to undermine their own reasonable needs. It has been my conviction for some time that Mrs. Edge and the Governor have learned to love Morven and might want to continue to make it their home. Even though the Edges have wholeheartedly offered to make their gift effective immediately, I would recommend that in accepting the property we provide appropriate assurance that no one, not even the State of New Jersey, has a right to interrupt or even trouble the residence of Governor and Mrs. Edge at any time so long as either one of them desires to make his or her home in Morven.

"In order to carry out these purposes, I have today requested the majority leader in the Senate to introduce appropriate legislation.

"Respectfully submitted,

"ALFRED E. DRISCOLL,
Governor

"ATTEST:
"PAUL T. STAFFORD,
   Secretary to the Governor"

On June 18, 1951 the Legislature took the desired action in:

"A Joint Resolution to accept the gift of former Governor Walter E. Edge and Mrs. Edge to the State of New Jersey of the historic Princeton property known as Morven, and to express the appreciation of the people of this State.

"Whereas Governor Walter E. Edge, while Governor in one thousand nine hundred and forty-five, purchased the estate known as Morven, located in the borough of Princeton, with the publicly announced intention of ultimately presenting the property to the State of New Jersey for use as an executive mansion or State museum; and

"Whereas, In pursuance of this intention, Governor Edge accepted a deed of conveyance of Morven from Helen Hamilton Stockton et al., and the deed vested a life estate in Governor Edge, then to the State of New Jersey in fee for certain exclusively public uses, as fully described by the deed recorded on February twenty-eighth, one thousand nine hundred and forty-five, in the office of the clerk of Mercer county, in Book 888 of Deeds at page 170; and

"Whereas Governor Edge has by letter of December eleventh, one thousand nine hundred and fifty, addressed to Governor Alfred E. Driscoll, formally offered an immediate deed to the property free and clear of all encumbrances, for the originally stated public uses; and

"Whereas, It is fitting and proper that the generous and enduring gift of Governor Walter E. Edge and Mrs. Edge be accepted by a grateful State; and it is the further desire of the Legislature, however, in recognition of his long service to the people of New Jersey covering as it does nearly half a century during which time he has occupied the highest offices within the gift of the people of this State, to assure that neither Governor Edge nor Mrs. Edge shall ever be interrupted, disturbed or even troubled in their residence at Morven so long as either of them desires to make a home there; now, therefore, Be It Resolved *by the Senate and General Assembly of the State of New Jersey*:

"1. The State of New Jersey hereby gratefully accepts from Governor Walter E. Edge and Mrs. Edge their gift of the property known as Morven, located in the borough of Princeton, and by its legal description in the deed from Helen

Hamilton Stockton et al., to Walter E. Edge, Governor, recorded February twenty-eighth, one thousand nine hundred and forty-five, in the office of the clerk of Mercer county, Book 888 of Deeds, at page 170, as the interest of the State of New Jersey is therein described.

"2. It is hereby made a condition of this acceptance of the said gift that Governor Walter E. Edge and Mrs. Edge shall have the exclusive right, free of any and all interruption, disturbance or breach of their quiet enjoyment, to occupy Morven as a home for their respective lives or so long as either of them shall desire to do so; *provided*, that during such use the property shall remain subject to taxation and they, or the survivor of them shall remain responsible for all taxes and costs of operation, maintenance, repairs and replacements.

"3. This joint resolution shall take effect immediately."

For eight years the Edges continued in the "quiet enjoyment" of Morven, which the foregoing resolution assured them. But when they left it for the South in November 1953, it was to return to it for only a brief stay, while they moved into the new house they had been building at the corner of Stockton Street and Elm Road, where the boundaries of Morven and Constitution Hill had once touched each other.

As Governor Edge left Morven for the last time, his parting wish was: "May the rich traditions of a glorious past inspire those who will follow."

# The Architecture of Morven

BY CONSTANCE M. GREIFF

DESPITE the interest it has engendered over the past century, the house called Morven remains something of a mystery. The activities of its various distinguished occupants are well chronicled, but information about the physical surroundings in which those activities were conducted is surprisingly sparse. Among Morven's many inhabitants only Sara Marks Stockton appears to have kept a diary, and hers covers only a period of four years in the mid-nineteenth century. If other recordings of daily events were made, they do not seem to have survived their authors. The voluminous correspondence of the Stocktons and their relatives contains few references to Morven. Presumably when major construction projects were undertaken, the owners were in residence and it was not necessary to communicate about work in progress. Bills or other records for the original building period must have been among the papers burned during the British occupation in December 1776. Early descriptions by others than members of the Stockton family are also unknown. Although Morven appears on most maps of the area after 1750, none of the many travelers through Princeton left a record of its appearance. In contrast almost all commented, some at length, on Nassau Hall. Nor is there any pictorial representation of Morven prior to 1849 known. By that time it had assumed approximately its present form. It can only be inferred that the architecture of Morven was in no way remarkable or unusual to the observer in the eighteenth and early nineteenth centuries.

Like many of Princeton's more cherished myths, the account of the buildings at Morven in the first edition of this book seems to be based on information derived from John F. Hageman's *Princeton and its Institutions*, published in 1879. By the late nineteenth century the idea that Richard Stockton, the founder of the Princeton branch of the family, had erected a house on part of the tract of land he purchased from William Penn in 1701 was evidently part of local folklore. The house familiar to Hageman and his contemporaries was accepted as the "dwelling plantation" bequeathed by Richard to his son John and passing in turn to his son Richard the Signer of the Declaration of Independence. Succeeding writers, following Hageman's lead, assigned construction of Morven to a date between Richard's acquisition of the property in 1701 and his death in 1709. When Hageman wrote, Americans were just beginning to view the building of their own past with some favor. The Centennial of the Declaration of Independence, although largely a celebration of a hundred years of progress, also served to awaken popular interest in the life of the colonial and Revolutionary periods. This first blush of enthusiasm was largely felt, however, not for buildings as architecture, but as objects connected with the life and activities of famous men. Dating building on the basis of property acquisition by a particular family was common; until the twentieth century few scholars attempted to construct a chronology of American architectural styles.

It was therefore perfectly natural for a man of John F. Hageman's era to accept Morven as the Stocktons' ancestral home because it stood on the Stocktons' ancestral lands, without considering whether it would have been likely for such a building to have been constructed in Princeton in the first decade of the eighteenth century. Viewed in the light of present knowledge of the history of American architecture nothing seems more unlikely. Morven, or at least its central block, the most consciously styled section, is clearly a Georgian building. It reflects the taste for a simplified version of the English adaptation of Renaissance classicism that dominated American architecture during much of the eighteenth century. In particular, the strong horizontality of the composition of the façade, the solidity of the building's massing, its clear and simple symmetry are characteristic of that phase of American

Georgian architecture typical of the period from about 1740 to the Revolution. No such building had been erected in the first decade of the eighteenth century in the vicinity of either Philadelphia or New York, the closest metropolitan centers to the backwoods Princeton then was. The most ambitious dwelling of the period, the Governor's Palace at Williamsburg, largely built between 1706 and 1709, was far less classical in character. Its irregularly spaced narrow windows, steeply pitched roof, and massive chimneys hark back to the seventeenth century rather than forward to the eighteenth.

Fortunately the question of the date of Morven's building need not rest solely on the evidence of its style. There is ample documentation to prove that until the 1750s the Stocktons lived elsewhere. When Richard Stockton wrote his will in 1709, he referred to himself as "of Middlesex," thus indicating that the "dwelling plantation" he devised to his son John was on the south side of the road that bisects Princeton, which since 1688 had served as the dividing line between that county and Somerset. That the house in which John Stockton lived, presumably the one left to him by his father, stood south of the road is confirmed by the so-called Dalley map of 1745 in the New York Historical Society. Properly titled, "A Map of the Road from Trenton to Amboy," it was drawn on the basis of a survey made to mark accurately the mileage along the much-traveled route across New Jersey's narrow waist, and clearly illustrates John Stockton's dwelling in the location where the house known as The Barracks still stands. No building is shown at Morven's location.

In his will, dated May 9, 1758, John Stockton provided "that the part of my Homestead Farm which lies on the South Side of the afd. Main Street or Highway be equally divided in Quantity between my two Sons Philip Stockton and Samuel Stockton; the Western Division thereof together with all the Buildings, Edifices, orchards and appurtenances I give unto my sd. Son Philip. . . ." Philip and Samuel were minors and John empowered his eldest son, Richard, to sell as much of the land left to them as might be necessary to further his younger brothers' education and advancement.

Accordingly Richard, in May 1764, sold to Ezekiel Forman "the plantation commonly known by the name of the homestead farm of John Stockton, Esq. deceased. . . ." No deed covering this sale has survived, but the transaction is described in a deed dated May 1, 1765, by which Forman conveyed some of the meadowland in the tract to Richard Stockton. That this is the property shown on the Dalley map is confirmed by a map drawn by Azariah Dunham in 1766 and entitled "A Map of the Division line between the Counties of Middlesex and Somerset." The house appears as in the possession of Ezekiel Forman. Although the county line illustrated, and described in the surveyors' notebooks from which the map was prepared, generally paralleled the road, it dips to the south at this point so that the house falls within the bounds of Somerset County. Probably this deviation had been made to accommodate John Stockton, whose major landholdings were in Somerset rather than Middlesex, and who had played some part in the civic affairs of the former county.

A little less than four years prior to making his will, John Stockton and his wife had deeded 150 acres across the road from the homestead to their eldest son, Richard. The consideration was a token five pounds plus "the Natural Affection and Respect which they bear unto the said Richard Stockton their Son." Again the language of the deed clearly indicates that John Stockton's dwelling was on the south side of the road. The property deeded to Richard is described as "Being on the North Side of the Main Street in Princeton," with the bounds beginning at a point identified by "the bank of Prim Oppisite the Dwelling House of sd. John Stockton." The tract includes the land on which Morven stands today.

Although some structure such as a tenant house may have been erected on the tract previously, it seems reasonable to assume that no major building activity was undertaken until its acquisition by Richard, since John lived elsewhere. Just when he began to erect his own dwelling cannot be determined, but it was undoubtedly completed by the time his first child, Julia, was born in 1759. Like the house formerly his father's, it appears on the Dunham map of 1762, and the name Morven is used on family correspondence in the 1760s. Whether, however, the building presently standing on the site is the one erected by Richard in the 1750s is uncertain. John Pintard, writing to his daughter after a fire damaged the house in 1821, noted that the entire building had burnt in 1770. This comment is given some validity by the persistent, if later, tale of the burning of the east wing or library by the British during the occupation of Princeton in December 1776, although no contemporary reference to such a fire or such a wing exists. Benjamin Rush, Richard Stockton's son-in-law, who visited Morven a few days after the British left, while cataloging extensive damage to the grounds and contents of the house, makes no mention of a fire or any damage to the building itself. The tale seems to have been concocted through confusion of the 1770 fire with the destruction of Richard Stockton's library. The cause may be a matter of semantics. In the eighteenth century the word "library" generally referred to a collection of books, only rarely housed in a special building or room. By the nineteenth century, as the story found its way into print, the architectural connotation of the word had almost displaced its earlier meaning. In any event, the possibility of a disastrous fire in the main part of the house rather than a wing is given further credence by marked discrepancies between the plan of the basement of the central section of Morven and that of the first floor. Although the present outer walls and chimneys coincide with the foundations, the inner partitions of the first floor do not rest on those of the basement. The total destruction cited by Pintard at least suggests the possibility that the original mansion at Morven may have been of frame rather than brick or stone. The latter would have been apt to survive fire, as the walls of Nassau Hall did, and even the former would not have been apt to be "entirely burnt down." In any event, the strong possibility remains of major changes in Morven's internal arrangements. The floor plan of the basement indicates a plan somewhat less formal than that of the existing house. In a manner somewhat akin to Stenton, John Logan's house in Germantown, Pennsylvania, three rooms of almost equal size, the middle one perhaps serving as an entry, may have been ranged along the south front of the house. Two smaller rooms and a stairhall may have occupied the rear. The remaining evidence, however, is so slight that any attempt to reconstruct the earliest house can only be conjectured on the slimmest foundation.

If, indeed, there was a major eighteenth-century fire at Morven, rebuilding was swift. There can be little doubt, both from the surviving remains, and from written documentation, that at the time of the Revolution Richard Stockton and his family occupied the brick house at Morven. Its appearance, however, was somewhat different from that which has become familiar in the last century. Numerous additions and alterations have obscured, although not obliterated, the major features of the original construction. Fortunately brick is a fairly enduring material and one relatively difficult to alter without leaving traces of what has been done. The elevation of the eighteenth-century house can, therefore, still be read, through layers of paint, in the walls of Morven. The extent of this house is defined by the use of Flemish bond brickwork. Several brick bonds were used in eighteenth-century America, but two types predominated in central New Jersey. In one of these, known as common bond, a row of headers, the short end of the brick, appears over every three or five rows of stretchers, the long side of the brick. Flemish bond, with its more intricate pattern, was preferred where greater elegance was sought. In this, headers and stretchers alternate in each row. The headers are centered over a stretcher in the row beneath, to produce a checkerboard effect. Frequently this effect was enhanced by the use of headers burned or glazed blue or black, but this does not seem to have been the case at Morven.

The entire façade of the central block of Morven, up to a course of brick just above the lintels of the second story windows, is of Flemish bond. So too is approximately two-thirds of the west wing. Using the dimensions dictated by the brickwork, it is possible to begin to perceive the appearance of Morven as a typical house of the third quarter of the eighteenth century as shown in the view in Fig. 1 (p. 174). The veranda must be thought away, as must the present doorway, which is of a type common in the vicinity in the closing years of the eighteenth century and the first two decades of the nineteenth. In its place should probably be imagined a pedimented doorway of more robust proportions, without pilasters, but with an eared or crosseted architrave. Perhaps, as in the surviving mid-eighteenth-century doorway at Maclean House, an arched fanlight was incorporated into the rectangular space between the doorhead and the pediment. The splayed lintels with projecting keystones over the windows are not uncommon in the area and are probably original. Usually in Princeton these were made of wood scored to simulate stone. It seems fitting, however, that those on the home of Richard Stockton, the town's wealthiest citizen, should actually be of cut stone, like those on Philadelphia houses of the period. The belt course, a projecting horizontal feature marking the delineation between the first and second stories, is also of stone.

At the roofline, the south wall of the house was some seven or eight courses lower than it now is, so that the crowning cornice pressed closely on the second story windows, cutting, in fact, through their central keystones. This was the original configuration of the roofline at Nassau Hall and Maclean House, as well as at Bainbridge House. In keeping with the restraint of the other exterior detailing at Morven, this cornice probably consisted of a few simple moldings, capped by a row of modillions, or curved brackets. The roof probably reached to the present ridge, thus having a somewhat steeper slope than it does presently. It was undoubtedly covered with wooden shingles. Slate, which had to be imported, was very expensive, especially when transported inland. Its use therefore generally was restricted to the most ambitious buildings in port cities.

The mute testimony of the brickwork also reveals the original appearance of the west wing. Like the central block, its roof was once considerably lower, the demarcation between the Flemish bond of the original and the common bond above still showing clearly a little above the center line of the sash of the present windows. The wing also was originally somewhat shorter in length. The line of the addition shows clearly; the westernmost portion being laid up in the same random bond utilized for the east wing. Despite its small size, the west wing always encompassed two full stories. The outlines of the original windows and door are still visible in the brickwork, and are shown on the conjectural drawing of the reconstructed façade. Like the openings of the central block, these were crowned by splayed flat arches, here constructed of brick, however, rather than stone. Two of the small-paned, thick-muntined sash from these windows were probably reused in construction of the so-called "slave quarters." Sash with panes of like size and similar width were undoubtedly originally used in the larger openings of the main block.

The conjectural drawing shows Morven as it appeared at the time of the Revolution. One wing only is shown, since the similarity in brickwork and style, as well as the scant written documentation that exists, suggest that the west wing, although not the east, is contemporary with the central block. A structural peculiarity reenforces this hypothesis. At the eastern end of this wing, in the wall it shares with the central block, is a large fireplace. The massive support for this construction remains in the crawl space under the west wing, and much of the masonry for fireplaces and a chimney remains on the first and second floor. At the latter level, however, the flue cuts across to join the west chimney of the central block. Such an arrangement would not have been particularly difficult to construct if the west wing had been built before, or at the same time, as the central block. On the other hand, if the west wing had been added later, this configuration would have necessitated rebuilding a considerable portion of the common wall, and it seems safe to assume that practicality would have dictated a different location for the chimney.

Although the west wing is thus probably coeval with the central block, the east wing can only be viewed as a later addition. The legend that it burned during the Revolution is without foundation and there is positive proof that the fire of 1821 occurred in the main part of the house. Furthermore, the materials of which it is made differ markedly from those of the rest of the house. The brickwork of its façade, like the additions to the west wing, is of random bond. Surviving details within and without, as well as its general proportions, bespeak a date in the nineteenth century. The surviving fabric at Morven indicates, therefore, that the house Richard Stockton built consisted of a main section with a single, lower wing. This was a common arrangement for houses of the period in central New Jersey, as witnessed by the dwellings built by Richard's cousins, Robert at Constitution Hill and Job at Bainbridge House. Richard's more imposing house differed only in scale and enrichment, not in concept.

The internal arrangements of Morven have also been altered greatly over the centuries. At present the first floor of the main section is organized around a great T-shaped hall. The stem of the T runs through the house from front to back. Originally there was direct access to outdoors at each end offering vistas of the gardens that adorned both fronts. One arm of the T contains a stair; the other now serves as a passageway to the west wing. On the second floor, however, the latter space is occupied by a small room, so that the hall

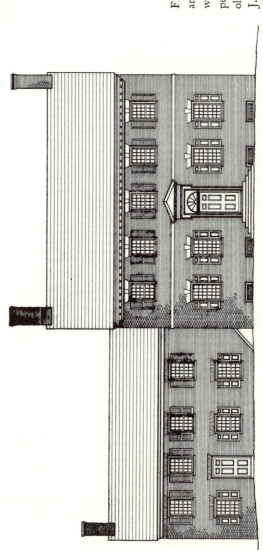

Fig. 1. Conjectural elevation and plan of central block and west wing of Morven as it appeared at the time of the Revolution. (Drawing by Michael J. Mills)

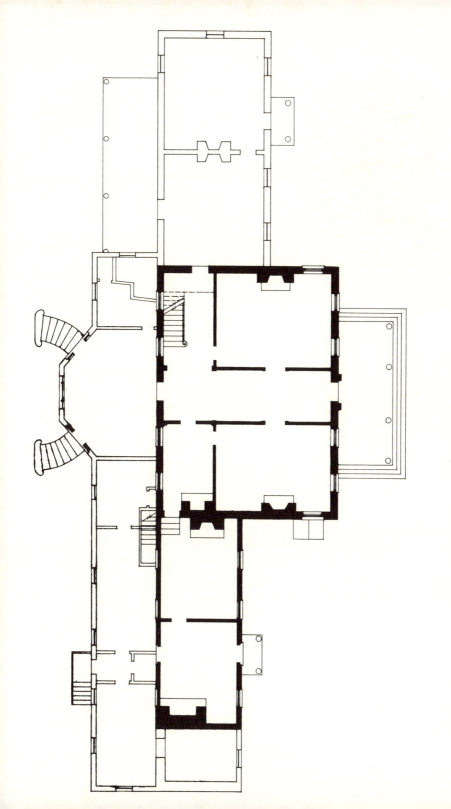

is L- rather than T-shaped, and there is some evidence that this was also the original plan of the first floor. Such a plan is suggested by the inventory of Richard Stockton's personal property made by Annis after his death in 1781, which also confirms the extent of the house as it existed in the eighteenth century. Two bedchambers are described, each containing a bed, dressing table, looking glass, nine pictures and six chairs. One was also furnished with a chest of drawers; the other with a bureau with glass doors, or what today would be called a secretary. Evidently the furniture of any other bedrooms was not worth listing, or was considered the property of the children occupying them.

The other rooms described were evidently on the first floor. One was the front parlor, furnished with a large, gilt-framed mirror, eight chairs with seats covered in crimson damask, and two mahogany card tables. This amount of furniture would not have gone far toward filling the two large rooms on either side of the hall. It is likely that the space described is the present hallway to the west wing. Like the other two rooms, this contained a fireplace, the fittings for which are included in the inventory. When the French cartographers with Rochambeau's Army mapped Princeton in 1781, they showed the drive into Morven leading from Bayard Lane rather than Stockton Street. The eighteenth-century visitor traveling by carriage or horseback would thus have arrived and been greeted at the north entrance to the house, rather than, as today, at the south, so that this small room would indeed have been at the front. The remaining two rooms were larger. The dining room held a mahogany sideboard, a relatively new type of furniture and therefore to be viewed as a species of luxury, a dining table, a tea stand, and eight more chairs. The walls were hung with a mirror and ten pictures. The back parlor was also devoted to gustatory pleasures. It held a small and a large dining table, as well as a large tea table. When Annis entertained the Continental Congress in 1783 she would have had no difficulty in arranging a large party to sup or dine, although chairs might need to be brought down from the chambers. In addition to the three major rooms downstairs, Annis listed "kitchen furniture," including tubs for washing and for curing meat. These domestic necessities must have been accommodated in the wing, the only structure on the property with fireplaces large enough for cooking and heating large quantities of water for laundry and washing up.

Subsequent remodeling has destroyed almost all vestiges of the original interior treatment of Morven. To establish where paneling may have been utilized would require removal of the present detailing and probing of the underlying structure, and even then much of the evidence may have been destroyed in the course of later alterations. Two surviving eighteenth-century features, a door to a chimneybreast closet and a door now hung between the present dining room and the back hall suggest that the interiors were carried out by a competent, if not remarkable, carpenter. Full paneling of rooms was not usually employed in the Princeton area. Carved wooden trim was confined to the area around the fireplace, cornices, chair rails, and the enframements of windows and doors. In the more highly finished houses, like Maclean House, built to accommodate the presidents of the college, the principal rooms were adorned with a paneled wainscot reaching from the floor to chair rail height. Morven's ample proportions and the quality and kind of furnishings listed in the inventory of Richard Stockton's estate indicate a certain pretension of elegance on the part of its owners. On the other hand, the simplicity of the exterior detailing suggests that workmen capable of executing sophisticated carving were not available in the Princeton area. Nevertheless, it can probably safely be assumed that paneling and moldings akin to that at Maclean House were once part of Morven's accouterments.

Although Morven is not an unusual house in the context of American architecture of the eighteenth century, it was, at the time of the Revolution, the largest and finest house of its kind in the immediate neighborhood. As such it stood in marked contrast to the houses erected by previous generations, including the dwelling known as The Barracks, occupied by Richard's father and grandfather. The early houses of colonial America, despite regional variations, shared some common characteristics. Medieval in concept, they were designed on an additive principle, with the location of rooms based on convenience and utility, rather than on any pre-conceived plan. Rooms served multiple functions, with beds a common item of furniture even in the parlor. The most important, sometimes the only, room in such a dwelling was known as the hall. It served the combined functions of kitchen, dining room, family sitting room, and bedroom. To this, other rooms might be added, usually laterally. No hallways, or as they would have been called in the eighteenth century, passageways, connected these rooms. One passed from one to the other, without regard for the privacy of the occupants. When, as at The Barracks (which, it must be remembered was originally approximately twice its present width), the building was built to a height of two stories, the resulting verticality of proportion is distinctive. This is often emphasized by the manner in which the building's walls rise abruptly from the ground without an exposed foundation or basement. Generally, ornament in the form of molded cornices or elaborate doorframes was at a minimum. Door and window openings were often assymmetrically placed, echoing the informal and utilitarian arrangements of the interior.

Buildings of this type, reflecting English medieval traditions with which colonists had been familiar before they emigrated, were built in America prior to 1700, and indeed often well into the eighteenth century. In the seventeenth century, however, English architecture itself was beginning to change dramatically. The Renaissance rediscovery of the principles of Roman architecture, which had begun to inform the work of Italian architects in the fifteenth century, was introduced into England by design books in the late sixteenth century, and beginning about 1620, in the buildings of Inigo Jones. By the eighteenth century this style with its classical references and rational ordering was the favored mode in England for both public and private buildings. Although its introduction predated the succession of the Hanoverian dynasty, this English manifestation of Renaissance architecture has been dubbed Georgian.

Characterized by a system of "proper" proportions, symmetry, and balance, Georgian architecture depended not on traditional forms passed on from builder to builder, but on a firm geometric base. The central theme of this aesthetic was the "orders," the organization of a building around a carefully regulated relationship between the base, shaft and capital of a column and the entablature it supported. Buildings were composed of rectangles drawn to a pleasing proportion, circles, and their sections. Even when no motifs directly derived from antiquity were employed, classical principles and Euclidean geometry, underlay architectural design. Because Georgian buildings were based not only on experience, but on prescribed rules, books played an important part in the dissemination of the style. These not only detailed the mathematics of constructing architectural components, but illustrated plans and elevations of actual buildings. Such publications, along with emigrant craftsmen, transported the Georgian style to America. Volumes such as Palladio's *Four Books of Architecture*, translated into English in 1715; Colen Campbell's *Vitruvius Britannicus*; James Gibbs' *Book of Architecture*; William Salmon's *Palladio Londonensis*; and the many books by Batty Langley, were purchased for gentlemen's private libraries, as well as by professional builders.

Like other elements of classical learning, some knowledge of architecture was considered part of the intellectual furniture of a well-educated gentleman's mind. Thomas Jefferson extended his interest beyond the usual practice by designing buildings for others, as well as residences for himself. But such contemporaries as George Washington and Benjamin Franklin played more than a casual part in planning their dwellings. When Benjamin Chew commissioned his country house, Cliveden, in Germantown, he first sketched his own ideas, based on an English publication, before calling in a local carpenter-builder to execute them. Richard Stockton's ideas, too, probably dictated the general design of Morven. If he sought professional advice, he may have turned to Robert Smith, whose acquaintance he is known to have made while the Philadelphia carpenter-builder was engaged on Nassau Hall, and who continued to own property in Princeton until 1765, or to the local builder John McComb, a cousin by marriage. No precise published prototype for Morven can be found, but this is by no means unusual. American Georgian buildings, with few exceptions, depend only in a general way on the published English models, which were too elaborate for colonial resources. What was derived from architectural books was the basic format of a classically balanced arrangement, and occasionally some specific details, adapted and simplified to conform to American tastes and capabilities.

Whatever the source of the design, the formal and architectonic composition of Morven stands in sharp contrast to the casual, vernacular arrangement of The Barracks. Rather than rising abruptly from the ground, Morven sits on a high basement, the exposed windows of which are now covered by the veranda, as on a firm base. The windows of the first and second floors are located directly over those of the basement and balance one another precisely on either side of the central axis marked by the doorway. The chief horizontal division of the house is clearly delineated by the stone belt course between the first and second stories. Originally, when the cornice pressed heavily on the lintels of the second story windows, the terminus of the façade was marked by an even stronger horizontal emphasis.

The formal balance and clarity of the façade are reiterated

in the plan. The house is bisected by a central hall or passage-way, affording a vista through the entire house. Rigid sym-metry is here abandoned, however, in favor of practicality. The hall to the east of the door is approximately a foot nar-rower than to the west, the additional space being allotted to the present drawing room on the east side of the house. Otherwise elements of the interior arrangement are paired. Balanced doorways give access to the large rooms on either side of the hall. Each of these in turn is organized around a fireplace centered on the exterior wall. The stairhall, too, was probably originally balanced by a small room of equal size across the hall.

The exclusion of the stair from the central passageway, while not unknown in eighteenth-century architecture, was not a common arrangement. It did, however, offer the advantage of an uninterrupted view of the grounds on both principal fronts of the house. To owners as interested in landscaping and gardening as the first master and mistress of Morven, this must have been a not inconsiderable advantage. Besides, the motif was one which enjoyed its chief popularity in the Delaware Valley. Separate stairhalls appear at the Trent House in Trenton as early as 1719, and in Penn-sylvania at Hope Lodge, the now-demolished Port Royal, and Mount Pleasant, the latter presenting the closest parallel to Morven.

The interior arrangements at Morven bespeak not only a formal architectural taste, but a formal life style as well. The medieval hall and other rooms of multiple purpose have given way to rooms set aside for special functions. Beds are confined to second floor chambers. There is a separate room for dining and another for cards and other forms of enter-tainment. The kitchen and other service areas have been relegated to a separate wing. The central passageway serves not only to organize the plan, but to set the rooms off one from the other, allowing a measure of privacy to the in-habitants. Morven in the eighteenth century was thus a commodious, elegant setting for a gentleman of the period. Its high-ceilinged rooms, if not exceptionally large, were gracious and dignified.

Yet the Stocktons, who often revealed themselves as conscious of both fashion and nobility soon felt compelled to make changes and improvements. One such general refurbishing appears to have taken place shortly after the Revolution. Evidently it was confined to alteration of details, rather than extensive construction. By the last quarter of the eighteenth century the sturdy proportions of the classical detailing illustrated in works interpreting Vitruvius and Palladio were no longer in vogue. The interest in antiquity continued unabated, but new discoveries engendered a taste for other aspects of classical vocabulary. Particularly influential were such works as Winckelmann's publications, in 1762 and 1764, of art unearthed in the course of the excavations of Pompeii and Herculaneum. The attenuation of form and the delicate linearity of these products of the later Roman Empire influenced such tastemakers as the Scottish architect Robert Adam and the English potter Josiah Wedgwood. In the post-Revolutionary period this taste for a lighter version of the classical vocabulary, like the Georgian style before it, crossed the ocean to America. At Morven it left its mark on the frontispiece of the main doorway with its attenuated flanking columns, dainty fanlight, and gouged decoration, and on a mantelpiece, moved to its present location the east wing from the second floor during renovations undertaken by the State in 1955. At this time, probably at the end of the decade of the 1780s, a piazza was added to the house, a feature that so impressed Annis with its novelty that she mentioned it twice in letters written in 1790. It is doubtful, however, that this was the present veranda. Its Tuscan columns and heavy proportions would not have been fashionable at the end of the eighteenth century and accord, rather, with the style of additional improvements undertaken some fifty years later.

On March 2, 1821, a well-documented fire broke out at

Morven. Contrary to many later accounts, this fire did not occur in the east wing. As reported in the Trenton *Federalist* on March 5, the house "took fire in an upper apartment. . . . The roof of the main building was destroyed, but by the exertions of the citizens, the fire was here arrested in its progress, so that no other essential damage was sustained by the building." The loss of the roof would have itself necessitated immediate repairs. It seems to have served also as the impetus for extensive remodeling. In this case it can be stated with some certainty that the work was entrusted to Charles Steadman, a local builder-architect. Although John F. Hageman cannot be regarded as a reliable source for eighteenth-century Princeton, or indeed any history related to the Stocktons, whom he viewed with an admiration little short of idolatry, his accounts of nineteenth-century affairs are more dependable. In particular his facts about those whom he served as clients in his legal practice are generally accurate. In a brief statement on Steadman's career Hageman noted that Steadman "built every house on Stockton Street, except the barracks, Mr. Tulane's (the present Lowrie House) and the original part of Morven, and perhaps one or two small ones."

Steadman's work at Morven consisted principally of raising the height of the central block and the addition of the east wing. Beyond this new construction, he was probably responsible for a number of alterations to the existing fabric. In executing this work, Steadman both harked back to the Adamesque taste of the turn of the century and forward to the new fashion that scholars have dubbed the Greek Revival.

The discoveries at Herculaneum and Pompeii only whetted the eighteenth century's appetite for information about the monuments of antiquity. With publication of Stuart and Revett's *The Antiquities of Athens*, between 1762 and 1816, attention shifted gradually from the sites of Rome to those of Greece. Greek prototypes were accepted with particular enthusiasm in America, where romantic associations with

Greek democracy reeinforced their appeal. At Morven the reference to Greek forms is confined to the cornice, installed on the main block when the roof was raised, with its triglyphs and metopes derived from the frieze of a Greek Doric entablature. However, the only other significant feature of the exterior dating from this period, the demi-lune windows in the gables, are Adamesque, rather than Federal.

Within, Steadman seems to have made numerous alterations in a rather old-fashioned style. The staircase with its square balusters, ramped railings and delicate scrolled detailing might readily be assigned a date in the late eighteenth century, were it not for its striking resemblance to staircases in such other Steadman buildings of the 1820s as 10 Nassau Street and the demolished Thomson Hall. The elliptical arches with reeded decoration that give access to the stair hall and to the present hall leading to the west wing, with their horizontally reeded moldings, are also of a form popular in the late eighteenth and early nineteenth centuries. They suggest that it was at this time that the former "front parlor" was converted to a passageway.

It may have been the expansion of the formal areas of the house through addition of the east wing that made it possible to eliminate one of the rooms in the central block. That the east wing is Steadman's work is indicated both by Hageman's statement and by the construction of the staircase. To balance the existing west wing, the east wing was constructed without a basement, that is with its first floor just a step above ground level. Its ceiling heights, too, are considerably lower than those in the central block. Access to its second floor is therefore achieved from a landing about two-thirds of the way up the main staircase from the central block, by a short run of stairs, with detailing identical to that of the main staircase.

Probably a general refurbishing of the interior also took place at this time. It is quite likely that whatever eighteenth century paneling Morven had was removed, to make way for the smooth plastered or papered walls favored in the early nineteenth century. Certainly the iron firebacks which remain in place in the dining and drawing rooms can date no earlier. Made in Burlington County, at Hanover Furnace, which began operation in 1791, they reveal a pattern of reeded ovals, which, produced at many furnaces, enjoyed enormous popularity in the 1820s and '30s.

It was probably also in the course of this remodeling that the brickwork at Morven was first painted. Although painted brickwork was not unknown in the eighteenth century, particularly in the post-Revolutionary period, it was not common. Certainly painting would not then have been applied to a façade carefully laid up in Flemish bond as Morven's was. There is every reason to believe that in the eighteenth century Morven followed the favored color scheme for high-style houses in the Delaware Valley and, indeed, in much of colonial America: red brick, with the pale line of the mortar emphasized by scoring, and pale buff or cream-colored trim. The decision to paint the brick may have been dictated by practicality. Some form of coating on the brick would hide any charring from fire, as well as disguising the discrepancy between the different bonds used in the original construction and the addition. Certainly the rather sloppily executed random bond of the east wing was never meant to be exposed. In addition, a color other than red would have been far more appealing to nineteenth-century taste. The fashion for the Greek extended not only to the use of classical motifs, but to what was (erroneously) believed to be the hues of the ancient monuments, pristine white or pale stone colors. There is some indication that the finish applied to Morven was some sort of stucco or masonry wash rather than paint, since the brick has been hacked to receive such a coating. Without scraping and actual physical analysis, however, it is impossible to determine the sequence of coatings and colors utilized at Morven in the course of well over a century.

That restless individual, the Commodore, was undoubtedly

responsible for the last of the major alterations made to Morven by members of the Stockton family. Between bouts of creating a transportation system, sponsoring innovative ships and naval ordnance, and expanding his country's boundaries, the Commodore devoted himself to domestic building projects, commissioning a handsome series of houses for his children. It is therefore not surprising that his daughter-in-law Sara in describing a visit on January 14, 1848, during which they had enjoyed "much amusing small talk," reported that the Commodore had "decided to build upon Morven." Although it is impossible to determine whether such elements as the extension to the west wing and the porches along the north side of the house were executed at this time or during the rebuilding following the 1821 fire, other features can be ascribed to the Commodore and his architect with some certainty. Among these should be counted the two small, square, one-story appendages attached to the north side of the house at the conjunction of the central block and the wings. These differ in construction from the remainder of the building, having brick, rather than stone, foundations and thinner walls. One contained the famous bathroom which, if not the first installed in Princeton, was at least an early local example of indoor plumbing. The function of the other appendage is undetermined.

If the Commodore retained an architect to assist him, he undoubtedly turned to John Notman, who was occupied with projects for the college and members of the Stockton and Potter families in the decade between 1845 and 1855. Most of Notman's work at Princeton was executed in what is known as the Tuscan Revival or Italianate style. Much as the eighteenth and early nineteenth centuries had looked to ancient Rome and Greece, the architects of the mid-nineteenth century turned to other past eras for inspiration. Notman, in particular, utilized the forms of fifteenth-century Italy returning to the Renaissance version of Roman forms, in contrast to the use of the Greek orders favored in the previous two decades. The bold and heavy interpretation of the Tuscan order, used on the veranda across the south front of Morven and the small porticos on the wings, reflects the taste of this period rather than the more tentative handling of classical forms typical of the eighteenth century. The roof of the west wing may have been raised to match the height of the east wing at this time. Certainly the solidity of the modillion cornices on these matches that of the veranda and accords with the treatment of the columns. To this era too belong certain features of the interior, including the parquet floors and the somewhat heavy-handed arched openings that give access to the drawing and dining rooms from the hall and to the morning room from the stairhall.

Although other alterations have been made to Morven in the more than a century and a quarter since the Commodore decided to "build upon" it, particularly on the north side, the south front remains today much as it was when Benson Lossing sketched it in the winter of 1849.

If the architecture of Morven was always rather conventional, the same cannot be said of the landscaping. The view of antiquity that manifested itself during the eighteenth century, and the several architectural revival styles of the nineteenth, was strongly tinged with romanticism. A longing for the unfamiliar in time and place, an admiration for brave men and deeds of derring-do, an appreciation for the beauties of nature—all manifestations of a romantic spirit—infuse Annis Stockton's poetry. More concrete expressions of her romanticism can be found in her name for her house, derived from the stormy and remote Gaelic kingdom described in James MacPherson's *Poems of Ossian*, and her choice of Alexander Pope's garden at Twickenham as a model for the landscaping of the south front of Morven. Pope's design would have been outmoded in England by the 1760s, but its irregularity, naturalism, and the inclusion of a grotto and antiquarian relics would have been a novelty in America. Indeed, the Stocktons' garden was probably one of this country's first planned romantic landscapes.

In contrast, the north front, according to Rochambeau's cartographers, was laid out in the formal continental style with *parterres*, an *allée*, and perhaps a terrace. If this were the case, it is unlikely that the building known as the slave quarters was part of the scheme. In any event, its proportions, the manner in which the brickwork is laid up, and the covering of stucco scored to simulate stone all bespeak a date in the mid-nineteenth century, although building components of earlier periods were reused in its construction. The eastern end, containing the ice house, may have existed in the eighteenth building, for a small, low building or pavilion would not have been an incompatible feature of a formal garden. Such a garden would have appeared hopelessly outmoded by the Commodore's day. In keeping up with the latest fashion, he evidently laid out his estate in the picturesque manner of an English gentleman's park. Some of the majestic trees planted for this purpose still adorn those properties that were part of the Morven estate before its subdivision at the end of the nineteenth century.

One reason that the architecture of Morven poses so many thorny problems is that from its inception its owners, and the architects and builders they retained, have conceived it within a uniformly classical frame of reference. Although almost every generation expanded the house or otherwise remodeled it to meet the requirements of their life style, Morven never suffered an accretion of additions and ornaments in conflict with its basic simplicity and solidity of composition and decoration. Were Richard and Annis Stockton's ghosts to return to see the house they built and named, they might have some difficulty in recognizing it, so all-encompassing have been the changes. Yet they would not feel uncomfortable, for the alterations have been faithful to the spirit, if not the precise forms, of the original. Morven stands now, therefore, not as a pure example of any particular architectural style but as a symbol of the continuity of taste successors. If the building is significant largely for its association with occupants who achieved a remarkably long record of leadership in the affairs of their community, state, and nation, it is no less interesting as a reflection of changing American views towards the classical style.

Morven Incumbents
An Informal History
by Bolton F. Schwartz

# ROBERT B. MEYNER

For more than 225 years the occupants of Morven had been members of the Stockton family. Beginning in 1928 the Mansion was home, for 17 years, for Gen. Robert W. Johnson, who had leased it from the Stocktons. For the next eight years the home folks were Governor and Mrs. Walter E. Edge, who had bought Morven from the Stockton heirs under a deed that expressed the Edges' intention to present the property to the state.

The Edges moved out in 1953 and New Jersey took over as the new owner. Since then, nobody can buy it nor can anybody rent it. The only way to get to live in it is to be elected Governor of New Jersey, for the Mansion is the official residence of the state's chief executives.

The gift from the Edges left it to New Jersey to decide whether the Mansion should be a residence for governors or a museum. Upon taking office as Governor in 1954, Robert Meyner appointed a committee to study the question. Members included Mrs. Jennie Moore, widow of former Governor A. Harry Moore, and Mrs. Mattie Driscoll, mother of former Governor Alfred E. Driscoll. Rejecting the museum alternative, the committee prepared to make Morven habitable. Armed with $250,000 in available funds the committee engaged Edgar Williams, an architect reputed to be expert in colonial construction, to make certain the historical values were preserved. Williams, who lived in Rutherford, was a brother of William Carlos Williams, the well-known poet.

The process of rehabilitation, from the appointment of the committee to the day Meyner moved in as the first governor to occupy the Mansion under state ownership, took three years. He didn't gain the right to occupy Morven without a struggle. The first step was a victory over former Congressman Elmer Wene in a bitter primary with Frank Hague, the Hudson County boss, backing Wene and fighting to retain his hold on his county and on the state.

Meyner was projected into the contest by a coalition of county chairmen, including John V. Kenny, who had challenged Hague and had already defeated him for the Jersey City mayorship. Meyner carried only four of the 21 counties in the primary, but he eked out a victory by a scant 1,500 votes in an election in which 236,000 Democratic ballots were cast. The result marked the end of Hague's rule, confirmed the ascendancy of Kenny, and underscored the emergence of the county chairmen as the top echelon of the party leadership.

With that victory under his belt, Meyner faced Paul L. Troast, who had won distinction as chairman of the commission that built and operated the highly-successful New Jersey Turnpike, in the general election. Aided by revelations of underworld activity in rock-ribbed Republican Bergen County and by the "Fay Letter" (a plea by Troast for parole consideration for Joe Fay, a labor leader convicted of extortion) Meyner, who began as the underdog, forged ahead to win by more than 150,000 votes. The election started the Democrats on the way back to dominance.

Robert Baumle Meyner was a 45-year-old bachelor when he won the governorship. He was the son of Gustave Meyner of Manchester, N.H. and his wife Sophie, who had come over from Switzerland. They settled in Easton, Pa., where Robert, one of three children, was born. The family lived briefly in Paterson and then moved to Phillipsburg. Meyner went to local schools in Phillipsburg and after being graduated from high school went to Lafayette College for his arts degree. He earned a law degree at Columbia University in 1933.

Politics attracted the youthful Meyner and he made an unsuccessful run for a state senate seat in 1941. World War II broke out and Meyner went into the Navy, serving as a gun crew commander and, frequently, as defense counsel in courts-martial. After the war, in 1946, he made an unsuccessful run for Congress, losing to J. Parnell Thomas, the incumbent, by 49 votes. In 1947 he won a senate seat. Four years later he lost the seat, by 61 votes, to Wayne Dumont whom he had defeated in the earlier election.

As Governor, Meyner, like his predecessor Governor Driscoll, and in contrast to all the others before, was a full-time occupant of the Chief Executive's office. While Morven was being rehabilitated, Meyner maintained a suite at the Hildebrecht Hotel, although he frequently went back to the family's domicile in Phillipsburg.

Most authorities agree that Meyner ran a tight ship. He had the reputation of being frugal with the state's money as well as with his own. He made generally-good appointments. He was known to be exceptionally stubborn. And he relished the pun as a high form of humor.

In office only a few months, Meyner was advised by one of several business groups he had pressed into service that irregularities had been uncovered in the Division of Employment Security, headed by former Governor Harold G. Hoffman. Meyner suspended Hoffman pending investigation and then refused to discuss the situation despite charges by editorial writers and some leaders of both political parties that he was "persecuting" Hoffman. The pressure mounted. Hoffman, an accomplished after-dinner speaker, was well-known and popular. But Meyner kept his own counsel. No action was taken because the missing funds were difficult to trace. Hoffman died in a New York hotel room. He had written a letter to his daughter in which he confessed embezzlement of state funds. The contents of the letter, made public, contained statements by Hoffman that he had used the money to finance his campaigns and to pay off a public officer who, he said, was blackmailing him.

Meyner appointed a series of lawyers to personal counsel spots as the openings arose. Among them were Joseph Weintraub, who later became Chief Justice, and Brendan Byrne, who became Governor.

Handsome, in his middle 40's, and in a position of

eminence, Meyner was a great "catch" in the matrimonial market. His name was frequently linked with those of women of prominence, notably Grace Kelly, Margaret Truman, daughter of the President, and various movie stars. He steadfastly refused to answer questions about his dates. He was finally "smoked out" in 1956.

The Democratic National Convention was being held in Chicago and the faithful were flocking into the Windy City from all over the nation. A large group from New Jersey was enroute by train and as it was pulling into the station Hortense Fuld Kessler, Public Utility Commission Chairman, advised a reporter friend to take a good look at the "Stevenson Girls" on the platform because Meyner was going to marry one of them.

It was a good tip. The girls were whooping it up for Governor Adlai Stevenson, of Illinois, and they surrounded Meyner. But there were no overt signs of courtship. It soon developed, however, that Meyner admitted he was attracted to one of the girls. She was Adlai's cousin, tall, beautiful, 28-year-old Helen Stevenson, a native of New York, and a graduate of Colorado University. She had been a Red Cross representative during the Korean War, had been a travel consultant for an airline, and had served in Adlai Stevenson's political headquarters.

Adlai lost the election (for the second time), but the romance flourished. The engagement was announced later that year and the marriage took place next January at Oberlin College, in Ohio, where Helen's father, William E. Stevenson, was president.

After a two-week honeymoon, the couple moved into the by-now ready Morven, the first governor's family to occupy the old house under state ownership. Among Mrs. Meyner's first visitors were her father and mother. She gave them the "grand tour."

Mrs. Meyner confessed later that she was somewhat overwhelmed by the 21-room mansion, the first home of her

married life. To her parents she pointed out the many items
of historic interest. Her mother was ecstatic. Her father's
reaction was: "Well, it's a roof over your head," which Mrs.
Meyner regarded as quite in character.

In the tradition of the old mansion, which had passed its
250th birthday six years earlier, Morven became the center
of official hospitality. The new First Lady set up regular
hours during which New Jerseyans were invited to visit for
tea and tours. A number of distinguished guests were entertained, among them Senator and Mrs. John F. Kennedy,
already running for the presidency. Adlai Stevenson, of
course, came to visit. Others included the Mayor of Amsterdam, Senator Joseph Clark, and Dean Acheson, State Department Chief.

The two last-named appeared at a reception the Meyners
gave for Fidel Castro who was visiting the United States after
the revolution that enabled him to take over Cuba. He had
been invited to speak at Princeton, and the organizers had
requested the Governor to give him a party at Morven. It
was a harrowing event for Mrs. Meyner who, it appeared,
was running around ceaselessly with trays to prevent acci-
dents, and in one case, to keep a still-lit cigar from being
ground into the red carpet.

A more rewarding event was the day dedicated to entertaining members of the United Nations. For the most part,
those who came were from the smaller nations, but it was a
good party and well-remembered by the guests, including
U Thant, executive secretary. Meyner said he met U Thant
several times later and found him very appreciative of the
occasion.

Neighbors and many others dropped in occasionally and
were welcomed. The pool and the tennis court were great at-
tractions. Both the Governor and Mrs. Meyner were avid
tennis players, and the court was in use whenever the weather
permitted.

Leadership groups from the Legislature were entertained

at Morven frequently and, in most cases, they were augmented by cabinet members or key personnel from the Governor's staff, as the Governor worked to win support for his programs. At least once a year the Meyners had as guests the entire Senate and the entire Assembly. The Supreme Court and members of the lesser judiciary were also entertained as were also men and women who served on important committees.

Twice each year the Meyners entertained the press, along with the Governor's staff and cabinet officers. The summer parties were held at Morven. The Christmas events, because of the problems of weather and numbers, were held at the National Guard Armory in Lawrence Township. Twice, when the guest list for a party was likely to be larger than Morven could accommodate, a tent was rented and set up in the gardens behind the house.

Spouses of the reporters were invited to both parties and although the Christmas event was the more elaborate, they preferred to go to Morven which had a strange fascination for them. The press corps did its share to enliven the parties, presenting miniature "gridiron dinner" shows. Mrs. Meyner became aware that her husband's romantic progress was depicted in one of the annual parodies. First it was "Hark the Herald Angels Sing, When Will Meyner Buy the Ring?" After the betrothal, it was "Meyner's Fin'ly Bought the Ring." And then it was, "Meyner's in the Well-Known Sling."

Helen made Morven glow at Christmas with parties and with candles lighting up each window.

It was not too long after the wedding that Meyner began campaigning for re-election. With a good record behind him and a beautiful bride at his side, he had no difficulty in being renominated or in winning a second term in November. His opponent this time was Senator Malcolm S. Forbes, publisher of the powerful *Forbes Magazine*.

Meyner's margin of victory rose to more than 200,000, and the Democrats made substantial gains in the Legislature. The Republican margin in the Senate was narrowed to a single seat, and the Democrats took control of the Assembly for the first time since 1937.

Looking forward to four more years at Morven, the Meyners began to enjoy life more. The Governor had retained his naval connection and was now a lieutenant commander in the Reserve. In that capacity he made two training trips each year to keep his Reserve standing. Every year the Meyners attended the annual National Governors' Conference held in such places as Hawaii and Puerto Rico, as well as at various locations within the United States mainland.

In 1959 the in-fighting began for the Democratic nomination for president. On the strength of his two victories in a state regarded as "normally Republican," Meyner was recognized as a possibility.

The Governors' Conference chose 1959 as the year to mount a good-will tour to Russia. Nine governors, Meyner among them, were chosen to make the trip. Mrs. Meyner went along, one of two women to make the journey. The governors spent 22 days in Russia, traveling from Moscow to Alma-Ata and went briefly into Siberia. It was clear the Russians believed Meyner had a good chance to win the presidency. Wherever the governors went, the Meyners generally got the best accommodations, although LeRoy Collins, of Florida, was the chairman of the expedition.

Returned from Russia, Meyner became involved in preparations for the 1960 presidential election. Frequent strategy sessions were held at Morven. It was clear that Senator Kennedy's support in New Jersey was growing, particularly in Hudson County where John Kenny, now in firm control, was working for him. Some Democrats, however, had misgivings about Kennedy's religious faith, remembering that the then-popular Al Smith had been unable to overcome the handicap of his Irish Catholic background. Meyner, by the way, had been born a Catholic but had never been interested in religion.

Despite his two losses, Adlai Stevenson still had support. Several New Jersey businessmen were committed to Lyndon B. Johnson, of Texas. Meyner's name was included in the list of possible candidates.

The New Jersey delegates voted to make Meyner New Jersey's "Favorite Son," which meant they were pledged to vote for him on the first ballot, at least. Determined to have what he called a "deliberative convention," Meyner resisted all pressures and refused to endorse any other candidate. There was speculation in the press that he was holding out to keep Kennedy from a first ballot nomination to aid Stevenson and Johnson, although he let it be known there would be more than 30 Kennedy votes on the second ballot.

The Democratic convention was held in Los Angeles. The New Jersey Democrats chartered a plan to take them there, and, appropriately enough, it was named "The Meyner Liner." At boarding time a large number of delegates wanted to support Kennedy and the plane was full of complaints against the Governor.

Dennis Carey, the Essex County leader, told reporters, as he was mounting the airplane steps, that he received a telephone call at midnight from a woman who said she was a fortune teller. She warned Carey not to get on the plane because "Meyner's enemies are going to shoot it down." Carey told her with the proper epithets, "Go back to bed, you old fool; all Meyner's enemies are on the plane."

Throughout the convention Meyner was under constant pressure to withdraw in favor of Kennedy. The pressure turned into verbal abuse, but Meyner wouldn't yield. He was nominated and the New Jersey delegation, albeit unwillingly, unanimously cast its votes for the New Jersey Governor on the first ballot. When it became clear Kennedy would win, Meyner sought to switch the votes to Kennedy, but the chairman of the convention refused to give him the floor and another state supplied the crucial votes.

Back in New Jersey Meyner was approaching the final year of his second term. As a lame duck, now, he found his powers curtailed. But he threw himself into the election and helped Kennedy carry New Jersey by about 22,000 votes.

Ineligible for a third term as governor, Meyner held conferences at Morven to take part in the selection of a Democratic nominee to succeed him. His first choice was Grover C. Richman, who had been his Attorney General, and the county chairmen's coalition agreed. Richman suffered a heart attack and Meyner was for William F. Hyland. But former Judge Richard J. Hughes was favored by the county chairmen and Meyner warmly accepted that selection. He worked hard to help elect Hughes.

In preparation for leaving Morven the Meyners bought a house in Princeton, retaining, however, the old Meyner home in Phillipsburg.

Meyner's Administration was marked by fiscal toughness and efficiency. He formulated a number of programs that were stymied in the Legislature but were enacted by his successors. Among these was the county college concept which became a reality under Governor Hughes in 1962. There were various law enforcement ideas, such as statewide grand juries, witness immunity, and the police training program, which were discussed but never brought to fruition.

Meyner inaugurated the "commuter benefit tax" under which New Jersey was able to recoup millions of dollars of the income taxes New Jerseyans who worked in New York paid to that state. He integrated state pensions with social security benefits, but that idea was overturned under his successor. And he took the first step to safeguard New Jersey against future water problems by persevering with the Spruce Run-Round Valley Reservoir project after he lost the plan to build a reservoir at Chimney Rock.

Meyner handed over the Chief Executive's office and

Morven to Richard Hughes in 1962, and resumed his law practice, taking with him as a partner Stephen Wiley, who was his last personal counsel. Once out of Morven, Helen Meyner embarked on her own career. She began to write columns for the *Star-Ledger* and to conduct television interview programs. In 1974 she won a congressional seat in the 13th district, newly-created and tailored for Senator Joseph Maraziti within rock-ribbed Republican Morris County. She was re-elected in 1976.

Meyner made a second try for the governorship in 1969. He won the Democratic nomination in a crowded primary contest but he lost to William T. Cahill in the general election.

# RICHARD J. HUGHES

Richard J. Hughes, like Meyner, was a Democrat, but there was a perceptible, albeit gradual, change in governmental philosophy in the Chief Executive's office shortly after the changeover in administration. Operations in the Meyner years were pragmatic in the main. Under Hughes the tenor of thought was liberal. The new Governor regarded himself as attorney for the poor and handicapped who, he believed, had never before been adequately represented.

At Morven, the changes were immediate and even more drastic. The 250-year-old mansion, home for the last five years for the childless Meyners, had to be adapted to house a family with nine children and a tenth on the way.

Hughes was 52 years old when he was elected Governor. He had been born in Florence, in neighboring Burlington County, but most of his life was spent in and around Trenton. His father had been of some prominence in the Democratic party and had served, for some time, as warden of the Trenton State Prison.

The younger Hughes was graduated from Trenton High School, attended St. Joseph's College, in Philadelphia, and won a law degree at New Jersey Law School (now part of Rutgers) in 1932. Becoming politically active in the Trenton area, Hughes made an unsuccessful run for Congress in 1938 and shared the Democratic county leadership with Thorn Lord. The two succeeded in turning strongly-Republican Mercer County into the Democratic column.

For six years Hughes served as Assistant U.S. Attorney for New Jersey. In 1948 Governor Alfred E. Driscoll appointed him to the County Court bench. Two years later, his wife, the former Miriam McGrory, died.

In 1954, Hughes, a widower with four children, met, fell in love with, and married, Mrs. Elizabeth Murphy, a widow with three children. She was a native of Trenton and a graduate of Douglass where she had majored in journalism. Her husband, Capt. William M. Murphy, died when his plane crashed in the Azores a few years earlier. Richard and Elizabeth Hughes had three children together.

Hughes was a surprise selection as the Democratic nominee for Governor in 1961. The coalition of Democratic county chairmen, which had taken over as the top echelon of the party eight years before, had settled on former Attorney General Grover C. Richman. He suffered a heart attack, however, on the eve of the announcement. The coalition had another meeting, and the decision to support Hughes was made known.

Hughes came into the election as an underdog. The Republicans had selected James P. Mitchell to carry their banner. He had been Labor Secretary under President Dwight D. Eisenhower and had developed an impressive reputation. Eisenhower had carried New Jersey by a record 750,000 votes in 1956.

Although John Kennedy had broken the barrier with a victory in the 1960 presidential race, there was still doubt that an Irish Catholic could win for Governor. Kennedy had carried New Jersey but only narrowly—by 22,000 votes.

Hughes started his campaign with a press conference at which he said that in his law practice he had been a lobbyist for railroads, removing that issue from the election. Naturally gregarious, blessed with an outstanding sense of humor, and accompanied by a wife with similar characteristics, Hughes proved to be an excellent campaigner. He won in a close election with a 35,000 vote majority.

The first thing Betty Hughes did in preparation for moving into Morven was to have the third floor turned into a dormitory for the children. Later she had a washer-dryer combination installed up there to enable the youngsters to do their laundry without having to run up and down the stairs. As good an organizer as she was a mother, Mrs. Hughes assigned chores to the older children and saw to it that they were performed.

It was a matter of great concern to Mrs. Hughes that there was no fire escape at Morven. She proposed that one be added but a spokesman for the overseeing commission said such an addition would ruin the colonial appearance of the building. There were no fire escapes in the glory days of Morven, Mrs. Hughes was informed. When she persisted she was told that her "excess children" could be housed in what used to be the slave quarters, which could, of course, be renovated.

"I have no excess children," Mrs. Hughes replied coldly, and in the end a fire escape was installed, hidden in the rear of the building so as not to offend the history buffs. Several years later Mrs. Hughes had cause to wonder about her "victory." It developed that the fire escape became a means of surreptitious exit and entrance for the older children.

It was inevitable that the large number of children would lead to some jokes. In the State House the favorite version told of Betty Hughes calling upstairs to the Governor to "come down; your kids and my kids are beating up our kids."

The number of children reached ten a few months after the Hughes family moved into Morven. Thomas More Hughes was born with a heart problem and impaired sight. The heart responded to treatment. The eyes did not.

Hughes had resigned his judgeship a few years before because he felt he could better support his large family in private practice. He found the Governor's salary, $35,000, also far below his earnings potential as a lawyer. Mrs. Hughes embarked on a career of eternal vigilance to keep costs down, to be as certain as possible that the youngsters, and particularly Thomas (whose sight would always be impaired), would be provided for in the future.

The money provided by the state to cover expenses at Morven—$30,000 first, and $35,000 later—was no more adequate than the Governor's salary. A certain amount of entertaining was dictated by custom. For example, Mrs. Hughes continued the practice begun by Mrs. Meyner of setting aside Tuesdays for tea and tours for interested New Jerseyans. Although Hughes was only the second Governor to occupy the Mansion, it seemed that custom already required that groups of senators, or assemblymen, or judges, had to be invited. It developed soon that these gatherings were incumbent on the Hugheses not only to conform to custom but also to obtain support for administration programs.

Twice a year, once in summer and once at Christmas, the Governor gave parties to which were invited his cabinet, his staff, and the State House press corps, with spouses. There was no room at Morven for large parties and most of these were held in a tent, rented for the occasions, in the garden. Mrs. Hughes convinced the powers that it would be cheaper, in the long run, to buy the tent rather than rent it. The cost could be recouped from rent savings in two years, she demonstrated, and the purchase would obviate the necessity of putting it up and taking it down for each party.

The Christmas parties, because of size and weather problems, were held at the Armory in Lawrence Township, a practice begun by Driscoll before Morven, continued by Meyner, and adopted by Hughes. Aside from the tent costs, the Morven parties were expensive, requiring the services of a caterer and a good supply of drinks. There were occasions when Mrs. Hughes, assisted by her secretary, prepared the food and with the aid of the Morven staff and some of the youngsters put it on the tables.

Hughes' first term in office was not spectacular. The Legislature was, in the main, under Republican control and he had as much difficulty as his predecessor in getting favorable action on his programs. He did, in the first year of the term, get the bill to create the county college system passed. And through the first four years, although he lost a number of bond issue approvals on referendums, he succeeded, in 1964, in winning support for a $50 million issue for institutions.

But Hughes completely captivated his party and a considerable portion of the public. He had no difficulty in gaining renomination in 1965 and his re-election seemed inevitable. The Republicans, in trouble again, resorted to an ad hoc screening committee to pick a candidate and wound up with Senator Wayne Dumont.

The general election was notable. Dumont proclaimed his support for a sales tax, the first time a candidate had openly espoused a broad-based tax. Hughes said he would prefer an income tax but made no move to press for one at the time.

The campaign centered about Eugene Genovese, a minor Rutgers teacher, who asserted he would "welcome a North Vietnamese victory" in the war in which the United States was involved in Vietnam. Dumont demanded Genovese be fired. Hughes defended his right, under academic freedom, to make the statement although he deplored it. Dumont won great applause wherever he attacked Genovese. But Hughes stuck to his guns and won easily by a record 350,000 votes.

The 1965 election was the first held under the gun of the U.S. Supreme Court's "one man, one vote" decision which put an end to the 21-member New Jersey Senate format based on one senator for each county. The number of senate seats was increased to 28 and, riding on Hughes' coattails, the Democrats won enough legislative contests to give that party control of both houses of the Legislature for the first time since 1913.

Supported, now, by a Democratic Legislature, Hughes broadened and intensified his program. He won approval for the so-called "striker benefits bill" admitting strikers to unemployment payments, a highly unpopular measure, which brought about another turn around, back to Republican control, in the next legislative election.

Hughes gave the State its first broad-base tax. He argued for an income tax but said he would accept a sales tax. On the verge of supporting the income tax, the crucial Essex delegation changed its mind and voted for the sales tax which was enacted into law.

Help for the handicapped, children particularly, became

virtually an obsession with the Governor and he worked ceaselessly to get the funds. He organized tours for reporters to bring them face to face with the problems of institutions he was determined to rectify. Unable in his first term to get support for a $750 million bond issue, he succeeded in 1968 in winning approval for three issues totalling more than a billion dollars, including more than $300 million for institutions. Also, he won approval for New Jersey's first lottery, the profits to go to education and institutions.

Before his term was over Hughes won approval for the "witness immunity act" and for a plan by the Port Authority of New York and New Jersey under which the Trade Center was built in New York and the Hudson Tubes were taken over by the Authority to become the PATH system.

Meanwhile, at Morven, life continued along its well-established ways. Groups of convicts were brought in for a day at a time to perform the outdoor work, and competition for places on the crews was keen. Selection meant not only a day out of prison but also excellent food.

John Hughes, third son of the Governor, won a law degree and took a bride—Miss Claudia Salvatore, whose father, the well-known Dr. Joseph Salvatore had died, and who was given in marriage by her uncle, Judge Arthur Salvatore. The reception was held at Morven, the first wedding celebrated there since former Governor Edge's daughter was married in 1952.

The Governor spent a few weeks in the hospital in Philadelphia for eye surgery to remove cataracts. The annual Christmas party went on without him, but he delivered a happy, humorous Christmas speech by telephone that more than made up for his absence and completely convulsed the guests.

Mrs. Hughes began in 1967 to make use of the journalism degree she got at Douglass. She began writing a column which was snapped up by the *Herald-News* and sold to several other newspapers. Now Morven began to ring with the sound of Betty's typewriter. Her horizon broadened. In August she packed eight of the children and her husband into two station wagons for a trip across the country to Los Angeles where Hughes was to attend the annual National Governors' Conference. The rigors and humors of the trip were recorded in her column.

Not long after, at a tea given by Ladybird Johnson, Betty Hughes sat in stunned silence with other guests while Eartha Kitt, a Black singer, sharply criticized Mrs. Johnson who, she said, fostered discrimination. Mrs. Hughes recovered and delivered a defense of Mrs. Johnson together with a criticism of Miss Kitt. The front pages told the story the next day.

The column continued to feature the kids and the problems at Morven. Soon Betty Hughes was writing magazine articles and winning national attention. Television was the next step. A Philadelphia station engaged her to become hostess on a "talk" program. In that capacity she interviewed many of the nation's greats in politics, government, and the arts, and, incidentally, made a considerable amount of money.

Presidential election time came along again in 1968, and among the visitors entertained at Morven was Vice-President Hubert H. Humphrey, seeking the nation's highest office. Humphrey was nominated at the convention in Chicago and there were rumors that he would pick Hughes as his running mate. The choice narrowed down to Hughes and Senator Edmund Muskie, of Maine, and Humphrey chose Muskie, apparently with Hughes' endorsement. In November Humphrey lost to Richard M. Nixon, who carried New Jersey in compiling the electoral votes he needed to win. There were some analysts who believed that the result would have been different had Humphrey chosen Hughes to run with him.

Back in New Jersey Hughes was approaching the final year of his two-term incumbency and the Hugheses were preparing to move out of Morven. They bought a large house on West-cott Road, in Princeton, and began the task of remodeling and modernizing it.

Another gubernatorial campaign was in progress. The Democrats had a large number of aspirants but the nomination went to former Governor Robert B. Meyner, who prevailed in spite of the enmity of John V. Kenny and his Hudson County followers. Richard and Betty Hughes worked hard for Meyner and appeared with the Meyners on a television program the day before election. But the polls pointed to a victory for William T. Cahill, the Republican candidate, and the polls were right.

Mrs. Hughes, concerned about the time television was taking from her family and worried about her health, turned down an offer for an enhanced television series and retired to the simpler life. The Governor joined a Newark law firm as its head and settled back into practice. He was appointed by the American Bar Association to head a national committee on prison reform.

Four years later, after Brendan Byrne was elected Governor but before he took office, Governor Cahill, with Byrne's agreement, named Richard Hughes New Jersey Chief Justice.

The Hughes family had at least one further connection with Morven. Michael Murphy, one of their sons, won a law degree and took for his bride another lawyer, Marianne Espinosa. The marriage was celebrated at Morven although all costs were born by the bridal families. To Mrs. Hughes it was evidence that a tradition had evolved—a tradition that the children of all governors could be married at Morven whether or not their fathers were still in office.

# WILLIAM T. CAHILL

William T. Cahill was 57 years old and in the middle of his eleventh year as a congressman when he was elected Governor in 1969.

He won the Republican nomination in a tough five-man primary contest with another congressman, Charles W. Sandman, as his nearest rival. The scales turned in Cahill's favor when he was endorsed by the Bergen County Steering Committee, headed by Nelson Gross. With a resulting victory in Bergen, Cahill went on to defeat Sandman by about 14,000 votes.

Cahill had considered dropping out of the race when one of his daughters, Patricia, was seriously injured in an automobile accident. It took a unanimous vote in a family conference to prevent his withdrawal.

It was the second time Cahill had sought the party nomination. He was one of three finalists in 1965 when the Republicans created an unusual steering committee to pick the candidate. He withdrew before the decision in protest against the selection process and Senator Wayne Dumont won over Sandman.

In 1969 Cahill faced former Governor Robert B. Meyner in the general election. Meyner, twice before elected Governor, had won the nomination over five other contenders and was regarded as favorite. Cahill swept to victory by a record half-million votes carrying even Hudson County, the longtime Democratic stronghold, by a decisive 30,000 plurality, a reflection of Meyner's unpopularity in that county. Cahill resigned from Congress as was required and prepared to move into Morven with his family.

Cahill was a native of Philadelphia who spent most of his youth in Camden schools and most of his adult life in Camden County. He attended St. Mary's Grammar School and Camden Catholic High School in preparation for matriculating at St. Joseph's College in Philadelphia. Graduated in

1933, he taught for four years in the Camden school system while working for a law degree in the Rutgers South Jersey Law School in night classes.

After getting his law degree in 1937, Cahill served for a time in the F.B.I. as a special agent in Washington, Little Rock, and St. Louis. Returning to Camden he became city prosecutor, then assistant county prosecutor, and later a special deputy attorney general.

In 1951 Cahill was elected to fill one of the three Camden County seats in the Assembly, and served through 1953. He was a member of the legislative committee named to inquire into why Deputy Attorney General Nelson Stamler had been fired. The hearings turned up evidences of underworld involvement in rock-ribbed Republican Bergen County and were later recognized as the first step in the GOP defeat in 1953.

Cahill married his school sweetheart, Elizabeth Myrtetus. He bought a home in Collingswood. The Cahills had eight children. Fortunately they followed the Hughes family into Morven. Blessed with ten children, Mrs. Betty Hughes had caused the necessary preparations to be made to house a large family as well as could be expected. The third floor rooms had been made into dormitories and a fire escape had been installed. Nevertheless, the new occupants found that several things had to be done. Although the mansion had 21 rooms, there were never enough to accommodate guests properly. After discussing the problem for some time, the new Governor had the old slave quarters, near the pool, repaired and refitted to provide guest room space.

The driveway in front of the mansion was rehabilitated; the trees lining it were cared for; and some new ones were planted, including trees in honor of Eileen, Teresa, and Patricia, three of his daughters. A rose fancier made the Governor a present of a newly-developed bush and Cahill had it planted in the garden, near the pool, in memory of his mother, Mrs. Rose Cahill.

Cahill's greatest complaint with Morven was the lack of room for large dinners or conferences. At one stage he contemplated breaking through some of the downstairs rooms to make a sort of hall for entertaining. But that idea died almost aborning under the frowns of the members of the Morven Overseers.

The need for large conference accommodations was never more apparent than in Cahill's incumbency. He had a varied and innovative program that frequently necessitated convening large groups for counseling or for the presentation of programs Cahill wanted passed. He invited state employees to Morven (for the first time) and entertained groups of 300 and 400 at a time.

When he came into office, Cahill found it necessary to increase the three percent state sales tax to five percent to take care of a $300 million deficit he inherited from the previous administration. As a result, Cahill gave a lot of thought to effecting economies in government and to increasing state revenues.

Cahill's first action was to call on industry to supply and support a group to study the operations of state departments. The group became the Management Study Commission and the recommendations implemented by Cahill saved the State, the Governor announced, more than $40 million.

Cahill won wide acclaim for his handling of a riot at the Rahway Prison. The disturbance was put down with no bloodshed, and the result was contrasted with New York Governor Nelson Rockefeller's actions in the Attica prison melee.

It is probable that the greatest conference activity ever seen at Morven came with the advent of Cahill's bid for an income tax. Cahill named a bipartisan committee, headed by Senator Harry L. Sears, who had been Nixon's top New Jersey supporter and was one of Cahill's rivals in the primary, as chairman to study the State's tax system.

In a five-volume, in-depth report, the Sears group presented a complex plan for complete revenue improvement with an income tax as its base. Cahill embraced the program and fought for it but was unable to get it through the Legislature. His tax stance haunted him in his quest for a second term.

Among the innovative ideas put forward in the Cahill incumbency was the concept of "no fault" insurance for vehicles. A somewhat similar method of dealing with divorce was adopted by the Legislature and Cahill, after wrestling with his religious beliefs, signed it into law. Attempting to compensate for the lack of a commercial television channel in New Jersey, the Cahill Administration created and funded the Public Broadcasting Authority.

The 1969 election which made Cahill governor approved a state lottery for New Jersey. Cahill undertook the task of making the lottery work and did it so well that New Jersey's lottery became a pattern for those in other states. It grossed more than $250 million in its first two years of operation.

It is widely believed that the greatest achievement of Cahill's Administration was the creation and success of the Meadowlands Sports Complex. Conceived as a combination of a football stadium and a horse racing track with State Treasurer Joseph M. McCrane among its chief sponsors, the concept was approved by the Legislature despite strong opposition. David A. "Sonny" Werblin, with wide experience in both football and racing, was named chairman of the Authority and set out with the Governor and McCrane to activate the plan. Working together the three managed to survive New York attempts to block the sale of Complex bonds and then lured the New York Giants to make the Complex the team's home base. Under Cahill's successor, the track, which opened first, became an instant success, soaring far above expectations. There was talk of additional construction to accommodate other sports events, expositions, and conventions.

In contrast to his immediate predecessor, Richard J. Hughes, who had no chance to make a Supreme Court appointment, Cahill had opportunity to make five appointments to the State's highest tribunal. Among the openings was one created by the resignation of Chief Justice Joseph Weintraub. To succeed him Cahill appointed his personal counsel, Pierre P. Garven, who had left a Bergen County judgeship to take a place in Cahill's Administration. Garven, who suffered from a kidney ailment, died after only a few months in office. Cahill, the first man to name two Chief Justices, named former Governor Hughes to succeed Garven.

Throughout his Administration Cahill was constantly entertaining groups whose support he was seeking for projects he believed were in the best interests of the State. A number of the meetings took place at Morven, but when the groups were too large, other quarters were used. For the most part those entertained were legislators or members of committees Cahill created. But they also included newspaper owners and publishers. And twice a year there were the now-traditional parties for the State House press corps, augmented by the Governor's staff. Some national figures were guests at Morven, notably Nelson Rockefeller, but they were few.

Cahill was fiercely proud of his family and of his Irish Catholic heritage. He delighted in singing Irish songs with reporters of Emerald Isle background as a wind-up of the press parties. Although he had what was known as a "short fuse," Cahill was a delightful host and a warm friend.

Cahill's eldest daughter, Mrs. Neil Tully, was married when the Cahills moved into Morven. His eldest son, William T. Cahill, Jr., earned a law degree in 1972 and married Miss Jane McManimon, daughter of a Bell Telephone executive. Young Cahill later began to practice law in the Camden area, where his father got his start. Perhaps the best news Cahill had when he was coming to the end of his term was that his daughter Patricia, so sorely injured in 1969, was making an excellent recovery.

Cahill was reluctant, at first, to run for re-election. Entering the primary he found Sandman already in the lists. Playing on the income tax and aided by the overhang of Watergate, Sandman won the primary. It was the first time an incumbent governor had been refused re-nomination.

Sandman was defeated by Byrne in a landslide. The Cahills bought a house in Princeton and moved out of Morven. Cahill returned to private law practice, becoming of counsel to an established Princeton firm formerly headed by John McCarthy.

# BRENDAN T. BYRNE

Brendan T. Byrne was the fourth incumbent governor to occupy Morven. He won the right to move in with victories in the 1973 primary and the general election later that year. Despite a late entrance in the primary, Byrne became an instant favorite to win upon his declaration of candidacy. Two formidable candidates—Richard Coffee and J. Edward Crabiel—withdrew, leaving Mrs. Ann Klein and Ralph DeRose to contest the race for the nomination with Byrne.

Byrne won easily by about 80,000 votes, while Congressman Charles W. Sandman was defeating incumbent Governor William T. Cahill for the Republican nomination. In the general election in November, Byrne defeated Sandman by more than 720,000 votes, a record majority for New Jersey gubernatorial races. Although he had never run for office before, Byrne was an almost unanimous choice of the political analysts to win. His credentials were impeccable. They included a well-publicized comment by an underworld figure whose lament that Byrne "couldn't be bought" as Essex County prosecutor became Byrne's campaign slogan.

The income tax issue, regarded then as of first importance since it was related, by most political writers, to Cahill's defeat, was vitiated by Byrne's statement that he believed New Jersey didn't need an income tax for the foreseeable future.

Byrne was born April 1, 1924, in West Orange. His father was a local official of Democratic persuasion. Graduated from West Orange High School, Byrne attended Seton Hall College where his stay was cut short by World War II. Enlisting in the Air Force (then the Army Air Corps), Byrne became a bombardier and served in the Eastern Theatre.

Discharged in 1945, Byrne completed his college education at Princeton and went on to Harvard where he earned a law degree. He was admitted to the New Jersey Bar in 1951 and served his clerkship with Joseph Weintraub, who later became New Jersey's Chief Justice.

A few years after he began private practice, Byrne was called into state service by then-Governor Robert B. Meyner who first appointed him assistant counsel and, the next year, acting executive secretary. In 1956 Meyner sent him back to his native Essex County as a special deputy attorney general and then as prosecutor.

Governor Richard J. Hughes called him back to state service as chairman of the State Board of Public Utility Commissioners in 1968. Governor Cahill, a Republican, appointed Byrne to a judgeship and not too long after that Byrne was designated Assignment Judge of Morris County.

That was the background Byrne brought into the 1973 campaign. Following his election, the State House press realized that, like his two immediate predecessors, Byrne was of Irish Catholic descent and included in the 1974 "Gridiron Dinner" a parody proclaiming "You've Got to Be an Irish Cath'lic, to Be Elected to Govern the State."

Mrs. Byrne was the former Miss Jean Featherly, a graduate of Bucknell University with a master's degree from New York University. She was teaching in the West Orange school system when she met Byrne. They were married June 27, 1953, and have seven children; six were with them when they moved into Morven.

They found the old Mansion in need of some repairs. Some of the toilets needed attention. The ceiling in the bedroom of one of the Byrne daughters fell down, but, fortunately, injured nobody. The tent used by the two previous governors to entertain guests was discarded, the Byrnes believing it was both expensive and unsightly. Instead, Governor Byrne directed that a roof be built over the patio to make possible increased use of that area. The gardens behind the house were spruced up.

As Governor, Byrne won immediate kudos for his handling of the gasoline emergency which erupted almost as soon as he took office. Then he began a three-year quest for enactment of a state income tax which, for the first two years, brought him a considerable amount of abuse. He persevered, however, and in 1976 became the first governor to gain approval for an income tax. The plan adopted was engineered by the Legislature and it barely cleared. Byrne signed it into law. In its final form, it was a tax reform program, providing over $1 billion, covering increased state school aid funding, and other rebates, and some relief for renters. It was designed to hold the line against increasing local property taxes.

Byrne was responsible for a number of additional innovative programs, among them the "thorough and efficient education" law, defining what the Constitutional phrase meant. The law provided for an increase in state aid to education, and for a revision in the formula for distribution of the aid, in conformity with a Supreme Court mandate.

The Department of Public Advocate was created under Byrne's direction and its head became, in effect, the state's ombudsman. To open up governmental operations to the people Byrne called for adoption of the so-called "Sunshine Law" and the Legislature passed it. He also won legislative support for a plan to finance gubernatorial campaign funds with public funds. The plan was signed into law and became operative, for the first time, with the 1977 election.

All these programs generated a considerable amount of movement at Morven. People were coming and going all the time, it seemed, to attend committee meetings, to consult with the Governor on political problems, or, if they were press people, to interview either or both of the Byrnes.

Morven became a center for hospitality, resembling to an extent what it was during the Colonial years. The Governor, and Mrs. Byrne, too, were avid tennis players, and the Morven court attracted a considerable number of local devotees. Miss Althea Gibson, a former Wimbledon champion, was a frequent visitor, and Byrne designated her as "Honorary Tennis Pro" for the Morven court. Later Byrne appointed her State Athletic Commissioner. She was the first woman and the first Black to hold that post, which she gave up in 1977 to make an unsuccessful run for a state senate seat.

Visitors to Morven included President Jimmy Carter, who was there for a reception in 1975 when he was "Jimmy Who?" Byrne helped raise $5,000 for Carter, the sum needed in each of 20 states to permit the former Georgia governor to qualify for federal campaign funds. Jody Powell, Carter's press secretary, paid a visit later.

Senator Lloyd Bentsen and Congressman Morris Udall, like Carter candidates for the Democratic nomination, were also at Morven during the campaign year. Ethel Kennedy, widow of former Attorney General Robert Kennedy, who was martyred by an assassin's bullet, was among the Byrne guests.

Internationally famous visitors included Cardinal Josef Mindzenty and the rulers of Monaco, Prince Rainier and Princess Grace, along with their children, Caroline and Albert.

Princeton has a large colony of literati, and members of that group visited Morven from time to time. Among them were Peter Benchley, author of the highly successful book *Jaws*; John McPhee, J. P. Miller, and Rose Franken.

Frequent guests were dramatist Sidney Kingsley and his wife, actress Madge Evans. With Kingsley, Byrne developed a plan to bring the motion picture industry back to New Jersey, where it began in the early years of the twentieth century. He named a committee to negotiate with film producers and Kingsley served as chairman.

From the performing stage came Madame Maria Jeritza and Jerome Hines, opera stars, along with Joseph Smith, known to fame as a member of the famous "Smith and Dale" vaudeville team, and singer Andy Williams.

Anita "The Face" Colby, a beauty from the modeling field, was among the guests.

Sports figures were frequently invited. Among them were

Bill Bradley, Princeton University and New York Knicker-bocker basketball great, and David A. "Sonny" Werblin, one-time executive partner of the football Jets, but better known as chairman of the New Jersey Sports Authority.

The 1976 Rutgers football team was entertained at Morven, underlining the Governor's devotion to sports since Rutgers was a long-time rival of Byrne's alma mater, Princeton. The Seton Hall team was entertained in 1977, and the Governor was made an honorary member of the team and assigned number 19.

In addition to being the first Governor to succeed in getting an income tax, Byrne inaugurated innovative means of reaching the public. These included person-to-person talks with New Jersey citizens who were encouraged to contact the Governor to express opinions or to ask for information. Byrne used the phone conversations to make points for the income tax.

Byrne reached the last year of his first term in 1977 with opinion divided, within his party, as to whether or not he could win again, and, in fact, whether he should run again. Cited against him, primarily, was the income tax. But he geared up for a fight, defending the tax and, in fact, using it as a tool for attack, demanding to know how critics would raise the money to operate the government without it. He faced nine opponents in the primary, conducting his campaign as if he were the underdog. He won a decisive victory, soundly defeating Congressman Robert A. Roe, his nearest opponent, and entered the campaign for re-election against Senator Raymond H. Bateman, who won the Republican primary. Polls taken after Byrne had challenged Bateman on the income tax indicated a shift in public opinion in the Governor's favor, and they were confirmed when he went on to win re-election in November by a substantial margin. He thus became the third Democrat to obtain an eight-year lease on Morven.

Adams, Charles Francis: *Life of John Adams*, Boston, 1856.

Adams, John: *Works of John Adams*, Boston, 1856.

*American Archives*, 5th Series, Vol. III.

Architects' Emergency Committee: *Great Georgian Houses of America*, 2 vols., New York, 1933, 1937.

Atterbury, Rev. W., D.D.: *Elias Boudinot: Reminiscences of the American Revolution*, New York, 1894.

Bayard, Samuel John: *A Sketch of the Life of Commodore Robert F. Stockton*, New York, 1856.

Bill, Alfred Hoyt: *Rehearsal for Conflict, The War with Mexico*, New York, 1947.

Boudinot, J. J.: *Life of Elias Boudinot, LL.D.*, Boston and New York, 1896.

Boyd, George Adams: *Elias Boudinot, Patriot and Statesman, 1740-1821*, Princeton, 1952.

Butterfield, Lyman H.: "Annis and the General," *Princeton University Library Chronicle*, Vol. VII, No. 1, Nov. 1945.

———: "Morven, A Colonial Outpost of Sensibility," *Princeton University Library Chronicle*, Vol. VI, No. 1, Nov. 1944.

Chastellux, Jean Francis, Marquis de: *Travels of the Marquis de Chastellux in North America*, London, 1787.

Collins, Varnum Lansing: *The Continental Congress at Princeton*, Princeton, 1908.

Cowen, David L.: "Revolutionary New Jersey, 1763-1787," *Proceedings of the New Jersey Historical Society*, Jan. 1953.

Cutler, William Parker and Julia Perkins: *Life, Journals, and Correspondence of Rev. Manasseh Cutler, LL.D.*, Cincinnati, 1888.

*Dictionary of American Biography*, New York, 1935.

Eberlein, Harold Donaldson: *Architecture of Colonial America*, Boston, 1927.

Edge, Walter Evans: A Jerseyman's Journal, Princeton, 1948.

Ellet, Elizabeth F.: *The Women of the American Revolution*, New York, 1850.

*Encyclopedia Americana*, New York and Chicago, 1952.

*Encyclopædia Britannica*, 11th Edition.

# Bibliography

Feld, Rose C.: "Guest House of Many Presidents," *New York Times Book Review and Magazine*, June 25, 1922.

Franklin, Benjamin: *Works of*, Boston, 1856.

Gauss, Katherine: "Two Hundred Years of Morven I Record," *The House Beautiful*, July 1927.

Glenn, Thomas Allen: *Some Colonial Mansions and Those Who Lived in Them*, Philadelphia, 1899.

Goldmann, Sidney: *Morven and the Stocktons*, typescript, 1945.

Gosnell, H. Allen: "U.S.S. Princeton," *Princeton Alumni Weekly*, Mar. 5, 1943.

Hageman, John Frelinghuysen: *History of Princeton and Its Institutions*, Philadelphia, 1879.

Halsey, W. F., 3rd: *Commodore Robert F. Stockton*, student thesis, Department of History, Princeton University.

Harland, Marion: *Colonial Homesteads and Their Stories*, New York and London, 1912.

Hone, Philip: *Diary of*, B. Tuckerman, ed., New York, 1889.

Hunter, C. W.: "Morven, the Princeton Home of the Stockton Family," *Proceedings of the New Jersey Historical Society*, New Series, Vol. IX, 1924.

Ives, Mabel Lorenz: *Home of Richard Stockton*, Upper Montclair, N.J., 1932.

Kemmerer, Donald L.: *The Path to Freedom, The Struggle for Self-Government in Colonial New Jersey*, Princeton, 1940.

Kimball, Fiske: *Domestic Architecture of the American Colonies and of the Early Republic*, New York, 1922.

Lane, Wheaton: *From Indian Trail to Iron Horse*, Princeton, 1939.

Lathrop, Elise: *Historic Houses of Early America*, New York, 1927.

*Letters of Members of the Continental Congress*, Edmund C. Burnett, ed., Washington, D.C., 1923.

Lockwood, Alice G. B., ed., *Gardens of Colony and State*, New York, 1931.

Marquand, Eleanor C.: *The Trees of Guernsey*, typescript in Princeton University Library, 1937.

# Bibliography

Mills, W. Jay: *Historic Houses of New Jersey*, Philadelphia and London, 1902.

Moreau de Saint Méry: *Voyage aux Etats Unis de l'Amerique, 1793-1798*, New Haven, 1913.

Morrison, Hugh: *Early American Architecture from the First Colonial Settlements to the National Period*, New York, 1952.

Myers, William Starr: "New Jersey Politics from the Revolution to the Civil War," *Americana*, Vol. XXXVII, No. 3.

Nelson, William: "Biography of Richard Stockton," *New Jersey Archives*, 1st Series, Vol. X, p. 427.

*New Jersey Archives*, 1st Series, Vol. IV, p. 98, and Vol. X, p. 424.

Pintard, John: *Letters from John Pintard to His Daughter Eliza Noel Pintard Davidson, 1816-1833*, New York, 1940-41.

Quincy, Josiah: *Figures of the Past*, Boston, 1901.

Rush, Benjamin, M.D.: *Autobiography*, George Washington Corner, ed., Princeton, 1948.

——: *Letters of*, L. H. Butterfield, ed., Princeton, 1951.

Sanderson, John: *Biographies of the Signers of the Declaration of Independence*, Philadelphia, 1823.

Savelle, Max: *George Morgan, Colony Builder*, New York, 1932.

Scott, William Berryman: *Some Memories of a Paleontologist*, Princeton, 1939.

Sloane, James R.: *Princeton Personalities*, privately printed.

Smith, Robert C.: "John Notman's Nassau Hall," *Princeton University Library Chronicle*, Vol. XIV, No. 3, spring 1953.

Stockton, Bayard: "Morven," *The Princeton Book*, Boston, 1879.

Stockton, Helen Hamilton: *The Trees of Morven*, typescript in Princeton University Library, 1937.

Stockton, John Wharton: *History of the Stockton Family*, Philadelphia, 1881.

Stockton, Mrs., *A Quest for a Garden*, typescript.

Stockton, Robert Field: "Defense of the System of Internal Improvements of the State of New Jersey," pamphlet, Philadelphia, 1864.

Stockton, Thomas Coates, *The Stockton Family of New Jersey and Other Stocktons*, Washington, 1911.

# Bibliography

"Stockton Mansion at Princeton, The," *Appleton's Journal*, Vol. XIV, No. 353, Dec. 25, 1875.

Symmes, Frank R.: *History of the Old Tennent Church*, Cranbury, N.J., 1904.

Van Doren, Carl: *Benjamin Franklin*, New York, 1938.

Washington, George: *George Washington's Diaries*, John C. Fitzpatrick, ed., Boston and New York, 1925.

———: *Writings of Washington*, John C. Fitzpatrick, ed., Washington, D.C., 1931-34.

———: *Writings of Washington*, Worthington Chauncey Ford, ed., New York and London, 1890.

Waterman, Thomas T.: *The Dwellings of Colonial America*, Chapel Hill, N.C., 1950.

Wertenbaker, Thomas Jefferson: *The Founding of American Civilization, The Middle Colonies*, New York, 1949.

———: *Princeton, 1746-1896*, Princeton, 1946.

Whitehead, John: *Judicial and Civil History of New Jersey*, Boston, 1897.

Williams, Carl M.: *Silversmiths of New Jersey*, Philadelphia, 1949.

By far the greater part of the manuscript sources of this book are to be found in the Princeton University Library, where many of them can be located by use of the card catalogue. But many others are to be found there only by searching through the voluminous "Temporary Deposit" of Stockton papers which, since it is a loan to the library, has never been catalogued.

The library's collections and the "Temporary Deposit" contain many letters and papers of Richard Stockton, "the Signer," and Annis, his wife; Annis's letters after her husband's death; a manuscript book containing thirteen of her poems; and letters of her brother-in-law Samuel Witham Stockton.

Bearing upon the life of her son Richard, who was called "the Old Duke," are a considerable number of his personal letters and papers; letters from his ill-starred son, Richard, Jr.; letters from his sister Julia Stockton Rush; from his brother, Lucius Horatio Stockton; from the Reverend Andrew Hunter, Mary Stockton Hunter, and their sons Lewis and Robert.

The personal letters and papers of Commodore Stockton are disappointingly few. There are none of his wife's, except her will. Here, however, are to be found the illuminating letter book of his business agent, William H. Gatzmer; the schoolboy journal of his son Richard; the vivid diary of his daughter-in-law Sara Marks (Mrs. John Potter) Stockton; more letters of Mary Stockton Hunter, her son David, and her daughter Mary (Mrs. Samuel Witham Stockton); the commonplace books of the Commodore's aunts Mary Harrison and Annis Thomson, and the diary of the former.

The best of several genealogical tables of the Stockton family, together with much useful background material, is included in the Records of the Princeton Chapter of the Daughters of the American Revolution, which are also in the Princeton University Library.

In the Historical Society of Pennsylvania, the Balch, Wayne, Coryell, and Canorroe Papers and the Dreer Collection contain several interesting Stockton letters and other items relating to the Stockton family.

The New-York Historical Society has letters of Lucius Horatio Stockton to John Pintard, a letter of Richard Stockton, the Signer, to Joseph Reed about the Stockton coat of arms, and a letter of Mrs. Mary Stockton Hunter describing the British occupation of Washington in 1814.

# Manuscript Sources

The New Jersey Historical Society collections contain, notably: a brief typescript, *Alexander Pope at Morven*, by Helen Hamilton Stockton; *The Stockton Genealogy* (blueprint) by the Reverend Elias Boudinot Stockton, dated December 7, 1909; and *The Stocktons of Morven, by a Descendant*, a typescript of some one hundred and thirty large pages, dated "Princeton, May, 1929," which gives an interesting and generally reliable account of the family.

Among the manuscripts in the New York Public Library are a letter from Richard Stockton, the Signer, describing the progress of his fatal illness; an official letter of Commodore Stockton; and the log of his flagship, the *Congress*, 1845-49.

The deposition of Richard Stockton (the Old Duke) in the case of the defamation of his daughter's character is to be found in the New Jersey State Library.

The Trenton Free Public Library collections contain interesting lists of the names of New Jersey tories.

Most important among the Stockton items in the possession of Mrs. C. Welles Little, of Hagerstown, Maryland, is the agreement between Commodore Stockton and his farmer at Morven, dated 1862, and a cloth-bound volume of his letters to the *New York Evening Post* in 1864 in reply to attacks on the monopoly of the Camden and Amboy Railroad Company.

Highly informative also is a large collection of newspaper clippings and other Stockton memorabilia belonging to Mr. Arthur Conger, of Princeton.